PRACTICAL H

By: Felix Joseph

Practical Hippie Shit

Copyright 2024 © Felix Joseph

All rights reserved. No parts of this publication may be reproduced, stored in a retrieval system, or transmitted in any form, or by means including electronic mechanical means. Photography and recording— without the prior written permission of the publisher is prohibited

Dedication

I dedicate this book to every family and friend whom I loved dearly and who passed away before they could write down their thoughts so that we could benefit from their wisdom.

In writing this book, I have only one aim: that somewhere in it, there is one concept, lesson, idea, practice, or exercise—whether new to you or one that you are reminded of—that improves your life. If I can achieve that, then the book has done its job.

Acknowledgements

Thank you to Ray McLennan for pointing out that I had a spiritual problem, not a business problem, and pointing me to this path.

Thank you, Daniel Mangena, for all your knowledge, friendship, and support, but most importantly, for the conversation that created the title of this book.

Thank you to Michael Davu, not only for being the best friend a guy could have but being the person who pointed out that even though I was into this hippie shit, at least I took a practical view of it and, in doing so, giving me the idea to write this book, even though I didn't know at the time.

Claudia Burnett, because you already know this shit.

To Goedele Leyssen for the same reason

To Dr Mahdi Brown for our long, insightful talks and because you know this shit better than most.

To Sharon George, for introducing me to 'the king' energy and the purple light.

To my bredrin Mr Maph, the definition of God before religion. Every time we link, our conversations go deep; your wisdom is a blessing, fam.

Thank you to Robert Longdon, whose common sense and practical approach to life have informed my worldview and enabled me to look for common sense in the woo-woo.

To Natalie Bent Mason, who is the definition of a practical person who knows hippie shit.

Thank you to Kevin Campbell, whose hours of debate surrounding concepts of the law of attraction helped sharpen my philosophy.

Thank you to my wonderful children Kamau and Makini, who suffer every new discovery that I make by having it foisted on them by a loving parent who constantly wants to improve their lives.

Thank you to my wife, Sharon, for finally finding a way to put up with my many, many investigations into hippie shit without frustrating and blocking them.

Thank you to Andrea Goya, my friend and compadre, who introduced me to many of these concepts long before I was ready to accept them.

Thank you to Jonna Samson not just for her unwavering support of my companies but also for your work in editing and creating the first transcription of this book, which was too perfect and helped me realise just how imperfect I wanted this book to be.

To anyone I missed, you know I'm a scatterbrain, so I know that you won't take it personally.

And to you, the reader, thank you for your trust. Now that I'm halfway through transcribing this book, I know I will not be satisfied. The topic is just too big, and I do not have sufficient knowledge to do it justice. But what I can do is be sincere and give you an honest account of my opinions and experiences regarding this subject matter and something tells me that for most of you reading this, that will do just fine.

Sections and Chapters

Introduction 1
   Before We Get Started 1
   An Introduction 1
   Another Introduction 3
   Why I Wrote This Book 4
   The Other Reason I Wrote This Book 5
   How You Learned To Hate The Woo-Woo 7
   Consensus 13

Science 17
   Science And Hippie Shit 17
   You Don't Know What You Don't Know 19
   The Miracle Of Birth 22
   The Subconscious Mind 25
   The Brain Explained 26
   Computer Programs And Our Brain 29
   Early Reading List 33

You 34
   You Are Broken, Sorry!! 34
   Too Cool For School 38
   Act As If 41
   Be Happy, Here's Why 43
   Celebrate Your Losses And Rejoice In Your Bad Days 48
   Celebrate Your Losses And Rejoice In Your Bad Days, Part 2 50
   Belief And Paradigm 51

Faith And Belief	53
Belief And Effort	57
Beliefs Create Your Reality	58
Truth And Belief	61
Your Decision Graph	64
Smile At Children	67
Ground Zero And Gratitude	69
Love Yourself First	73
Telling Yourself You Love Yourself	76
Love Yourself, Again	80
Practical	**82**
First Thing In The Morning	82
The First Hours Of The Day Should Be Yours.	85
Doing Things In A 'Different Way'	87
Focus... It's Not Just A Song By Xzibit	88
How To Rewire Failure So That It Leads To Success	90
The Athlete Example	91
The Will Vs. The Way	96
Anger	104
Angry Again?	106
Self-Defence Is No Offence.	107
The Two Wolves	109
Your Influence	113
Shoot Where They Are Going To Be	116
Negative Thoughts	120
Two Plans	125
If You Have To Be There, Be There	126
Your Perfect Day	129

Hug It Out	131
Breathing	132
Food	133
Sleep	134
Exercise	134
Scratch The Record	136
Hippie Shit	**139**
Why Do It? Why Not?	139
Manifestation, The Reticular Activated System And Segment Intending	141
Repetition	144
Affirmations & Self-Talk	146
How To Listen To Self-Talk	151
Self-Talk Addendum	154
Self-Talk Exercise	155
Belief In Your Statement	157
Imagination	161
Imagination Pt 2	164
Fuck It Til You Make It!	165
Dohavebebedohavehavebedo?	167
Manifestation	172
Be Unrealistic	175
Different Types Of What And How	176
God's Delays Are Not His Denials, Aka, I Planted The Seed Yesterday; Where The Hell Is My Tree?	181
Inspiration From Meditation	194
Three Types Of Meditation	196
How To Use Technique 3 To Achieve 2	199
Meditation Addendum	200
Positive Thinking Again	201

Rewiring Worry 202

Gratitude Questions 205

Nature 209

Tree Hugging Hippie Shit 210

Resistance: The Hapkido Example 213

Three To One 216

Right Action. It Comes Four Times Before The Word Chameleon. 218

Practical Karma 221

Forgiveness 223

Make Yourself Happy 225

Woo Woooo!!!! 228

Talking To The Universe 228

As Below Above 231

Fear Addendum 233

Weight Control 234

Happy Accidents… No, Not What You Think 236

Do Bad Things Really Happen? 238

The Rights And Wrongs Of Right And Wrong 242

Prayer And Affirmation 243

Dreams 244

Aliens 246

Time 247

Parallel Universe Surfing 248

The Matrix 249

The Projector Example… All The Way Down The Rabbit Hole 250

If It Is Done, Then What Should I Do 252

Life 255

Conclusion 256

x

Practices & Exercises 259
   Practices 259
   Invoke Happiness 259
   Segment Intending 260
   Gratitude List 260
   Listen To Self-Talk At Night 262
   Exercises 262
   Rewire Worry Exercise 262
   Counteract Your Negative Thoughts 264
   Be Less Reactive 266
   Get 'The Happy' Feeling 267
   Shadow Boxing, Aka Mental Rehearsal 267
   Tell Yourself You Love Yourself 268
   Got A Problem? Ridiculise It 270
   Gratitude Questions 272

My Personal Experiences With The Woo Woo 275
   My Personal Examples 275
   The Mr Maph Experience 279
   My Early Warning System 280

About The Author 282

INTRODUCTION

Before We Get Started

In the famous words of the Strafe song 'Set it Off,' 'Y'all want this party started right', or in 'legalese', allow me to set your expectations correctly. This is a book of my experiences and opinions; everything within it is up for debate, and you are more than welcome to disagree with any point I make. My experiences are my own; they are what I perceive to have happened in my life. And my opinions, well, opinions are like arseholes; everybody has one; this is mine, and I'm showing it to you. So, I apologise in advance if anything in this book proves to be demonstratively wrong; as I said, what you're reading is just a book of my experiences and opinions about those experiences. If you already know what I talk about in this book, it can still be helpful. Repetition is the mother of learning, so treat this book as a refresher course on all the things you already know, but are probably not using. If you know the subject matter better than me (of whom there will be many), then feel free to reach out to our Practical Hippie Shit community and help others who, like me, are just trying to piece this stuff together.

An Introduction

During one of our business meetings, while discussing property finance, my good friend Daniel Mangena mentioned something about manifestation. I distinctly remember responding, 'Yeah, I respect you, bro, but miss me with that hippie shit.' There are not many moments in my life when I have said something so memorable that it would come back to haunt me. But those words, without a doubt, did just that.

Years later, after using sheer willpower to push my way through business, overcoming obstacles, and keeping my ventures alive through brute force, hard work, ingenuity, and skill without ever relying on anything that could be seen as esoteric or otherworldly, I decided to seek mentorship. At the time, I was based in Spain and would fly to England once a month to be mentored by a group of business professionals.

After a few months of this, I remember expressing my frustration to one of my mentors. I said, 'Ten years ago, I was a multimillionaire with a multi-million-pound property business. I lost it during the recession, and that's fine; shit happens. But I don't understand why it's taking me so long to succeed again. I know ten times more now than when I made all that money. I know I'm more knowledgeable about business, yet I can't seem to reach the same level of success.'

Ray McLachlan, my mentor, replied, 'Ah, you don't have a business problem. You have a spiritual problem.' In my mind, I thought, *What the fuck? Say what now?* This response was shocking because Ray McLachlan, a well-known, hard-nosed business financier, was the last person I expected to talk to me about spirituality.

I was absolutely blown away. Then, two months later, I spoke with another mentor, Gavin, another hardcore business professional, and shared my frustrations with him. He responded, 'Sometimes you just have to ask the universe.' Again, I thought, *Motherfucker, say what now?* Another tough, no-nonsense businessman with a reputation for finance was telling me that my problems were spiritual.

What freaked me out the most about this experience was that it wasn't entirely unfamiliar. I had previously been very spiritual; I was involved in the arts twenty years before, and I had done lots of meditation and visualisation, but in my mind, I had compartmentalised spirituality as an artistic avenue and business as a non-spiritual one, believing the two could never meet.

This experience is why I've decided to write this book: to show people who think that spirituality and business don't mix that they can. My aim is to take some of these spiritual concepts and put them into a practical context for you to understand, and to take some common-sense practical life concepts and show their spiritual dimensions.

Another Introduction

So why 'Practical Hippie Shit'? Well, because all spiritual teachings, at least from a beginner's perspective, seem to start with the same requirement. This requirement is to switch off your analytical brain, turn off all common-sense concepts, forget everything you know about reality and how the world works in practice, and just believe. Just believe what I'm saying on faith.

The problem is that many people don't want to do that. We've spent a very long time building up our common sense, analytical abilities, and practical view of the world, and these abilities have served us well in surviving and thriving. These skills are the cornerstone and foundation of how we interact with the world. Plus, it's always seemed like a cheap shot to me. Whenever I was around someone from a religious background or in a spiritual class at school, and someone asked the teacher a complicated question that they couldn't answer, they would say, 'You have to believe; you have to have faith.' To me, that was just a cheap cop-out.

This book aims to provide you with some practical answers—or at least, what I hope will be practical answers—to some of those questions. Things that, if you genuinely have an interest in, you can use this as a starting point to dig your teeth into and find out more. They will provide you with a place to start using some of these concepts and viewpoints that I believe would benefit you without suspending all common sense and practicality, throwing away acquired knowledge, or jumping off a cliff into an abyss of blind belief. Because, you know, throwing away all common sense and acquired knowledge and jumping off a cliff into an abyss of blind belief is how you end up in a cult, right!!!—Believing everything people say and following the teacher without question, ignoring society's norms and your accumulated wisdom leads you right to Waco. That is why you need a foundation for why anything makes sense, and I'm hoping this book will be just one brick in creating that foundation for you.

Why I Wrote This Book

So before starting this exploration into Practical Hippie Shit, I just wanted to point out the obvious. I'm not a guru. I haven't had life-altering experiences like Dr Hawkins, Dr Joey Dispenza, Deepak Chopra, or any of the many Indian gurus. I wasn't contacted by alien intelligence or interdimensional beings like Bashir or Esther Hicks.

That's the point of this book because I appreciate that all those things are highly questionable to people who look at life from a practical standpoint. All of the above seem somewhat suspect for people with reality-based or science-based paradigms. So, I'm not a guru. In fact, like most things, much of what I say here may well be debated even by people who follow similar philosophies. So why write this book? Well, I really wanted to write the book that I needed to read when I was starting out on this journey.

I really needed an introduction to these concepts from a place where they could be seen practically, where I could be eased into them practically. I needed a book from a down-to-earth, practical standpoint, from a logical point of view. Where I was not just told to have faith or belief or that I was disillusioned and delirious because I was living in an illusion (take the Red Pill!!), and the real world was something else, and science was nonsense.

I wanted someone who could take me through these concepts, starting from a point of practicality and common sense. Not starting from way out there, woo-woo ism, treating the whole process just like organised religion, treats everything, i.e. we're right, you're wrong. You are deluded; we know stuff you don't know, and we have the secret. We will have a better life than you are now and a better life than you will in the future.

This attitude is the opposite of what practicality and your common sense tell you. This attitude of, 'and if you don't believe me, boohoo Oh, ye of little faith'. 'You just need to believe, but I will give you no practical evidence.' This is what kept me away from this worldview for so long.

So that's the gap that this book is trying to fill. I'm feeling very weird because I know I am not the best-placed person to do this. I apologise in advance for failing to explain any of the concepts. But I do believe that the sincerity of my intention will shine through. This is not supposed to be the definitive answer to any of these questions, concepts, theories, or philosophies. It is just a starting point to allow people to see that maybe there really is something in some of these ideas and then try the exercises and see if their life improves. And if their life does improve, they may find their guru, teacher, philosopher, or spiritual leader of choice to delve more into these concepts to their satisfaction and benefit.

The Other Reason I Wrote This Book

I also wrote this book because my good friend and local neighbourhood genius, Dr Mahdi Brown, introduced me to human engineering.

Well, he was actually the second person to do so in a week, and as I will go on to explain, when coincidences like this appear, I tend to take them as a sign from the greater power and follow through.

So, I went to the website and did the test. The results said that based on the information I put in, my purpose in life was to take complicated concepts and explain them in a way that everyone could understand. Now, this was one of those experiences, like doing my horoscope for the first time and discovering that I'd already been living all the traits of the Leo for the previous 15 years. Then, doing my Chinese horoscope a few years later, I found out that the typical traits of a dog (my Chinese Star sign) are traits that I had exhibited all my life.

When it came to my human engineering, it was precisely the same. Sure, it could all be absolutely bullshit, and I totally understand the idea of what mentalists do, which is to probe you or find traits that are so common to everybody so that you believe what they tell you is specific to you because actually, on some level is specific to everyone. I totally get it.

But for me, there was no doubt I'd spent my whole life trying to communicate with people. Communication was my thing. At 12, I used to draw comic strips about my school friends. I had attempted to write my first book at the age of 13. My favourite type of music was rap music, an art form closest to speaking, making it the most effective form of musical communication. I've been told in university by my friends I had the art of eloquence, which was the ability to give good speeches and to explain things to people in clear and entertaining ways, or, as my wonderful friend Sophia Aziz once put it, 'I could talk the hind legs off of a donkey'.

Strangely enough, when I initially tried to pursue a career in sales, I was the worst salesman on the floor. This painful experience and many identical ones that followed taught me that although I could maybe talk the hind legs off of a donkey, I couldn't do it just for material gains and definitely not if it was not to the donkey's benefit. I couldn't do it if I was lying or trying to trick them. Sure, I could talk the hind legs off a donkey, but only if I was telling the truth and saying something beneficial to them. I couldn't apply the art of eloquence to lies.

So, although I'm not a guru or an expert in any of the topics presented in this book, I have always believed that your life experience is valid. Before the advent of social media, I used to tell people, particularly people of a certain age, that they should write a book. As a young man in my 20s, I used to love talking to people in their 60s and 70s. Soaking up their experiences of life, how things were for them, how things were in the world before I was born or before I could understand what they had been through. I listened intently to what they had learned; it was like my favourite thing. I told so many of them that they had a book in them and that they should write that book. If they didn't want to write it, they should dictate it to somebody, just share their lives with the world.

Then social media came along, and as technology does, it has sped up that ability. Now, people get to write their books daily through social media posts.

My point is that although I'm not a guru or an expert or a sage at any of this stuff, I genuinely hope that my experience is helpful to other people. And suppose I have truly been blessed with the art of eloquence, and it is truly my destiny to take things that some people may find complicated and explain them in a simplified way. In that case, my wish is that this book does exactly that and helps people see a practical aspect or viewpoint of concepts which they may otherwise have passed over as hippie shit and, in that way, embellish and improve their lives.

How You Learned To Hate the Woo-Woo

So, you were living your life based on the same paradigm of reality that almost everyone has. We all have to subscribe to it because we live in a world that we all have to share, and in order to share the world, we have to agree on the nature of reality.

We are aware that gravity exists and if you pick up a pen, hold it high in the air and let go of it, it will fall. We know that our senses are the tools we use to send information to our brain. So, if the sun shines, we might feel hot. If we fall into the water, we'll feel wet. Suppose I use my eyes, and I see one car crash into another. In that case, I've witnessed a car crash, and anybody else in that same environment would have witnessed the same thing. We agree on the consensus of a 12-month year with varying numbers of days, even though a much more logical approach would be to have a 13-month year with exactly 30 days. We even take this as far as to move time every year. It is a bizarre system by which we put our clocks forwards and backwards, leaving anyone who disagrees with this consensus an hour early or late for six months because everybody else is now on a new timescale. These are some of the consensuses we all agree on and abide by to live together.

Then, on top of this consensus, we have society. Society gives us our rules; some are moral, and some are legal. One legal rule, for example, is that if I take something from somebody that does not belong to me and refuse to return it, that's called theft. Legally, that person can go to the police, who were established by the government, to take me to the courts, which is one of the systems that we put in place to recover stolen goods and penalise me. These rules vary from society to society.

I know this is all pretty obvious, but I wanted to establish a baseline from which we can work.

Then, we have moral rules, which vary from place to place. A common moral rule is that children who do not have the mental capacity of an adult are not able to make certain decisions. We cannot consider that, in their undeveloped and uneducated state, they are not fully capable of giving consent. So, it is wrong to assume consent from a child. It's morally wrong for us to try to get them to make certain decisions, such as smoking nicotine, taking drugs, drinking alcohol or engaging in sexual activity. We believe in this so strongly that we made this moral rule a legal rule.

Then, there are moral 'rules' that were not legal. For example, a 70-year-old man shouldn't date an 18-year-old girl. Even though there's nothing legally wrong with this in most countries, we still judge whether it's right or wrong. We make a moral judgment that a mother shouldn't date the best friend of her son, or a man shouldn't date their best friend's ex-wife and definitely not his daughter. There's no law against it, but many consider these things morally wrong. These are just a few ideas regarding the consensuses we all sign up for when we agree to be a part of society.

The strange thing about this consensus is that we're forever meeting people who don't agree, and the funniest thing about the people who don't agree is they're the people who change the world. Without going too deeply into it, notable examples would be people like Galileo Galilei, Charles Darwin, Albert Einstein and Nikola Tesla, Rosa Parks, Emmeline Pankhurst, Mahatma Gandhi, Martin Luther King or Harvey Bernard Milk.

These people change the world because so many of the rules that we all agree to via consensus are about what we can't do and what's not possible. We live in a world that's very much based on an agreement of Cannot. You can't do this, you can't do that, you can't do this, you shouldn't do that. That is the vast majority of our consensus. Little of our consensus is about what we should do. Very little of it suggests that you should do this, or you should do that, or you can do this, and you can do that.

We live in a null-void consensus, which is why the people with the can-do attitudes, the people who are willing to defy the no's, the nots, the can'ts, I wouldn't dare, or you'll never make it. These are the people who change the world. Because once you grow that muscle of consistently being able to do that, the muscle that teaches you to say yes when everyone else is saying no. You begin to grow and gain momentum against the world of 'nots' and power and strength into the world of cans, coulds, wills and musts. And the more you achieve, the more you can achieve. In precisely the same way that the more things you think you can't do becomes an ever-decreasing circle of more and more things you think you can't do, the more you achieve becomes an ever-increasing circle of more and more things you can achieve.

But that's just laying out the playing field.

The reality of how we learn to hate the woo-woo is that one day while living in your world of nots, the world that everybody around you agrees with and lives within the parameters of, you meet somebody different. It may have been one of your friends who recently had a 'realisation' or maybe a stranger, but they had that glazed look in their eye, the one that slightly unnerves you.

So, whilst you were wondering if they were on drugs, they started to tell you about a different world and a different reality. Well, not a different reality per se, but a different way to see the exact same reality that you're living in. They start to tell you that the world you're living in is precisely the same one they're living in, but they see it completely differently. This offended your sensibilities because the basic concept of reality defines that there's only one way to see the world, the real way. The world only exists in one way, and it exists in the way that you see it. You know this because you see it the same way everyone else sees it, so it must be correct. The world exists within the legal lines that you accept and abide by and the moral lines that most people agree to and frown upon the people who step outside, even though they can't do anything legally against them. It exists within the physical lines regarding the things you can and can't see because they do or don't exist. Things such as aliens, ghosts, telepathy, and energy patterns don't exist. You know they don't exist because science has never proven that they do. It's never been on the six o'clock news for anybody to say that any of these things are actually reality. They're just fantasies from people who want to believe or the insanities of people who have not yet demonstrated their insanity to the extent that they're put in a nice, safe home with padded walls, a comfortable jacket that zips up from the back and kept away from the rest of society.

But this person, or these people who you met, not only annoyed your sensibility by challenging your view of what was real, they angered you with their stupidity for believing things outside of the paradigm of the society that everybody agreed on. This is bizarre because, within all of the rules, laws and morals that you live by, there are things that you disagree with. You don't agree with everything morally accepted, legally accepted, or outlawed. That is why laws change. I mean, the outrage from the requirement to wear masks and quarantine during the 2020 COVID-19 outbreak shows how many people disagreed with the so-called consensus. More and more people are diving down conspiracy theory rabbit holes simply because when they're introduced to the fact that they don't agree with the consensus in society, it's such a shock to them that they follow whatever that particular disagreement is down a trail that takes them to all kinds of places that they had no intention of going. Whether it is an anti-vaxxer, QAnon, a believer in the great reset, the Illuminati, or other worldwide government conspiracies, a simple society says this, but I'm not sure I will get them there.

I'm not saying any of these things are not true. Well, except for QAnon, which was complete and utter bullshit. I'm just saying it's been interesting for me to see people dive down these rabbit holes as they discover that they actually don't believe in everything they're told. As they finally separate themselves from the consensus and start to explore this newfound mental freedom, it's very easy for them to be manipulated and dragged very far away from where they started into mental places, which they never planned to be.

However, all they needed to do was simply understand that maybe the consensus they had been given wasn't perfect. Maybe everything that they had been taught wasn't correct. Perhaps they can be a bit more objective in how they look, not only at this one thing but at all things, including some of the things they were being told by this long-haired, googly-eyed exponent of the woo.

But they could not because this woo-woo person not only offended their sensibilities in terms of confronting beliefs which they had accepted their whole life, they also annoyed the living shit out of them. They were probably Pollyanna. They told them things like everything happens for a reason, not something you wanted to hear when your best friend or your child had died; your preacher didn't even tell you that one. They said to you that no matter what happens in life, everything turns out good again, something that nobody else in the world has ever proven. Even your parents didn't tell you that, and your parents told you that Father Christmas was real. They said that the route to success was not created by your work; it was an internal game of mastery over yourself; hmm, well, your boss never told you that, and he is in charge of promoting you. They told you that all life is energy that we can't see, but we can learn to manipulate it. They told you things that your best friend never told you, that your mom and dad never told you, that your auntie or your uncle never told you, the news never told you, your favourite TV show never told you, stuff that absolutely nobody fucking ever told you. And to top it all off, they had absolutely no proof.

And you said to yourself, 'We're sending rovers to the moon. We've built a telescope that can see a trillion galaxies. We have created artificial intelligence. We've done all these things, and yet you're trying to tell me that there are energy patterns in the world that I can't see that scientists haven't discovered yet, but somehow you know about.'

They told you that you had the ability to mould and define what happens in your life. This was probably the greatest offence to you because you said to yourself, 'Listen, dickhead, if I could mould and define what happened to me in my life, I wouldn't be in the shitty job, in the shitty situation, in the shitty marriage within the shitty apartment, driving a shitty car. I'd be driving a luxurious car, living in a luxurious apartment with my dream wife and doing absolutely nothing because I would have won the lottery.' They told you all these things that were so highly offensive to you. You were offended that they said them and offended that they believed them. No matter how much you argued with them about what was obviously the actual reality (aka the paradigm you share with everybody else) they consistently argued back that this was not the case.

They told you that there was another reality running absolutely parallel with the one that you existed in, a reality in which different people could live differently and do different things and that you could join them. Fuck them,' you thought. 'Fucking idiot, that guy's so annoying. That woman is such a pain in the ass.' They really annoyed you, and you never took a moment to think about why they annoyed you so much. They annoyed you so much because not only were they challenging your paradigm of reality, but they were telling you something that you knew deep down was true, and the inkling of the truth that you could not engage with is what caused the anger.

How do I know this? Because it has happened to me on more than one occasion, particularly when someone told me something true about myself that I didn't want to accept or acknowledge.

I remember my overriding thought was, 'How dare that person, who I barely know, knows me better than myself' and 'How dare they know that truth about me.'

I immediately went to indignation and annoyance. In fact, I went straight to anger.

I remember the first time I was told that everything that happens to you is your fault, which I'm still struggling with. I was absolutely outraged. Coming from the environment that I grew up in, with a lot of poverty, having friends who were rape survivors, people who got themselves into the wrong place at the wrong time and had been stabbed or robbed, and people who'd spend their lives fighting to get out of poverty, being told that everything that happens to you is your own fault was the most egregious offensive thing anybody could have said to me with words out of their mouth.

Maybe because the person who said it didn't have the depth to give it a good explanation or the skill to present it in a way that wasn't as offensive and would be more palatable.

But having grown up with domestic abuse as a child. Being told that the abuse I had to witness and suffer was my fault was not something that I wanted to hear. 'Fuck you,' I said. 'You fucking lunatic. Don't come to me with that fucking bullshit.' And so on and so forth.

That's how we learn to hate the woo-woo. That's probably why it took me so many years, and two tries to get to a point where I could actually start to see the practicality and engage in what I'd always previously thought of as woo-woo thoughts, beliefs, and practices.

That's the reason why it is so important to me now, even with the limited amount of knowledge I have to write this book. Let me repeat, I'm not a PhD, I'm not even a psychologist or therapist, I'm not a guru, or an enlightened master or even a dedicated follower. I'm not any of these things. But in one of my meditation sessions, I was given the inspiration, the intuition.

I didn't even ask what to do. It just came to me that I should write this book to give my own perspective on the practical basis, the practical foundations of what I call hippie shit. The woo-woo that so many people have been taught to hate because it was introduced to them by kale-munching, long-haired robe-wearing, people walking in Jesus creepers, who most people don't think represent anything to do with their real life. In fact, most people see them as people who live outside of normal society and, therefore, have nothing to teach them.

The aim of this book is to help people who would be reviled and turned off by anybody who looked like that and reviled and turned off by anybody who talked like that to see that there is something that they can learn and benefit from these types of spiritual teachings, particularly when used from their practical basis.

I will start with the most practical uses of these philosophies, the most practical understandings or interpretations of these philosophies, and then show how those practicalities can be scaled up to whatever level of woo-woo your mind can be comfortable with. Therefore, please feel free to stop at any point that the woo-woo stuff goes too far.

Because the point of this book isn't to drag you kicking and screaming into the world of woo-woo. This book aims to give you some practical advice, tips, tricks, and practices that improve your life, and maybe offer you a glimpse of another way of looking at the world. A way of looking at the world, which you can leave for good if you already have all that you need or explore more and scale up to varying levels of woo-woo until you find a level which makes you uncomfortable. At this point, you should stop and maybe return to that practice and not go to another level until you're more comfortable and willing to accept that new concept or paradigm of life.

Consensus

Just two more points on consensus for the previous chapter.

The problem with the consensus we experience through our eyes and ears, nose and touch, is although we are 100% resolute that that consensus is the reality, the science that we rely on actually proves that our senses are poor, or at least not perfect vessels for us to use in terms of creating that consensus in the first place. The best examples are the scientific proof that what we hear can be manipulated by what we see.

In the TV drama *The Irrational*, the professor plays an audio and asks his students to write down what they hear. They all agreed unanimously. Then, he replays the video with the audio subtitled. They realise that although it sounded like the crowd was saying one thing, with the changing subtitles, they were easily led to believe that the crowd was saying something completely different. He concludes, 'It's freaky, isn't it? You heard the same thing every single time. Our eyes and ears take in electrical signals, which our brains interpret based on our expectations. We don't see reality. We see our reality.' 'Wide-backed Virgina Camilla', anyone?

The same result can be achieved by people who look at drawings, which, from one angle, look like one thing, but when moved around, you realise that they are completely different.

Our brain is constantly trying to make sense of what it sees, hears, smells, and touches, but trying to make sense of these things based on previous information doesn't mean that the conclusions it draws are always correct.

The mere fact that your brain is using previous information to decide what it is seeing, smelling, touching, or experiencing is why it can be misled. Your previous information creates the foundations for your belief of what you are seeing, smelling, touching, or feeling, and this is what points to the fact that the bedrock of absolutely everything in your reality is what you were previously told.

There is a very good reason for this: in general, the brain is a deletion machine. When you wake up in the morning, you don't want your brain to look at the pillow that you've been sleeping on as if it has never seen it before, and it's a totally new item requiring you to spend an hour examining it.

And then when you get up in the morning, you don't want your brain to have to work out how to urinate again and spend half an hour doing that, making a mess on the floor every single day of your life. Your brain is super-efficient at learning things and accepting what they are. It knows what to do with them and how to use them and then includes that information into its database of knowledge so that it can use them and move on without having to reanalyse and pay attention to them every single day. This is one of the greatest aspects of the human brain, but it also creates limitations. The limitations it creates are that whatever's been programmed into it in the past will be accepted as the foundation and the blueprint for the reality of whatever's happening right now. And this is the reason why it's so difficult for us to break a consensus. Because if you wake up and look at an object and think, this is the pillow I've been sleeping on, but it actually isn't. It's something different. Your brain must take the time to make that differentiation, that it looks like a pillow, but it isn't, and then work out what it is.

And for most of us in our busy lives, there's really no time for this. It looks like a pillow, seems like a pillow, feels like a pillow, then it's the pillow. Let's move on.

The key here is, how much does this affect our life when we get it wrong? If we thought somebody was chanting a racist slur, but what they were saying simply 'sounded' like an offensive word. There is a huge difference between how we will respond and how we should. If We thought we saw a man hit a woman, but actually, what we really saw was a man trying to dust off a woman who'd fallen into a spider's nest and had been covered in spiders (something we didn't notice from a distance), again, our perception of reality will be flawed and so will our reactions. These are not particularly great examples, but now you get the point, I'm sure you can make your own.

It's evident that what we are led to believe by our programming, by our past, by the consensus that we were given from our environment, our teachers, our leaders, your town's folk, your parents, your teachers, your preachers, your best friends, everybody that you grew up with. The consensus we're given by them creates the basis for what we go ahead and believe in in the future, and this consensus can be anywhere from unhelpfully limiting to devastating and detrimental to our lives.

Limiting would be thinking that you can only reach so far in life because everyone in your life is average. Everyone in your family has been average, everyone in your town is average, and an average life is the best that anyone can expect. Devastating and detrimental could be somebody who lives just one town over, who believes that no one ever had a chance in his family and that everyone in his town is a criminal or corrupt. There are no good opportunities, and the only way to get through life is to take from other people, whether that means robbing, stealing, killing, raping, as their norm.

If robbing, stealing, killing or raping are normal, then this person's life is going to be detrimental, not just to themselves, but to everyone around them. This will be built on the consensus of what they grew up with, which led to a set of beliefs as to what the world is and a set of actions as to what to do in this world they believe they live in. The same world that you live in, just overlaid with a completely different belief set. Well, that's the key. The woo-woo does precisely the same thing, but in contrast, whereas that person has a belief set that is primarily negative in how they see the world, the woo-woo has a mainly positive worldview. In the way that the previous person's worldview is frighteningly negative, dangerously pessimistic and annoyingly destructive for any of us who have to come into contact with them, the woo-woo person's attitude of the worldview is, unreasonably positive, ridiculously optimistic and annoyingly cheerful to us when we come into contact with them.

But let's keep it real. If you had to deal with one of the two, which would you choose?

Felix Joseph

SCIENCE

Science and Hippie Shit

I love science. Above all, I see myself as a practical, common-sense type of person, which might seem strange to someone whose nature is rooted in the arts, but there you go. I've been in business for 24 years; before that, I worked as a senior technical consultant in the information technology arena. In that field, practical solutions to real-world problems and fixing things were the order of the day. None of this highfalutin 'How it should be? Wouldn't it be nice? Wouldn't the world be better? Shouldn't we just imagine, visualise, conceptualise, hypothesise?' No, none of that. It was more like, 'This doesn't work; it should be working this way. Get it done; we're losing money.' That's my IT background. Business is much the same; it's about making money, getting things up and running, making them deliver, and making them profitable. Or, if necessary, cutting losses, rationalising, and getting back within revenue margins; that's my business background.

So, for someone with this background, I'm always amazed at how little science actually knows. Now, admittedly, I'm not a scientist, just a science enthusiast, and ever since I left school, I've not had any real scientific study. When I worked in IT, I wasn't in development; I was in support. Someone else built the system; I learned how to maintain it, support it, fix it when things went wrong, and suggest improvements or integrate it into other systems. Now, in business, no matter how you cut it, the aim is to create a product that solves a problem, sell it, deliver the product, make a profit, run and scale the business, and manage the staff, all practical aspects. So, I didn't have much time to investigate science just because I loved the field.

Funnily enough, it was only recently, when I started exploring spiritual concepts to increase my business effectiveness, that I found time to investigate science. Many years ago, when I worked in IT, I stopped reading fiction and started studying for various systems accreditations. Then, when I went into business, I started reading about business. Then, as I delved into spiritual concepts, I not only read those books, but I also began exploring science. And when I did, I was bowled over by the realisation that although we are inundated with the extraordinary levels of the new scientific discoveries we have made since the eighteenth century, we don't know that much.

We say that gravity exists, but what gravity is is still being debated. We can harness electricity and understand that if current goes from positive to negative, i.e., electrons flow from negative to positive, we can use electricity to do many things. But again, we have yet to have a firm consensus on what electricity actually is. Imagine that? We have powered our whole world with this phenomenon that we can use, but we don't fully understand it.

This brings me to a crucial point: if so, much of what we consider the foundation of our scientific world, principles like gravity and electricity, are based on phenomena that we don't truly understand, why do scientists persist in belittling and discrediting religion and spirituality due to our lack of understanding of them? I'll tell you why: because they believe they can put these scientific principles, like electricity, in a laboratory and get a calculated and repeatable result. Meanwhile, when people talk about religion or spirituality and say, 'Do this, and you'll get that result,' those results often seem less repeatable or at least not scientifically reproducible. Or do they?

If you look at the work of people like José Silva, who taught spiritual principles of meditation and visualisation, he took a scientific approach and produced predictable and repeatable results. Dr Joe Dispenza also has years' worth of highly scientific experiments with repeatable results for meditation and visualisation. Yet, amongst scientific purists, these results were not widely accepted. The question is, why? I think it's because our society is at a turning point, much like a road-to-Damascus moment. Hypothetically, we are approaching a time when we'll discover that the Earth isn't flat—it is indeed round. And all the scientists who had previously devoted their knowledge and beliefs to the flat-Earth theory (i.e. those who ridicule all things spiritual) will soon be in for a rude awakening when they learn from more advanced and open-minded scientists that the world is, in fact, actually round (i.e. Spiritual Phenomenon is real).

I've always been interested in science and religion as interconnected fields because I was taught that this is how it was in ancient times. Egyptian, Sumerian, and Dogon cultures were cultures in which the scientist was also the chief priest. There are many writings about this in history. Some say it was 16th-century thinkers such as Galileo and Newton, others 18th-century philosophers such as Kant and Rousseau who caused science and religion to part ways and become separate disciplines. So, I've always felt validated in my view that science and religion should be the same thing. As we progress, more scientists are reaching conclusions that align with what religious people have been saying for decades, if not millenniums. Quantum mechanics, quantum physics, and string theory all suggest that the world could actually be a holographic 3D illusion. This concept was once dismissed by science as spiritual nonsense, fantasy or religious dogma, but now the same scientific investigations validate these ancient religious and philosophical teachings as fact.

You Don't Know What You Don't Know

So, if you're practical, it means that you don't believe anything that can't be proven; science is, after all, evidence-based theory. For most people, this means that they only follow things accepted by science because these things have gone through analytical hypotheses and rigorous testing and, as such, can be proven true. I love this way of looking at things because, as I said, I am a huge fan of science. But as I got to my 50s and started researching science out of personal interest and enjoyment, I was pretty amazed because one repeatable theme kept coming up. Things that I thought we knew, things that I thought had 100% been proven, were not. They were just the best suggestions we have yet, and most of them were still seriously being debated. Now, obviously, this may have changed from the time of writing, but today, if you Google or, better yet, ask an AI large language model such as ChatGPT, Co-pilot, or Claude, what is the controversy surrounding the understanding and definition of electricity you will get an answer similar to the following.

1. *Nature of electric charge: There's ongoing discussion about what electric charge fundamentally is. While we can describe its effects, the underlying nature of charge remains somewhat mysterious.*

2. *Is electricity energy or a force? Electricity is often casually referred to as a form of energy, but it's more accurately described as a set of phenomena resulting from the presence and flow of electric charge.*

3. *Wave-particle duality: In quantum mechanics, electricity exhibits both wavelike and particle-like properties, challenging classical definitions.*

4. *Field theory vs. action at a distance:*

    There are different ways to conceptualise how electric forces are transmitted - through fields or as action at a distance.

5. *Pedagogical debates:*

    There are ongoing discussions about the best ways to teach and explain electrical concepts, especially at introductory levels.

This absolutely blew my mind. We can send a rover to Mars, but we have no concrete idea what the electricity we use to power it is, only how to use it. This is absolutely mind-boggling.

Now, these controversies don't generally affect practical applications of electricity; I mean, everything we use in the modern world is 100% reliant on it, yet we, at a very deep philosophical level, do not yet fully understand it.

Okay, let's take it to the biological sciences. Can you provide a specific list of things science does not currently understand about 'How the brain works?' Again, let's ask one of the LLMs.

Your search will start by telling you, 'The human brain remains one of the most complex and mysterious organs in our body.'

Amongst the things that science still struggles to fully understand or explain:

1. *Consciousness: The nature of consciousness and how it emerges from neural activity is still a profound mystery. Scientists debate various theories, but there's no consensus on how subjective experiences arise from physical processes in the brain.*

2. *Memory formation and retrieval: While we know some basics about memory, the precise mechanisms of how memories are encoded, stored, and retrieved are not fully understood. Particularly puzzling is how the brain stores vast amounts of information in such a compact space.*

3. *Sleep and dreaming: Despite extensive research, the fundamental purpose of sleep remains unclear. Similarly, the function and meaning of dreams continue to elude scientific explanation.*

4. *Neuroplasticity limits: While we know the brain can rewire itself, we don't fully understand the limits of this plasticity or how to optimally harness it for recovery from brain injuries or learning.*

5. *Individual differences in intelligence: The neurological basis for variations in cognitive abilities between individuals is not well understood. What exactly makes one brain 'smarter' than another is still a matter of debate.*

6. *The placebo effect: While well-documented, the neurological mechanisms behind the placebo effect (and its opposite, the nocebo effect) still need to be fully explained.*

We can add dark energy, dark matter, and the recent discoveries made by the James Webb telescope to this list. And don't even get me started on Time or Gravity. Get the picture.

The point is that the more you investigate science, no matter the discipline, one reoccurring theme will emerge. Frankly, considering our extensive scientific knowledge, we don't really know shit.

And when you take this in perspective and really think about all the things that we don't really know or understand, things that we only know how to use, you will understand why this is my foundation for paying attention to some of this hippie shit. This is my explanation for my interest in some of this esoteric knowledge. Because just like electricity, or the human brain, or gravity, it becomes clear that you don't have to know exactly how it works. All you need to know is that it can be proven to work consistently enough to use it to get the results you are after.

The Miracle of Birth

While looking at what we think we know, aka science, I think I would be remiss if I didn't mention the miracle. No, not a miracle I am going to perform, although after bearing two of my children, I am sure that this a procedure that my wife would love to see me suffer. But alas, I do not have such abilities even if such a thing were possible. Yet this miracle occurs, as predicted by Google at the time of writing, 278 times every minute. I am, of course, talking about the miracle of birth.

The problem with the human condition is that, in mental terms, we are deletion creatures (more on this later). Through this constant deletion, we become so accustomed to the things around us that we no longer pay attention to the miraculous and begin to see it as ordinary. And by paying it less attention, we start to diminish its importance and promote the importance of much lesser things.

So it is with the miracle of birth. I love the miracle of birth and have used it for many years to help people who are depressed, believe that they are worthless or that they have no purpose and there's no point being here.

I use it to point out exactly how amazing they are just by being here before they have done anything. I point out that they beat approximately three hundred million other sperm ejaculated that could have made it to fertilise the egg. Out of all of that competition, they are the ones who made it through.

I explain that they went through all of the other obstacles and rigours of their growth as a foetus, along with the other potential dangers which could have aborted their birth. They passed all of that to be born into this world as an infant who had absolutely no ability to take care of themselves but were born to parents or given to guardians who (however poorly) raised them into a fully grown human adult, avoiding all the pitfalls, illnesses and other ways that they could have died along the way.

Their view of the world is, I don't matter, nothing's important, I'm no good, I'm no use. But if you put it in this perspective, these negative self-opinions are entirely impossible. The only way this whole process could have happened is if you are indeed important, you are special, you are needed, you are of use. A contradiction to this fact could possibly exist if it were something that came from your own mind. Because objectively, the facts very clearly speak for themselves.

Neil Degrass Tyson talks about all the people who never lived on this planet. He says, and I paraphrase…

'Most people who could ever exist will never even be born. If you look at the human genome You can make all kinds of people with the human genome. There are so many possibilities to rearrange it. The things that make us unique, such as tall or short, dark-skinned or lighter skinned, etc. So how many total humans are possible? Well, based on the potential it's a billion trillion, trillion or maybe even more. So, let's be clear, if you were born you are most definitely unique and one of the lucky ones.'

But as he was expounding on the views of Dr Richard Hawkins, I will paraphrase him as well…

'Most people are never going to die because they are never going to be born. The potential people who could have been here in my place, but who never exist, will outnumber the sand grains of Sahara and include greater scientists, musicians and artists than they world has ever known. Yet it is you and I, in our ordinariness that are here. We privileged few who won the lottery, against all odds.'

And just in case you have a scientifically biased mind, let's look at that lottery for a second…

Of the three hundred million sperm released during sex, all vying for the same goal, the chance to fertilise the egg and motion the potential for life. Each sperm and each egg carry a completely unique genetic code. The number of potential combinations of chromosomes in each sperm or egg based on generational possibilities gives rise to seventy trillion different potential genetic accommodations.

Now let's talk about your parents. Think about your lineage, parents, grandparents, and great-grandparents; think about each generation. Consider how many things had to go right for them to have been alive long enough to bear and raise you. They had to survive disease and endure famine and wars. Go back a few hundred years, and we can add predators, floods, Tornados, wildfires and ice ages to this list, just to have survived to be the parents of the parents of your parents.

Then add the potential combinations of the genetic material of these ancestors and look. I won't go into the numbers on the probabilities here, but I assure you that they run into thousands of zeros. But the most important zero you need to be concerned with is the fact that based on all of these immeasurable circumstances, the probability of you existing in your exact form is zero.

So, I think the final word in all of this statistical and probability talk should go back to Neil Degrass Tyson…

'So, no matter what your lot is in life, whether you are disabled or have a disease or in poverty or in mental anguish, whatever you are going through the key thing at the end of the day is not your problem, but the very fact that you're alive in the first place as opposed to not having ever been born. And you are not yet dead.'

So, if you ever feel down, useless, or unworthy, just remember that you have already won the hardest race imaginable.

And if I haven't beaten you over the head with this concept enough, can I add the final blow which is the age in which you were born. If you are alive in the 21st century, you were born into a veritable golden age.

Fast food, medical breakthroughs, cars, planes, and computers are all things that we take for granted. And if all of that wasn't enough, we have AI now, for god's sake. Even the poorest of us in the West have a better basic living standard than kings and queens 300 years ago, so to put it simply, we've never had it so good, and we have a lot to be grateful for.

We know that there are approximately seven billion people on this planet now, and our research shows that many billions of people have lived on it since the beginning of time.

But we don't talk about the trillions of people who could have existed but never did.

Those are all the people who you beat to the punch. They prove that you are special because they could have existed but didn't, and you do.

So, you have absolutely no foundation to believe that you are not important, special, or valuable. You are, you are, and you are.

The Subconscious Mind

Continuing with our exploration into science, I'm hoping you're aware of the trillions of bacteria in your body right now as you read this book. Like the functions performed by your subconscious mind (which we will get into in a moment), you have absolutely no idea what these things are doing. Generally, all that most of us are aware of is that there are what we call good and bad bacteria. The good bacteria are busily performing jobs that aid your digestion, general gut health, and other healthy functions of your body. In contrast, the bad bacteria can make you sick. Now, you have no control over any of this; it all happens without your active participation.

One of the most interesting things are the parasites in your skin, which again perform multiple functions without your conscious control or direction.

In fact, the only control we have over the majority of the things that go on with our body on a day-to-day, minute-to-minute basis is the control our mind has to will the limbs of our body to do things. If you tell yourself to jump over a gorge in a free running exercise, you can make your body jump over that gorge. You could jump and land after somersaulting to the applause of your friends, or you could miss your landing spot and end up in hospital. But when it comes to your body's actual day-by-day, moment-moment maintenance, you have very little to do. Let's be clear, you don't even know when to eat. Your body tells you with signals of hunger. You don't know when to sleep. Your body tells you when you become tired. You don't administer jack shit when it comes to running your body. Without your conscious knowledge, your body is regulating your temperature, controlling your heartbeat, breaking down food in your digestive system, detoxifying waste products from your body, regulating your cells and numerous other activities, all going on whilst you watch Netflix with the intent to get the person with you to chill. Understanding this just leaves you two potential conclusions: either this bizarrely complicated system, more complicated than any computer we've ever invented, runs by accident, or it runs by design. A deep explanation of the subconscious mind is far beyond the parameters of this book. But for a fuller understanding of it, I suggest reading *The Power of the Subconscious Mind* by Dr Jr Murphy,

The Brain Explained

Now that we have broached the subject of everything being run in your body by an intelligence that is not consciously yours, before we go any further, let's break down the possible architecture of the human brain. I say a possible architecture because, as I explained, our scientific knowledge is not only devastatingly limited but ever-changing and evolving, so what we think we know is only really what we think we know for now. Plus, as the great neurophysiologist Charles Sherrington is quoted as saying, 'What we know about the human brain would not change much if we just assumed that it was stuffed with cotton wool.' So there.

The best explanation of the brain I have heard comes from Emily Fletcher, founder of the M Word meditation program. She describes the brain as a computer network. She said, and I paraphrase, think of the brain as a computer network with a processor, database, and broadcasting/receiving station. This network is split into two parts.

The first part (the left side of your brain) functions like a computer. Its job is to analyse and calculate, processing the information it receives to find the correct answers to the questions asked. Your left brain is the part of the computer system that processes all the information. Just like a desktop computer, it has peripherals that feed it information. These are called your eyes, ears, nose, skin, etc., and your left brain processes the data given to it by these peripherals to make the best decision. You should be familiar with this part; this is the analytical brain we are all taught to rely on and use as our sole foundation for truth.

The second part of the brain (the right side of your brain) is like a Wi-Fi router. This is the broadcaster and receiver. That's what connects to the internet. In this example, the internet is everything that your brain can connect to, which is outside of itself.

It sends out messages like, 'I don't know how to do this,' or 'How can I solve that?' or usually just 'Help!!!!'—basically asking for information from outside sources, information that is not already on its database and not accessible via one of its peripherals. And when it sends out messages on the Wi-Fi, it receives responses like 'Go to the old inn, you will find your solution there', or 'Call your old school friend Tom, he will help you to get a job', or 'be careful driving around the next bend there is danger ahead'. In the realm of hippie shit, we might refer to this as intuition, connecting to the all, tapping into the collective consciousness (i.e. the thoughts and knowledge in the brains of other people), connecting with your higher self, even angelic beings, communing with the infinite intelligence, or messages from God,—whatever label you prefer. My personal belief is that we can use it to do all of these things.

How else could we intuit these things if they come from outside ourselves? I mean, if you have a computer, and you only have so much information about Plumbing on the hard drive and memory. If you wanted more information about Plumbing, you'd search on the internet. If you have a good browser and clear search terms, you can find more information about Plumbing on the internet. Then, if you wanted to, you could download the information to your hard drive to analyse and, if deemed valid, decide how you want to use it.

I think this is a really good way to see the balance between the left and right sides of the brain. The left side is a processing station for the information that you have already learned, and the right side is a broadcasting/receiving station that allows you to access information that originates from outside of yourself—information that you do not currently know.

This Wi-Fi gives you access to frequencies of reception that include but are not limited to, your own intuition, the thoughts of other people just like you, the intuition of your higher self, other entities (people refer to

Angels or Aliens), and finally, the infinite intelligence, which some believe is the universal power or God itself.

Now, does this actually exist? This is where some might argue that the spontaneous realisation of things that you didn't previously know is just coincidence.

Well, I appreciate the concept that your brain has receiving abilities is all a bit woo-woo. So, let's say that, at the very least, the Wi-Fi side of your brain has been scientifically proven to be able to receive transmissions from other human beings (commonly known as Telekinesis) and intuition from sources that we do not fully understand.

In practice, I think that most of us have experienced moments that suggest our brain is indeed a broadcasting and receiving station. Whether it's thinking of someone and having them call you or thinking of them and then bumping into them five minutes later in person, sensing danger just in time to avoid a car crash, or dreading something only for it to appear, we all have countless examples of this. Yet, we usually dismiss these experiences as coincidence because that's what we're taught.

But if we really took the time to analyse these moments, we might see something different; we might see that our brain has a broadcasting and receiving station. The left side processes and analyses, while the right side sends out requests and receives information or something like that. This is why musicians often say if you don't write down that idea for a song, someone else will. Even scientists have remarked that if they hadn't published a particular theory, someone else would have come up with it, eventually. This is where inventions come from. How many inventors have sworn that the solution to the problem came to them spontaneously? 'Eureka!!!!' they shout as a solution to their problem appears without their analytical intervention.

The information is out there, in the ether, and we pick it up from each other. This is the basis of the concept of 'use it or lose it.' The higher power wants these things to exist, so it broadcasts them out. You receive it, and if you don't do anything with it, then it will broadcast it to someone else, leaving you to see it created by them while you tell your friends, 'You know I had that exact same idea months ago.'

This brings us to the concept of frequency. Suppose you accept that the brain is a broadcasting and receiving station. In that case, it's easier to understand how the law of attraction works. More than just the law of attraction, there's the law of resonance, the law of expectation, and more. But I don't want to dive too deep into all of the universal laws; I mean, this is practical hippie shit, not a deep dive into woo-woo, woah-woah, hold on, you're going too far there, Hippie shit. But the point is that if your brain is sending and receiving signals, you must be on the right frequency to get the desired results.

You can't broadcast on FM and expect to receive a message on AM. For example, let's say that you've had a bad day. I mean, a real stinker and you are frustrated, pissed off, and mad. If this causes you to send out low-energy signals (let's call low-energy signals broadcasting on AM), and you're tuned into that same low-energy frequency. On that frequency, you'll only be able to receive things that align with that frequency, other things being broadcast on the AM frequency, such as frustration, anger, and disappointment.

But if you had a great day and are full of gratitude and, as such, you're broadcasting on FM, sending out high-energy, positive vibes, you'll receive things that match that frequency. That's the key to all this positive-thinking stuff. If you accept the theory that your brain is a broadcasting and receiving station, it's not a big leap to understand that you need to be on the right frequency to receive what you want. You'll never get high-frequency results from a low-energy state, and vice versa. These concepts will be explored more as we delve deeper into this book, so if this is feeling a little woo-woo to you already, buckle up.

Computer Programs and Our Brain

My final point about science is that I find its circular nature very interesting. The best examples I have of this are the modern computer and the human brain. I definitely find it intriguing that humans created an item called a computer, which actually works in a very similar way to the human brain (before we knew that the human brain worked like that).

I don't know if it's a form of egotism, but it does sound very biblical in terms of 'let us create something in our own image', and now we have AI taking this concept one step further. I hear very often how similar the brain works to a computer, particularly in terms of the hippie shit concept of programming the subconscious mind.

Whether you call it the subconscious mind or the impersonal mind, scientists still debate whether this aspect of the mind exists. Nobody debates that your body is performing millions of functions to keep you alive without being consciously instructed to; the debate only concerns if this is conducted by a subconscious mind, and if it is, then do we have access to it? But many of those from the scientific fraternity who accept its existence are quite happy to agree that it works by being programmed very similar to a computer. When I worked in Information Technology, there was a saying that we learned from the computer programmers, the saying was 'shit in, shit out'. This alluded to the fact that if you write a poor program and input it into a computer, then the computer will output poor results; well, this applies to the human brain as much as the computer. Suppose the human brain runs on programs that are given to it, and it is totally impartial to the programs (meaning that it doesn't judge their quality; it just carries out the program's instructions that it is given). In that case, its programming has a massive effect on our lives. Because if we program the subconscious mind with negativity and limitations, then negativity and constraints are what it will create.

Now, the woo-woo idea of the law of attraction suggests that your mind has the potential to bring external factors into your life by some kind of magnetic force, so if we put negativity into our minds, then it will bring negativity into our reality, i.e., attracting the things we don't want. But if this were true, the converse would also be correct. We could teach our minds to think positively on the subconscious level, thereby attracting positive things into our lives.

But even without that woo-woo law of attraction stuff and just working with the base concept of the shit in/shit out philosophy or SISO as it was abbreviated. SISO would suggest that if you tell your subconscious mind, the same controller that performs thousands of functions in your body every single second of every single minute of every single day without you consciously having to think about it. Suppose you tell this subconscious mind that you will fail at something. In that case, it will do what it needs to do to your body, your body's capabilities, your mental ability, and your effort level to ensure that you do indeed fail at that particular thing.

Similarly, if you tell that same control mechanism that you are going to succeed at something, it will do the opposite, and create the adrenaline boosts, the muscle twitch fibre, the energy levels and the focus to give you the best chance of achieving the aim.

As the Meerkats would say, 'Simples.'

And this is where it gets interesting. Suppose we accept that we can challenge the programming and change the programming of our subconscious minds. In that case, we are accepting that we have been given the ability to program ourselves to achieve anything we want.

Look at any high-performance person in any field, whether it's athletics, football, business, or the military. These are all people who have programmed themselves to be exceptional at something. None of those things happened by accident. It's all self-programming. Yet so many people are strongly averse to the concept of self-programming because it's hokey and woo-woo.

But the reality is, anything in the world that you achieve, if it hasn't been achieved by self-programming, then what the hell was it? If you have a degree, it's because you programmed yourself to study in a certain way to be able to regurgitate the information required when you sit for the exam. If you're a great athlete, it's because you have taught yourself to use your body in a certain way to get the result that you want in your next athletic meet. If you're a great orator, it's because you have programmed your brain to overcome the fear of public speaking and taught yourself to project your voice, enunciate and speak in a certain way to get your point across clearly with emotion so it resonates with your audience.

It's all programming. All learning is programming. Yet we don't seem to want to accept the fact that at a deeper level, there are programs that run not just our activities, but our lives. Programs that affect the way we see the world, programs which give us our worldview, our paradigm, what we believe, and the way behave in the world.

This is so important to me because the one statement I hate to hear most from any human being is 'I'm the kind of person who'. In my experience, that statement was usually always followed by an excuse for ignorance or bad behaviour. People would often say, 'I'm not accepting that because I'm the kind of person who…' and once you say, 'I'm the kind of person who…' you immediately cut yourself off from all forms of growth because you've already defined your limitations.

'I'm the kind of person who will punch you in the mouth if you speak to me in a way that I perceive to be disrespectful.' Say this, and you have already cut yourself off from every other possibility of how to deal with being disrespected.

'I'm the kind of person who never wins when it comes to sporting occasions', has already cut yourself off from any opportunity to be successful in sports.

It's all programming, and it's sad that so many people seem reticent to explore the deeper levels of programming.

We understand programming in terms of learning a skill to get a job, but we always seem reluctant to address our programming when it comes to changing our worldview, paradigm, belief systems, and the way we think or what we say to ourselves in our internal dialog. This is sad because these are the most important programs you'll ever run.

You can always get another job, learn another skill, or pick up another sport; these things are all superficial. The real programs that you want to be affecting are what you say to yourself about yourself, what you say to yourself about the world, what you say to yourself about your relationships with people, what you say to yourself about your abilities, what you say to yourself about your relationship with luck or success or hard work or overcoming obstacles.

These programs have a general effect on one's whole life, yet people are most reluctant to engage in them.

Early Reading List

In order to fully understand my personal view of the limitations of both religion and science, I recommend the following books as reading lists.

Thirteen Things That Don't Make Sense by Michael Brooks and *Quantum Theory Cannot Hurt You* by Marcus Chown. These books are brilliant yet show the limitations of our supposedly all-encompassing scientific knowledge, demonstrating just how preposterous its assumptions can be. Once understood, you will never be able to take a scientist laughing at the 'implausibility of God because it can't be proven' seriously again. Frankly, I spent my time reading these books just thinking, 'Really!!!' and laughing my head off.

And *God is Disappointed with You* by Mark Russell, which, although only it focuses on one religion, in my opinion, applies to all religions equally in highlighting how utterly ludicrous the strict interpretation of these written religious scriptures is.

Somewhere between these two philosophies of the world is the truth. I'm not saying that I know where it is. Like John Snow, frankly, I know nothing. I'm just saying I am confident that neither of these two extremes has it. The truth could not possibly be based on the level of ridiculousness and the hypotheses of beliefs with the levels of 'I can't explain it; just take my word for it and have faith' that both approaches require.

YOU

You Are Broken, Sorry!!

Okay, so I'm really sorry to tell you this, but regarding how to approach yourself, the first thing you need to accept is that you are broken. I know many people will disagree with this, and I also appreciate it's a very dangerous statement. I don't want you to take the words that you are broken and weaponise them against yourself or start thinking that you were broken, are now irreparable, and as such, have excuses for all kinds of self-destructive behaviour, the mistreatment of others, or any other type of foolishness. Please take it from this perspective.

You were born in perfection. Your genetics may have dictated whether you were short or tall, fat or thin, have a big nose, have eyes close together, or have a low jawline. Those are your genetics. You may even have what some people term a disability. Still, nonetheless, I truly believe we are all born in perfection.

When you were a baby, you were given to your parents or guardians, whose job was to take care of you. Like the big toys that adult humans are, you were given to somebody to play with and care for, as if you were a very expensive doll. If you had a very expensive doll, you would give it to your children to play with but tell them to be careful not to break it. Unfortunately, your parents, your guardians, didn't know enough about human psychology, so although they took care not to let you break physically, they played with you in the wrong way. They taught you the wrong things. They put you in harmful environments. They filled your head with negative self-taught the negative beliefs. They ruined your concept of faith. They did not understand the full power and potential of your imagination and how to encourage it. In fact, they did not understand your full potential and power and how to encourage you. All they did was fill you with their petty prejudices, hates, worries, fears, limiting beliefs, sense of lack and religious dogma, most of which has nothing to do with the beauty of the Creator of everything or your potential. Put simply, they broke you mentally.

This is what I mean by you are broken. Obviously, some people have been broken more than others. Some of us grew up in abusive households or maybe had parents who were people with alcoholism, drug addicts, Narcissists or Sociopaths, but this was just another layer on top of the basic foundation, which almost everybody is broken by their parents who, frankly, don't know shit. I mean, there's no examination that you have to pass to have a baby and no examination required to raise one.

Don't think you're broken? I had two experiences in the last 48 hours, which will bear my point out. The first was a conversation at lunch with a small group of friends. One friend was explaining that they had a parent who was fanatical about weight control and how this parent verbally abused them and their mother during their childhood, admonishing them for putting on weight. This, quite frankly, gave them a complex. There is no proof that this has occurred, but it would be a miracle if this person didn't develop bulimia. What most definitely was noticed was that they didn't eat at lunch. They only drank. Many people choose to drink alcohol to soothe their mental pains. Plus, you can't drink alcohol and eat food at the same time because you will put weight on, so most people who like alcohol, if they have to choose, don't eat.

But the second part of the conversation revolved around the fact that their mother didn't eat either. This is reminiscent of what Natasha Hamilton, a then-member of the girl band Atomic Kitten, said in that infamous interview when asked how she kept her figure and replied, 'We just don't eat.' After being criticised for putting on weight, the mother just took that approach, eating as little as possible.

Seriously. That child is broken. That child needs help to be repaired, and that child needs to repair themself.

My second example was another dinner, this time with some Caribbean friends. We were talking about our childhood, and as often occurs when talking to a group of people of Caribbean heritage, we got to talking about corporal punishment or, as we like to call it, 'beatings'.

Every single person at that dinner table had a story of being beaten by their parents, to the point that, as always happens when Caribbean people get together, we were comparing stories, trying to outdo each other on who got the most outlandish beating from our parents.

At the end of this, I said, 'You know, it's great that we can all look back on this and laugh about it, but on another level, this really is quite disturbing.' As a group of people, this is the one thing that we can all bond over. This is our one common experience.

We did not discuss how much our parents encouraged us, how many times they told us that they loved us or that they were proud of us, how our parents got us into sports or healthy eating, or how they encouraged us to pursue our dreams, although many of our parents did all of those things.

But those things weren't trauma-inducing enough for them to stick out in our memory, and there wasn't an almost guarantee that the other people at the table would have experienced the same thing. Being beaten, we knew, was the one thing that would be common to all of us because it's common to almost all Caribbean children of a particular generation, and so that is the thing that would stick in our minds.

The thing that would be stuck in our minds sufficiently so that we could recall the experiences vividly and humorously because we were all broken. All of us. Some of us went on to beat our own kids, saying it didn't do us any harm and repeating the cycle.

Others went on to say that we would never commit corporal punishment to our children because of what happened to us. But it was challenging for any of us to have a sensible, balanced view on how to discipline or punish a child or even an objective view on how we were brought up.

Our discipline was so overwhelmingly brutal that we had to make a joke out of it, but we never really dealt with it on any deep psychological level; Broken all of us.

Plus, to make things even worse, children are also, by design, selfish. They see everything through their own needs, meaning that it is almost impossible to satisfy them. So, as well as being broken by others, your memories as a child who was impossible to please mean that in many ways, you broke yourself.

These are just two examples from two lunch dates I had in one week. I'm sure if you examine your own life and the lives of your friends, lovers, workmates, and even strangers, you will find many more examples and much more drastic ones to boot.

So, I'm going to repeat: I appreciate that the idea of being broken is dangerous. I again need to clarify. I am not saying that you were broken beyond repair or that you are a bad or unworthy person. I am saying absolutely none of those things.

What I am saying is that you were born perfect—absolute perfection. You were given to a guardian and put in an environment that wasn't optimal. The guardians did their best but didn't know what they were doing, which wasn't optimal. They put you in the best environment that they could, but it was a destructive one.

Now, as you will see later in this book, I question if bad things really happen. And there is the rub. This is where the genius beyond any of our ability to fathom comes into play. Perhaps you were put in that exact environment so that you would be treated that way and broken in a specific way because, during the process of repairing yourself, you would create a specific result.

One of my favourite quotes is that diamonds are formed under pressure. Perhaps we're all put under pressure from a certain upbringing in a certain environment, which forms a cocoon around us. That cocoon stops us from being the beautiful butterflies or moths that we are supposed to be. And it's our job to break out of that cocoon so that we can finally spread our wings, fly around the earth, and spread our beauty as butterflies do. That could be what is going on here.

Nevertheless, it must be acknowledged that most of us were not raised in suitable environments by parents who understood the true results of their words and actions, and we are broken. We need to accept that we need some form of help and self-improvement. I now finally understand why it seems that everyone in America is in Therapy; we need it, all of us. We can't just go ahead replicating what we grew up in, the beatings or fat shaming or the domestic abuse or alcoholic abuse or the narcissism or the fear or the painful shyness. We can't just go on replicating that.

We must acknowledge that many things in our environment growing up weren't right. In understanding this and that they broke us, we are now predisposed to repeating that behaviour or to going completely in the opposite way and overcompensating, which is often just as bad. We have to acknowledge that neither of those is correct. Like an alcoholic or a drug addict, once you admit and acknowledge that you have a problem, you're much more likely to find the proper solution.

We must accept that we are perfect in design and creation. We've been broken by our parents and our environment, and now we have to find which self-improvement tools and practices work for us to repair ourselves. We need self-improvement practices to help us find that balance between the destructiveness of our past environments and the personal brilliance with which we were born.

By finding that balance, we will have the mechanism through which we can break through the cocoon that we were encased in and emerge the beautiful butterfly or magnificent Moth ready to spread its wings, take flight and shine its brilliance and beauty throughout the world.

Too Cool for School

There is a great story about the fact that the Basketball player Wilt Chamberlain dramatically increased his free throw average by changing his style to a Granny shot. This shooting method is to bend your knees, hold the ball with two hands and throw the ball up in the air with two hands in the underhanded way you do when throwing a ball to a young child. This also worked for Rick Barry, and it has been said that in tests, it apparently proved to be the most effective way to score a penalty shot. So, since this is so effective, how many players in the NBA do you see taking shots using this technique? None. Absolutely none in the NBA or any other basketball league because it looks so uncool. It makes that person look rather foolish. As I said before, the throw looks childish.

This is one of the best analogies for life ever. So much of our life is based around trying to look cool to others and ourselves. We're so concerned about this that we don't even take a moment to think about who set these standards of cool in the first place.

So, think about it. Who set these standards of coolness in the first place? I'll wait…

Most of the standards for cool, which we subscribe to, come from advertisers or dropouts. Advertisers who had a horrible product to sell told us that the product was cool. Products such as revealing clothing, life-ending drugs, life-decreasing cigarettes, and brain-altering alcohol. Any manner of things that, by any objective measure, are not good for the consumer or society. But get a Movie star to promote them or a Pop star to use them. By transference, they can get millions of people to do harm to themselves to look like, act like or feel closer to their idols.

And the other place where we learn cool is usually from failing people. People who aren't good at things and because they're not good at them demean those things and make those things seem as if they are not attractive to do. As if they're not cool, as if they are the dumb thing to do. Failures and dropouts define what teenagers think is cool based usually on what the person with influence cannot do. Instead of trying to improve at it, which for a short time would make them look foolish, they make themselves feel better by saying that they wouldn't want to do it anyway, it's stupid, it's dumb, and then spread this influence amongst their peers. This is the tall poppy syndrome, where you cut off the heads of those doing better than you to bring them back down to your level.

This is how education became so uncool. This is the root of 'too cool for school'. It's not because it's a good thing to be 'too cool for school'. Actually, it's nonsense. Education is a wonderful thing. There is much to be said regarding how education is administered, and lord knows the educational system could do with a complete overhaul. But learning should never be uncool. How would you get anything done if you never learned how to do anything at all?

But in the world in which we live, teenagers through to young adults are taught what's cool by people who were either too frightened to try things in the first place or tried a thing, discovered that they were not good at it, didn't have enough character to keep going and improve at it, so gave up and decried it as uncool.

If you're a brilliant basketball player, someone will tell you that basketball isn't cool, bouncing that ball around, getting sweaty, and looking stupid. If you're a fantastic male singer, someone will tell you that singing isn't cool. That's just for girls. You need to learn how to rap. If you're brilliant at art and handicrafts, someone will tell you that art and handicrafts are for old ladies, and that's not cool.

But guess what is cool? Hanging out at the mall, doing petty crimes, or even worse, doing major crimes, being rude and abusive or bullying other people. All these things are taught as cooler than activities such as sports, music, arts or education. And we fall for it, generation after generation.

I wanted to put this here to help you to challenge your view of what's cool. To help you challenge your views or learn what's hokey. Because a lot of the stuff in this book is going to seem uncool. I promise you that when you first start listening to self-talk, it will seem uncool. Doing affirmations will seem Hokey. Visualising what you want in your life will seem ridiculous.

So, I just want you to remember who gave you your version of cool anyway. You see, surely there's a society where visualising, affirming, and self-talk lead people to be nice to others, be positive in their outlook, and be happy more of the time than they are sad. These are all cool things. And I know on some level, deep down, you know that a world where being nice to other people, being positive and having a can-do attitude is undoubtedly cooler than the alternative, which, funnily enough, is the world we live in.

So, take a leap of faith, Take the granny shot, and get the result even if the process makes you look uncool to yourself or others. Because at the end of the day, getting the results you want is the coolest thing of all.

Act as If

I remember the first time I heard the term 'Act as if'. It was from Russ Whitney, the first major property training course I took, which admittedly was the first thing that helped set me on the path to becoming a property multimillionaire.

When I first heard it, I liked the concept, but a part of my brain initially rejected it. The idea of pretending to be rich and successful, pretending to be the boss of the company, or pretending to be a professional footballer or concert pianist seemed outlandish.

You see, as children, we are encouraged to pretend, but as adults, we're often admonished for it. People will outright criticise you if they think you're being childish and not accepting your adult responsibilities. Your adult responsibilities are facing reality and dealing with things as they are. If they believe you're pretending that things are not the way they demonstrably are. You're not confronting reality; you will be criticised and potentially sectioned under mental health issues. So, the mere thought that you could pretend to be something that you are not yet, something that you want to be, seemed at the least irresponsible and, at worst, potentially dangerous, making it initially worrisome to me.

But is there a practical way of viewing this? Well, here's how I see its practicality now. Let's say you want to be the managing director of your company. When someone says, 'Act as if,' no, they don't mean that you should walk into the current Managing director's office, sit down in their chair, pick up the phone, and start making multi-million dollar decisions. That would most definitely get you fired, and again, potentially even committed to a mental institution as they drag you away, out of the office screaming, 'You can't do this, I'm the boss!!'

But what you can do is adopt the demeanour and attitude of that person. You can adopt the demeanour and attitude of your boss. Nothing stops you from walking, talking, and behaving—within yourself, by yourself, for yourself—the way you would when you are the company's boss. More importantly, there's nothing to stop you from treating your work with the same level of importance and responsibility as the owner of the company does, even if you're just in the mailroom.

The difference between saying, 'I'm only in the mailroom, it doesn't matter. This work is unimportant, so I will do it to a low standard. In fact, they're lucky that I do it at all. I only get paid eleven dollars an hour for this, so why should I care about how I perform?' and the attitude of, 'I'm going to perform my daily tasks—reading the mail, sorting it into the correct categories, and placing it in the correct pigeonholes—with the same mentality, level of excellence, and sense of importance as if I were making decisions about the company's future, striking big deals, or making essential staffing decisions,' is stark. There's a world of difference between these two attitudes. Let's be clear: which attitude do you think will bring more opportunities? Which will lead to the kinds of promotions that could result in a person being offered the CEO job? You can bring that attitude of importance to the work you're already doing, which is what 'acting as if' means in a practical sense.

The best example of this is the story of Edwin Barnes, as told by Napoleon Hill. As the story goes, Barnes arrives on a train looking like a common tramp yet presents himself to the offices of Thomas Edison and boldly proclaims, 'I came here to go into business with you.' If this example seems too old and out of touch, allow me to present a more recent example. In the Netflix documentary *Headliners Only*, Chris Rock tells the story of his first meeting with a young, unknown comedian called Kevin Hart and how the then-unknown Kevin boldly proclaimed to the world famous and successful Chris Rock his intention to work with him. This interview was given not only after Kevin Hart had worked his way up to being one of the highest-paid and most successful film stars and comedians in the world but also at an interview for a comedy tour where Chris Rock and Kevin Hart would present a night of comedy at Madison square garden and work together.

So, what does 'acting as if' in practicality achieve? Many scientific experiments support the idea that people who believe their work is important experience numerous benefits. They gain psychological and physical benefits, and the quality of their work improves compared to those who think their work isn't important. My favourite example is the story of the three bricklayers. When asked what they were doing, one said, 'I'm laying bricks.' The second said, 'I'm earning five dollars an hour.' But the third said, 'I'm building the world's greatest cathedral.' The importance you place on your work most definitely affects the way in which you perform it and, as such, its quality. But most importantly, the importance you place on your work also affects the importance you place on yourself.

If you believe that you are important because you do important work, it will change your self-view. If you see yourself as an important person doing important work, you will achieve much better results—not just in the quality of the work you produce, but in the quality of the life you live. Numerous examples, particularly around retirement, show that when someone believes they no longer have value, their health rapidly deteriorates. Their mood, outlook, and the output of whatever they're doing deteriorate, and their overall quality of life deteriorates.

So, 'acting as if' isn't just some nonsensical outlook or fantasy. It's not about pretending like a seven-year-old (although, on another level of 'hippie shit,' living your whole life with the mindset and outlook of a seven-year-old is actually the high point of sensible living), but that level of hippie shit might be a bit too much for today. However, 'acting as if' allows you to borrow from the magic, power, freedom, and unlimited potential of having a childlike view of the world. A view formed a time before you were told what was and was not possible and were trained to behave accordingly. A view where you can still be anything you want and achieve anything you desire. 'Acting as if' lets you harness that energy and turn it into realistic, tangible benefits in your day-to-day life.

Be Happy, Here's Why...

The idea of just being happy is closely aligned with the concept of 'act as if,' but deserves separate analysis. 'Be happy no matter what happens.'

To me, this was most definitely one of the most offensive hippie shit credos—because, like many people, I grew up in an environment where many of the external factors were not the kinds that filled people with joy. There were relative levels of poverty. There was racial abuse, there was prejudice and forced limitation from our potential by gatekeepers, there was domestic violence, child brutality, and to add to this mix, to make our lives worse, there was the misuse and misquotation of religion to cause guilt, fear, and feelings of inadequacy. Then in the middle of this, some motherfucker comes and tells me, 'Just be happy.' Oh yes, I could have punched them right in the face.

So, what is the practicality of just being happy? Well, this deserves a book all by itself. Still, as this tome would not be complete without including this attitude, I'll make some very quick points regarding it. The first one, which took me many years to discover (I originally heard it from Anthony Robbins), is that happiness is not a feeling created by external circumstances. Happiness derives from a set of actions which you do in response to what you think the external stimulation is. You see, your brain and body indicate that you are happy through a series of thoughts and actions that create feelings and emotions that you call happiness. Well, guess what? You can create them independent of external stimulation.

For example, when somebody says, 'I love you,' you feel a warm feeling of importance and acceptance—your eyes water, your mouth creases into a smile, and maybe your breath becomes shallow. These are all physiological things you do when your brain tells you that happiness has occurred. But you can do those things without any external stimulation. One way to do this is to actually perform those actions to create happiness instead of only performing them when external stimuli have informed you that an action has occurred, to which happiness should be your response. If you know that your external representations of happiness are smiling, whooping, clapping your hands or dancing, then why not just do them when you want to feel happy.

This refers to the study where clinically depressed patients were told to laugh on order a certain number of times a day and were all found to have major improvements in their levels of well-being.

Another option to consider is reliving a happy memory. You can simply remember a time when you were happy, dive into that memory, and relive it as intensely as possible. Whatever method works for you—whether it's auditory affirmation, picture visualisation, or a kinaesthetic activity—you can dive into a time when you were blissfully happy and replay it to trigger those feelings.

But why should you just be happy? Well, I don't think you can always be happy, although I am still waiting for that to be proven incorrect. Truly, there are people, as suggested by Dr David Hawkins' Map of Consciousness, who are at a level of peace or love where they feel what we call happiness all the time. But bear in mind that, according to Dr Hawkins, only a minuscule percentage of the world's population exists at that level, and it's not something that most of us will ever experience. However, what we can do is find methods and mechanisms to counteract unhappiness.

Why would we want to counteract unhappiness?

Well, let's get straight to the point. Unhappiness is proven to affect your physical health, your lifespan, your platonic relationships, your productivity, your output, your sex drive and your sex life. Quite frankly, absolutely every single aspect of your life will be negatively impacted by how unhappy you feel.

So, the practicality of trying to be happy is about something other than responding to the stimuli in your world. It's irrelevant. Being happy, or trying to be happy in bad circumstances, is like trying not to be obese, give up smoking, control your anger, or learn a new productivity technique. Being happy is like something you read in Cosmopolitan—that article that promised that if you do this one thing, you'll send your sexual partner into a frenzy.

Unhappiness will affect all of these things. And if we are to believe that being happy is not something that is done to you, but something that you do to yourself, and in addition to this, not necessarily based only on outside stimuli, but something that you can self-stimulate, then I suggest that, just like with masturbation, we learn how to get on with it. So when there's no outside stimulation to create the result, we have a very effective mechanism for making the result ourselves. If we appreciate and accept all of the benefits it creates, we really don't have any reason for not self-stimulating if we can.

Lastly, why would you want to just be happy? Well, as a salesman, one of the tactics you come across in many sales courses is the concept of asking your client or prospect, 'Why?' They say, 'I need someone to help with my marketing.' You say, 'Why?' They say, 'Because I want to improve my marketing numbers.' You say, 'Why?' They say, 'Because we'll get more leads.' You say, 'Why?' They say, 'Because more leads mean more prospects.' You say, 'Why?' They say, 'Well, because more prospects mean a better chance of making more sales.' You say, 'Why do you want more sales?' They say, 'Because more sales mean we'll make more money.' And then you really get into it. You say, 'Okay, great. Why do you want more money?' They say, 'So I can have more things.' You say, 'Okay, great. Why do you want more things?' They say, 'Well, if I had more things, I'd be able to enjoy myself more.' You say, 'Why do you want enjoyment?' They say, 'Well, because if I had more enjoyment, I'd be happy.' And only then, finally, look at the prospect and say, 'Ahhhh, I see.'

The answer to almost any question you ask anybody about anything, if dug into just a few layers deep, is soon revealed to be rooted in their desire for happiness. Whether it's someone trying to make themselves a billionaire or someone who will give up all their worldly possessions to serve the poor and sick. The root cause of absolutely everything everybody does is to be happy. So again, returning to what I think is Anthony Robbins-ism or something I have heard elsewhere. If the root cause of absolutely everything you do in your life is to be happy, and you discovered a mechanism to be happy without any external stimulation or going through a process, why not just go directly to that feeling?

Lastly, moving more into the hippie side of things, if there was any truth in the concept that the level to which we vibrate has an effect on the things around us—if there is any truth in this concept—Well, if you can get yourself to be happy and spend most of your day in a happy state, then, you will attract happiness to you. This means the people around you will be happy, too. The people around you who are miserable will either be repelled from you, thereby not affecting your happy state, or be happy only when they interact with you because you're already happy, and your happiness rubs off on them.

The circumstances around you may even be happier. Things that were going to break won't break; things that were going to fail won't fail. Why would this be possible? Well, because in a happy state, you're closer and more akin to what we call a flow state.

Every athlete will tell you about the existence of a flow state, but first, let me tell you about the existence of a non-flow state. When you wake up in the morning and you've got a massive hangover, you feel tired. You go to reach for that cup, but you don't reach it properly and tip it over, causing it to fall. It smashes to pieces, making you late to leave for work, so you have to spend valuable time clearing up the mess, potentially even cutting your finger as you rush to clean up. Then you're driving to work, not really paying attention, and you bump into another car while reversing. You get to work and make that phone call, and even though you know what you're supposed to say when the client raises an objection, you're not focusing correctly, and you say the wrong thing, losing the sale. Have you ever had a morning like this? I bet you have? We all have, haven't we? Well, that's the opposite of a flow state.

That's the performance that you get when you're unhappy. But then, you have that day when you wake up, and you don't know why, but you just have the feeling that everything will go well. You go for your coffee cup, which slips out of your hand, but react quickly and catch it before it smashes. You're driving down the road, and some lunatic flies right by you, but you just hit the brake just in time and avoid a collision. Then, you make that phone call, and even though the client is tough, and you're thinking to yourself, 'I have no idea how the hell I'm going to close this client,' somehow, miraculously, you say the right thing and close the deal.

That is the flow state. The state where you perform to your highest level without consciously thinking about your actions. It feels effortless, and you don't quite know how you achieved the results you achieved. Well, I can't prove that happiness is guaranteed to put you in the flow state, but I think we can be confident that being unhappy, whether slightly down or absolutely furious, will take us out of it.

Celebrate Your Losses and Rejoice in Your Bad Days

'Celebrate your losses.' Why on earth would I want to do that? Well, here are a couple of practical reasons.

Let's start with the idea that there are only so many losses or wins you'll experience in your lifetime—or, to simplify it, let's say, in one year. Statistically speaking, all other factors aside, you will have a certain number of ordinary days, some big wins, and some days that are losses and feel terrible.

The best way to look at a loss, a bad day, or a disaster is that it's one of those terrible days in your life, gone. You were going to have one anyway, and now you've just had it. You can dwell on it and feel sad, and that's okay, but after you've gone through that process, the best thing to do is to celebrate it. Be glad that this terrible day has happened, is finished, and is gone. There's no point in thinking about it anymore. Just be grateful that one of the terrible days you were going to have this year is now behind you. I mean, come on, it's unlikely that every day in your life will be terrible, right!!

Even if you're in a bad situation—like going bankrupt, going through a divorce, or losing a loved one—you might feel like every single day is terrible. But to be honest, a lot of that feeling comes from carrying over your sadness, pain, remorse, and upset into days that are actually quite good. These are days you can't appreciate or enjoy because you're dragging the feelings of sadness and disappointment from days gone by into them.

Think of it on a level playing field. Statistically, you'll probably find that there are a certain number of great days in a year, some that are just okay and some that are horrible. Some days, you wake up and feel awful for no apparent reason. On other days, you wake up and feel great for no apparent reason. Some days are horrible because something external happens that you really didn't want to happen, something very upsetting and distressing. Other days are lovely because something you've been working hard toward finally comes to fruition, or something unexpected and beneficial suddenly presents itself. This is life. I think most people's lives look like this, and most people cannot circumvent this reality.

Since this will happen to you anyway, I'm not telling you to have a Pollyanna attitude and be happy about everything. But one way to see a bad day or a loss is to recognise that it's just one of the bad days, one of the unfortunate circumstances from the millions of random or not-so-random things that happen to all of us that were going to happen to you anyway. Now that it's passed, it's one less thing you'll have to face for the rest of the year. And that's a good thing, so celebrate it.

The other reason to celebrate your losses is that when I say 'celebrate,' I don't necessarily mean in the traditional sense of a party, but rather in the sense of acknowledging that it's a good thing the bad day is over. It's one less bad thing to happen to you statistically for the year so the way to celebrate it could be by doing something you enjoy.

It's funny that when we succeed, we tend to do something we enjoy—like calling our friends, partying, having a drink, or going out for a nice meal. These things add to the good feeling, but you're only adding to an already good feeling. That's not to say you shouldn't do that—you absolutely should try to make yourself feel as good as possible. But what about when bad things happen? This is why comfort foods exist: we instinctively know that when we feel bad, we want to do something that makes us feel better. But surely other things can help us feel better, things other than Ice Cream.

So, when you do feel bad, sometimes you're smart enough to call your friends and talk to someone you love. You don't even have to talk about the problem; sometimes, just hearing their voice and talking about something completely different—something totally irrelevant—makes you feel better. Often, for many people, eating something they enjoy takes the sting out of a horrible day. For far too many people, having a drink they enjoy takes the sting out of an awful day, so they use alcohol or other substances that change their body chemistry and how they feel.

So that's what I mean by 'celebrate.' You can have a horrible day and decide, 'Okay, you know what? I will go for a nice meal at a restaurant that I enjoy. I'm going to celebrate the fact that this bad thing has happened, and it's gone. I'm going to use a slap-up meal at my favourite restaurant to make myself feel better.' That way, you don't get caught in a negative mindset and carry it into more days than necessary. You want to make yourself feel better by doing something you enjoy and then carry that positive energy into the next day.

Obviously, there are other methods. You can exercise, which always changes your mood. You can give yourself a celebratory workout—punch it out if you like boxing or martial arts. Punching out your aggression is one of the best methods to eliminate anger and frustration I have ever found. It can be quite profound, and I have in the past burst into tears as I hit the heavy bag, which I used to represent the overbearing, insurmountable problem I had at the time. Fighting the intangible issue is a very powerful tool. You can get that stress and frustration out of your system and help yourself overcome the bad things that happened. Alternatively, as I mentioned before, you can connect with friends or loved ones, go to the theatre, watch a movie, or do something else you enjoy that takes away the sting of your shitty day. The goal is not to get caught up and dwell in that negative feeling and vibration. As Dr David Hawkins explains masterfully in his book *Letting Go*, give in to the anger and despair, scream, shout, and imagine all the destructive thoughts you like. Just get it out of your body and mind once it's finally left you. Celebrate the loss. Get it out of the way, and at least get back to what most people call a typical, average day as soon as possible.

Celebrate Your Losses and Rejoice in Your Bad Days, Part 2

There is a last reason to celebrate your losses and rejoice in your bad days. If you are moving towards achieving a goal, and your loss is part of your effort to achieve it. Even if that attempt was unsuccessful, you've still made progress. Like the concept of your life regarding overall statistics, you've taken another step in crossing off the list of things that don't work. This means that if you continue in the same vein, you're one step closer to finding the thing that will work and achieving success.

This is very much an 'Edison attitude', having made one thousand attempts to create the incandescent light bulb. He could have given up after attempting two hundred, thinking that it would never work. However, as Edison himself is quoted he said, 'I have not failed; I've just found nine hundred and ninety-nine ways that don't work.' Every single one of those experiments was essential to him finding a way that would work. This is more or less true for every business, although having that kind of perseverance is very hard.

Don't get me wrong—it's not always the right approach to persist with every idea. Some ideas are just dead ends. Some are simply bad ideas that shouldn't be pursued because they aren't going to work. But what you can always pursue is your end goal.

For example, let's say you want to be a business coach, and you decide to coach unemployed people who don't want to start a business. You try nine hundred different ways to attract these kinds of people, and you might eventually discover that unemployed people who don't want to start a business aren't a great target market. However, those nine hundred attempts might not only reveal that they're not a good target market but also help you to define who a good target market is.

Maybe you'll find that unemployed moms who want to start a business or unemployed people who say they don't want to start a business but secretly do (they're just too scared to admit it or don't know how to begin) are a better target market. Your failures will help you refine not just your business model but also your marketing strategy and target audience.

Your end business might not be exactly the one you envisioned at the start—your definition of your target market and product might evolve. But by celebrating and rejoicing in every single loss and failure, you'll maintain the motivation to keep going until you finally define a target market that's interested in what you're selling, with people you want to work with, and a product or delivery method that they're happy to pay for.

Belief and Paradigm

Now, I understand that when people talk about paradigms, self-conception, and self-image, it can sound like a lot of woo-woo nonsense.

After all, you know yourself, right? You look in the mirror and see who you are. You know your experience and level of knowledge, and they tell you what you're capable of. That's your worldview.

But I want to share a few personal stories that I didn't realise were related to self-conception until many years later when the concept was taught to me.

I was always chubby as a child, growing up in a tough neighbourhood where physical fitness was highly valued. I was surrounded by super-fit, athletic kids—something I was definitely not. However, I remember the day (or at least the feeling) when this began to change. I don't recall the exact date, but it was the first time I played football with those kids and noticeably contributed. Usually, they would run rings around me, making me feel stupid, and I only played to be included. But one day, for some reason, I put in more effort, kicked the ball really hard, and scored a goal. Everyone cheered.

At that moment, my self-concept changed from someone who couldn't play sports to someone who could actually participate and succeed. My skill level and physique hadn't changed, but my self-image did. This shift led me to want to play more because I now saw myself as someone who could contribute. The more I played, the better I got, and within a few years, I was even selected for the school football team.

The second story involves mathematics, which I struggled with throughout my schooling. My friends teased me because every time my teacher asked me to solve a problem, I would furrow my brow and scrunch my face, trying to show how hard I was thinking, yet I still couldn't grasp the concepts. This continued all the way through to my university degree, where I failed math consistently every year. In all probability, I earned my University math pass mark in effort, if not merit.

Despite this reality, when I started working in property, I discovered something strange. No, I wasn't doing calculus, but I was doing math, and I found that I could quickly learn and apply mathematical formulas. This was especially true when calculating whether a business venture would be successful. In fact, I became very good at it. I would analyse deals and find things others had missed, earning a reputation as the go-to person for deal analysis. What changed was my belief in my ability to do math when it mattered to me, leading to a shift in my paradigm.

The third story involves technology. I graduated with an economics degree, while most of my friends had technical degrees and went into IT. But I hadn't anticipated the recession of 1992. In 1992, there was a severe economic recession, and nobody wanted to hear from an economist. After some time out of work, I pivoted to a technical job because IT was booming. I took a six-month course and got a job in information technology. I'll never forget how one of my university friends couldn't stop laughing at the idea of me working in IT. He remembered how, similarly to my struggles with math, I once needed his help to fix a bicycle chain because I couldn't do it myself.

I was known for my artistic abilities—I could write, make music, and excel at anything creative. But I had absolutely no aptitude for anything technical. However, during the recession, there were no jobs in the arts, and being an economist wasn't exactly popular given the circumstances. So, I went into IT despite being terrible at it. Through nepotism, a friend, Robbie, got me a junior position in his IT department. But a few weeks later, he left the company, and I was the only person left in the IT department. I had two choices: run away or step up. I chose to step up. Within months, I had the entire department running smoothly. I learned quickly and on the job because I had no choice; it was either that or the whole business would come grinding to a halt. I eventually left that position and moved on to another IT job. Within a few years, I became a Senior Technical Advisor for ICL (now Fujitsu), working on one of their biggest accounts, liaising with heads of departments from companies as large as British Telecom and rolling out new technology across the UK.

This from a guy who couldn't even fix a bicycle chain. What changed wasn't just my knowledge but also my beliefs and paradigm. I started to see myself as someone who could learn and excel in technical fields, and that belief made all the difference.

Faith and Belief

When I was growing up, I was interested in religion. And I believe that the worst damage that was ever done to me in terms of religion was when the priest, Imam or whoever I was talking to at the time couldn't answer a question which I had asked them or didn't have an answer to the analysis that I had made about a particular scripture, belief, practice or custom. In those instances, when I questioned them about its validity, they would say, 'Well, you just have to have faith,' or 'You just have to believe.'

In one way, it was the best thing because I called bullshit. If you couldn't answer my questions, it meant you didn't know, and if you didn't know, you probably didn't have any right to teach me the Religion. This kept me from blindly following dogma for the majority of my life. Even Islam, which was purported by the people teaching it to me at the time as a scientific religion where everything could be questioned, was the same. I would find myself in the same place where the Imam or the teacher, when presented with a difficult question to which he had no answer, would tell me to, 'Just have faith and believe.'

When I went to Christian churches, I heard this a lot because many of Christianity's teachings were contradictory. As I questioned these contradictions, having faith and believing seemed to be the answer to everything that couldn't be answered by the priests I spoke to (although I'm sure there may have been priests who had more knowledge or better answers).

So, in one way, this was great. It taught me to always analyse things and understand that when you hit a point where someone didn't have an answer, that person wasn't someone to follow. This means that I never followed any of these religions, and I still don't to this day.

But the damage it did, which I didn't realise until much later when I started my spiritual journey for the second time, the journey which led to the writing of this book, was the fact that it taught me that faith and belief were dirty words. They were just words used by incompetent proponents of religions who didn't have the answers to difficult questions, so they used those terms as proxies for real answers. They were just terms used to cover up a lack of knowledge or the fact that these people were blatantly promoting and teaching bullshit. Words to cover up the fact that they knew what they were taught was potentially wrong, so they were used to covering it up because they had absolutely no evidence to defend their point.

This made faith and belief dirty words in my life. I wouldn't have faith in anything; you had to prove everything to me. I never thought of myself as someone with a scientific brain. If I did, I think I would have gone into the sciences because that was how I approached everything. I wanted Proof, and if you couldn't prove it to me, then I wouldn't be interested in hearing it.

This is why, during my very early days of understanding spirituality when, an atheist friend insisted that there was no God and wanted to debate the fact with me. I remember telling him that God was an 'experience good', and I stick by that view to this very day. I can't convince you that God, the Infinite Intelligence, a higher self, the universe, or any outside power exists. I wouldn't even want to waste my time trying.

If you have experienced it, you know; if you haven't, then you don't. However, I do not think that is strictly true because I know we've all experienced 'something'. If you haven't acknowledged the experience, then there is absolutely nothing I can do to convince you that it exists.

If you are open-minded, I can give examples of when something beyond your efforts created results. Still, these scenarios are what most people would just call coincidence, happenstance, or unexplainable things.

But in my experience, tracking and analysing this collection of coincidences, happenstances, serendipity, fortunate accidents, and the unexplainable finally led me to accept that the probability of these things all being chance was too high. As such, it was time for me to accept that something else was going on.

Faith and belief are two of the most powerful things in the world. It's sad that religion has used them in such a derogatory way because faith and belief are key to achieving anything.

Firstly, your beliefs are the foundation for absolutely everything you do in your life. So rather than just believing in something you are told, destroying the true meaning of that word, you should choose your beliefs meticulously. Your beliefs are the foundation for absolutely everything that happens to you. More importantly, your beliefs are changeable and should constantly be challenged because they should always be proven, at least to you. There's no point believing something that you can't prove or defend. So, when someone tells you that, you just have to believe they're actually using the word in the complete opposite way it should be used. You don't follow what someone tells you to 'just believe' you believe because you have tried and tested your belief and found it to be true over and above all of the other things that you have tested. And every time you retry and retest your belief, you find that, at least in your opinion, it holds up against all criticism and objection and, in your opinion, is still objectively true.

Faith is even more critical because faith is using that belief to ignore all external sensory input, circumstances, opinions of others, and all evidence to the contrary. Faith is continuing to live and act, pushing forward as if the thing that you want to happen will occur even though all the evidence may be to the contrary.

This is probably the most important feeling that anybody can have because this is the creator of miracles. I can think of so many times when all of the evidence indicated that a bad thing would happen. If I had lost faith and started to accept that the bad thing was inevitable. I would have been guaranteed to create a self-fulfilling prophecy, causing a circumstance where the bad thing would indeed occur.

Human beings are so rare that we spend so much of our time and effort, our thought process, and our energy in accepting that a bad thing will happen, only for it not to occur. And when it doesn't happen, at the very least, our lives will be worse off for spending so much time thinking about it. At the worst, we will have worked ourselves into a frenzy of real emotional and physical bad health.

Faith is confronting all the evidence that the negative thing is going to happen and the positive thing won't happen and yet going forward with the actions preparing for the positive thing to happen and the negative thing not to happen because you have faith that you can overcome all of the obstacles and circumstances that would create the negative.

This type of faith creates everything. Most people in the process of achieving anything, whether it's a minor sporting improvement or a massive world-changing invention, will come across obstacles at some point. If they don't have faith that they can overcome these obstacles, nothing gets achieved. So again, being told to 'just have faith' when the version of the faith they're trying to tell you to have is just to follow what you're told blindly, be part of the dogma and ignore what your research and logical senses are telling you is the total wrong use of faith.

The purpose of faith is to get you through the hard times. The purpose of faith is to help you push on through to the successful achievement of your lofty and worthy goal. The purpose of faith is not to appease a lack of knowledge or Proof and evidence due to a lazy proponent of a religion or belief system.

Belief and Effort

Henry Ford reportedly said, 'If you believe you can, or you believe you can't, you're right.' So, if you approach any hippie shit practice such as affirmations, visualisation or manifesting with the belief that it won't work, you are effectively telling it not to work.

Think about that for a second. How many things can you do while telling yourself they won't work and still be successful? Or look at it another way: since we're focusing on practicality, what is the probability of you trying to dunk a basketball while continuously telling yourself that you can't do it? Do you think that will increase your chances of achieving it, or do you think it will decrease your chances?

On the other hand, if you try to dunk a basketball over and over, and every time you fail, you say to yourself, 'I can do it, I know I can do it, I know I can do it,' even from a simple, practical view of effort, wouldn't you think that one of these days you're going to succeed? At the very least, this belief will push you to keep trying. And from a basic statistical perspective, taking nothing else into consideration, the more times you try, the greater the probability of succeeding. Conversely, the fewer times you try, the more likely you are to fail.

The concept is very simple: if you believe you can or you believe you can't, you're right. This means that if you don't think something is possible, you will try it fewer times and put less effort into it. But if you do believe something is possible, you will keep trying with maximum effort until you achieve it.

Let's take another practical look at this. Consider something you've done before. You know from experience that you have tied your shoes in the past, but let's say you've had an accident that affected your hand-eye coordination or motor skills, and now you're having difficulty tying your shoes. Since you know it's something you've learned to do before, you have every reason to continue trying because you know 100% as a fact that it is achievable.

Another example could be, let's say, after many attempts, you finally dunk a basketball. It might have been 100% pure luck, but it doesn't matter because now that you've done it once, you have a foundation for the belief that you can do it again. With that belief as a foundation, you have every reason and impetus to keep trying until you succeed a second time and a third until you build up enough skill and muscle memory to learn how to do it on demand.

So, whether you believe you can or can't—you're right. This can be understood from a purely statistical and effort-based perspective. All hippie shit aside, if you think something can be done, you'll put more effort into doing it and attempt it more times based on the belief that it's possible. And if you tell yourself it can't be done, you'll put less effort into it and try fewer times, based on the belief that you're wasting your time by even attempting it.

Beliefs Create Your Reality

A favourite and pretty core hippie shit concept is that your beliefs create your reality.

That sounds very woo-woo. I agree. Your beliefs can't create your reality because reality is just reality, right? It doesn't change based on what you believe. It just is. If I'm in a room and I'm looking at my desk, the desk is just a desk. What I believe about it doesn't change it. I can't believe the desk is a banana and have the desk become a banana.

Well, I agree. That's why this is one of my favourite topics to get some practicality on. I totally agree. You can't look at a desk, believe it's a banana and have it turn into a banana. Or can you?

The point I want to make here is the American History X example of how beliefs shape your reality. I like the movie American History X. It's a beautiful redemption story, but more importantly, it's a story that I've been through myself. In fact, I think a lot of people, if they're lucky, will have been through an experience where they had a belief system that they held firmly. Maybe because it was part of the culture they grew up with, or perhaps it was given to them by their environment, but either way. They firmly held this belief, and one day, they had it challenged. They had it challenged, and the challenge to that belief ended up changing it, and their reality shifted.

Well, this is what happens with Derek Vinyard, the character played by Ed Norton in the movie *American History X*. Derek Vinyard is a guy who grows up as a White Supremacist, hating all non-white people because he believes white people are superior. This terrible thinking leads to him killing somebody just because they are black, and he ends up in prison. Now, during his incarceration, he falls out with the Aryan Brotherhood, the people who are supposed to be protecting him. He becomes alienated and alone, which makes him vulnerable.

Then, he makes friends with a black inmate named Lamont. Now, his previous belief was that black people were all bad, beneath him, and they were definitely not people to befriend. Well, that belief created one reality for him, because anybody who believes that will not go into situations where there are black people and would not interact with black people or other people of colour. They would not have anything to do with them. So, if those Black people had any way of giving them a benefit, they would never receive it because they wouldn't want to be around those people.

A lot of people have the same issue with rich people. They have a belief that rich people are all crooks and that to be rich, you have to be a cheat or a thief. They believe that no wealthy person would want anything to do with them other than to exploit them, and if they feel that, what do you think happens when they're in the presence of rich people? A rich guy could want to invest in you because you remind him of his son, and he sees you as somebody he can relate to. Or you remind them of themselves when they were younger, and they would like nothing better than to help you. But your belief is that no rich person has ever done anything for anybody else without wanting something back and that they will want to exploit you, steal from you, manipulate you and use you. So, with that belief as your base, you will want nothing to do with that person, no matter how much they want to help you.

Is that not affecting your reality? Is that not saying that a desk is a banana? If that rich person is a desk that wants you to help, saying, 'Put all your papers here. Do your work here so you'll be successful.' And you think, 'I don't believe that such a thing exists. I don't believe you are a desk; I believe you're a banana; you want to use your skin to trip me up so that I slip and fall; all you want to do is exploit me and take advantage of me.' Well, that will most definitely affect your reality, will it not?

It doesn't matter how many rich people approach you and ask if you need help. If your belief system says not to trust them, you will refuse and refute them all, and that will affect your reality.

So, reality isn't stable. Reality is what you make based on your beliefs and your decisions.

Now, back to *American History X*. As I said, Derek eventually made friends with a Black inmate named Lamont. Now imagine that not only did they become friends, but when he was released from prison, Lamont brought him into the community where his family and neighbours lived. This interaction would again change Derek's reality. It would change his day-to-day living. It would change what he ate, the music he listened to, and where he went out to have fun. It would change his whole life, giving him completely new experiences and perspectives from his previous life. Just by changing one simple belief about one group of people, all these things in his reality changed.

So, no, a desk is not a banana. You can't make a desk turn into a banana by simply believing it is. But you can make a one-hundred-and-eighty-degree change in the direction of your life by changing what you think about things.

If you believe television is bad or podcasts are a waste of time, that will affect your life. If you believe that courses are all scams and rip-offs, that will affect your life. If you believe rich people are crooks and you can only get rich by being a thief or manipulator, that will affect your life. If you believe that all women are money-grabbing hoes and it's impossible for you to get into a relationship with a good woman because all they want is to find rich men to live off of, that will affect your life. If you believe that all Black people or Mexicans or Chinese or Arabs or any nationality of people are all untrustworthy, that will affect your life, and if you believe that all White people are racist and disingenuous, that will affect your life too.

Whatever you believe will affect the day-to-day reality you live in. So, I suggest that you take the time to develop beliefs that work for you, empower you and benefit you rather than just adopting the beliefs of other people, particularly those in your environment. The worst thing in the world you can do is blindly adopt the beliefs of your parents, your friends, your peers, your town, your race, your sex, and your nationality. These are usually the worst beliefs in the world because they are usually based more on tradition than introspection or analysis.

So, in doing this, by adopting the beliefs of these groups, you are allowing other people, often the most damaged people in society, to dictate your reality.

Truth and Belief

Is belief the same thing as the truth?

You see, I just realised one of the reasons that self-talk as a means of manifestation didn't work for me in the past. It's because back then, I thought everything I told myself had to be true.

There was a massive disconnect for me to hear myself repeat a statement, even in my mind, that was not, in my opinion, objectively true.

Now, obviously, this meant that I was severely restricted with regard to reprogramming my mind to do anything different because I could only feed my mind data based on my current sensory inputs.

But that's not how the mind's built to work. The mind is built to work in the exact opposite way. You give your mind a blueprint of what you want to create, and then it goes ahead and makes it. It creates the plan to achieve the results you want, it lays out actions for you as steppingstones in its achievement, and as we have previously mentioned, it quite possibly broadcasts information into the ether for other people who can help to bring the result about to receive and come into your life to assist you.

So now I have a new take on this. My new take is that truth and belief are not the same thing. I appreciate for some people that this has always been the case, so they might be thinking, 'No shit Sherlock,' but for me, it was a complete revelation. A revelation which changed the way that I look at the world.

I guess the internet, YouTube, social media, and the various rabbit holes that they have encouraged people to go down have aided my understanding of this. I mean, even before the advent of the aforementioned new technologies, creating modern cults like QAnon and Info Wars, before the so called Culture Wars, there has always been a huge disparity between belief and truth, which was probably the cause of my problem.

You see, some people have always been able to believe what they want, regardless of the truth. The truth is the hard facts around them, and the belief is what they choose to think is the reality, no matter how much it diverges from the hard facts presented by the external sensory inputs.

Some people believe that others have different intellectual abilities or moral characteristics based on their race; they continue to believe this, and no amount of scientific proof will change their beliefs.

In fact, most people believe things first and then go looking for scientific proof to confirm their beliefs. Confirmation bias is the technical term, I believe. The belief comes first, and then they look for scientific proof or otherwise to confirm it. So, truth and belief are related, but most definitely are not the same thing. Yet, as a truth seeker, I always tried to hold my beliefs open to question and analysis, meaning that I was willing, however grudgingly, to have them challenged, disproved, and replaced by whatever I could be convinced was the truth at that moment.

This approach brought many limitations, so now my new thinking is this. What you need to do is hone your belief. If you believe that you are meant to be a sprinter, but you are clinically obese, the truth is, you are clinically obese. There's no hiding that. If you wake up every morning, touch your body, look in the mirror or ask anybody else what they see. Everyone will tell you that you're clinically obese. But that's not the same as not believing that deep down inside, you are a sprinter. If you believe deep inside you are a sprinter, you can start walking every day, lifting weights, doing squats, and slowly moving that process into jogging every day and then running every day. That belief that you are a sprinter will manifest in you. That belief will direct you to the right continuous actions, which will have you shedding that weight, building the correct muscles, taking the right courses, getting the right training, going to the track, and eventually learning to sprint. The truth is that you were physically obese at some point, but your belief was that, deep down, you really were a sprinter.

The best example of this isn't just people who make themselves turn into things but people who regain themselves.

An example would be somebody who was an athlete but received an injury and had to stop their training regime and maybe put on some weight but never lost the belief that they are an athlete. The truth was that they had an injury, and they couldn't perform in the usual way. While injured, they couldn't perform their athletics. That is the truth. However, their belief as to what they are is that they are athletes. And as such, the moment their physical health allowed them to, they returned to training.

In fact, many injured athletes never stop. They either imagine and visualise themselves running again, remembering what it was like, reliving the feeling and imagining themselves in visions running again, calculating how they will improve and run differently in the future. Or they do whatever exercises they can with the injury in place. For example, a sprinter might do abdominal exercises or train the leg that wasn't injured and lift weights so that they don't get atrophy in their other muscles.

So don't be like the old me. Don't allow your objective truth to interfere with your belief. The Objective truth and what you believe do not have to be the same. The truth is, undoubtedly, what you can see, hear, smell, and feel. I'm not going to get any deeper than that because anything outside of that is undoubtedly hippie, hippie shit, but suffice it to say, the truth is represented by what you can pick up with your senses.

But your beliefs are not the same as these sensory inputs. You get to choose your beliefs. This is the concept of Be Do Have, being something as opposed to just doing it, which we will explore in more depth later in the book.

If you believe that you are something, then you will be that thing on the inside, no matter what the outside factors show. You will have the actions, mannerisms, and confidence of that thing, and this (fake it before you make it mentality) will drive you towards the actions of that thing.

You can choose to believe that you're anything. These are the roots of the great stories we hear about people who were in very difficult situations, such as prisoner of war camps, concentration camps, abusive relationships, people who grew up in abusive families or abject poverty. People who had every door closed in their faces and every opportunity denied them but always believed they were better than the truth that they were experiencing. They never allowed the truth that they were experiencing to change their belief of what they really were. These are the people who overcome seemingly insurmountable obstacles and, in doing so, give us jaw-dropping stories, inspirational anecdotes, hope and a glimpse into the indomitable human spirit, creating amazing legacies for us to learn from.

Your Decision Graph

Vishan Lakhiani has a brilliant idea of creating a graph showing all of your life's high and low points. This is truly a very useful document to create, but I've taken it one step further. Rather than charting the high and low points of your life, which makes the graph seem a little bit deterministic as if these points on it were guided by fate, I've created a decision graph.

This is a graph of the most influential decisions I've made in my life, which may or may not have created some of those high points and low points. Or maybe these decisions created some other experience in my life.

The point of the decision graph is this: every time you think to yourself, how did I get here? Admittedly, this will happen more times when you're having a very negative experience than when you have a positive one; it is well worth thinking back to the decision or decisions that got you there in the first place. Now, this technique adds putting these decisions on a graph so that you can look back and trace your good decisions, bad decisions, and their results, and use it as a tool to help guide you to not repeat the same mistake and make better decisions in the future.

I say this because I'm, quite frankly, in the middle of an absolute cluster fuck of a situation right now. And this business cluster fuck that I'm in, is genuinely the result of two or three decisions which I made four or five years ago. I can now quite clearly trace the decisions which I made that at the time seemed like good ideas, or were shortcuts, were done to benefit clients even though I knew they might be risky, were made out of laziness, or I didn't put a process in place to de-risk potential problems or were done to enrich myself at the time.

I am now aware that all of these decisions have led to this absolute monster of a problem I currently have to deal with. So, they're going to go on the graph, so I'll be able to see the effect that those decisions, which didn't seem so bad at the time, had on my future.

(Author's note: By the way, I feel compelled to inform you that this problem was resolved 24 hours after writing about its existence using a combination of the following: I used my willpower to control my mind, diverting it from panic, frustration and despair and keeping it positive. I then used meditation sessions before I contacted the people involved in the issue, which resulted in their cooperation and presentation of potential solutions which resolved the issue before I went to bed)

This is about more than tracking your Karma, which, contrary to popular belief, means right action, not what goes around comes around. It also aids in accepting your accountability for your actions and how they lead to your outcomes.

You know, one of my previous business partners had a fantastic talent, and I've only realised it recently. I didn't pay much attention to it then, but his talent was always finding a reason why whatever was going wrong wasn't our fault. The moment we had a problem, he would say, yeah, that's because of this. That's because of that. That would not have created this situation if he hadn't done this. The economy's done this. The government did that. The lawyer did this, and the other lawyer did that. For every single problem we had, he immediately had a response for it, and his response was never that we were to blame, even when we were. Obviously, this is something that he started developing in his childhood, so by the time I met him as an adult, he was an expert at it.

But I'm more aware than ever that almost all the problems you have in life can be traced back to your own decisions, attitudes, or beliefs.

So, as confident as this business partner was, it wasn't helpful. Deflecting everything bad that happened as somebody else's fault might make you feel good at the moment but doesn't help you improve.

You see, the cause of your current situation, whatever it may be, whether good or bad, most of the time is you—you and the decisions you made and the actions you took following those decisions.

So, make a decision graph. Then, you can look back on the big decisions you've made in your life.

You can start this any time. Probably, by the time you're old enough to read this book. You can start this graph. If you're a teenager, you could look at whether you decided to join that football team or not and the effect it had on your future. If you did or didn't decide to take that art class, if you allowed your friends to talk you out of joining that theatre group, if you asked out that person you were so attracted to. If you came out as a member of the LGBTQ community to your family or friends, if you decided to focus on studying to pass your exams because you were academically skilled and talented, or if you allowed your social group to convince you that academia was uncool, so you started hanging out and pretending to be a young thug or a gangster instead, just to seem cool by fitting in with the crowd. Or if you did the reverse.

These decisions are all going to lead to a point in your life, a point on that graph, and it's good to be aware of them. They might lead to great points in your life that make you happy and fill you with feelings of self-pride and accomplishment. And if they do, then you know these are the decisions you need to replicate.

But if they lead you to points in your life where you feel nothing but despair, stress, anger, frustration, sadness, or depression. Then, rather than using this graph to wallow in all that depression and sadness, it should be used as an obvious indicator of the kind of decisions and actions that got you there and the fact that you can probably avoid more unhappiness in the future, just by paying attention to the motivation behind those decisions and doing the opposite.

Smile at Children

By 2006, I had become a multi-millionaire through property investment. After several visits to Spain to examine opportunities to expand our property business, we decided to migrate to Spain altogether.

One of the main reasons we migrated to Spain was that we were 100% convinced that our children would have a much better upbringing in Spain than in our native UK, albeit away from their family, friends, relatives, and native language. We were convinced their lives would be better in Spain than in England.

One of the cornerstones of this belief was that every time we went to Spain, I paid very keen attention to the treatment of children in general.

Not just our children, all children. I used to say that 'being a child in Spain is like being a cow in India', a reference to the cultural phenomenon in India where cows are revered and treated almost as gods. This treatment is fantastic to see. For example, traffic jams occur because a cow wanders onto the road, and rather than being harassed and pushed off the road, all the traffic stops and waits for the cow to finish its journey. Additionally, I've been in parts of India where cows happily wander in and out of people's houses without being disturbed or ushered out. It has been twenty years since I was last in India, so this may have changed, but I saw these things with my own eyes, and it left an indelible imprint in my mind.

In Spain, well, in our experience in Andalucia, children were treated similarly. The first thing that I noticed was that everybody smiled at the children. Every child, whether happy, sad, angry, hungry, or frustrated, is greeted by an adult with a smile, and I often wondered to myself what kind of psychological effect this had.

Secondly, unlike England in the early 2000s, where fear of paedophilia or being accused of having untoward intentions created an environment where people avoided the children of other parents, most children were never given sweets by strangers.

I will never forget being in a DIY shop with a huge six-by-four plank of wood, waiting for the guy operating the wood Saw to cut it to my required measurements. While I waited, I had my son with me and as soon as he noticed my six-year-old, he smiled at my son and immediately produced a sweet to give to him, for him to suck on while we waited, Children are waiting hand to foot. I don't know if this spoils them, but I'm pretty sure that child depression and child suicide rates are lower than elsewhere, all because of this environment.

These children grow up in an environment where they are told and shown that they are important. The fact that people smile at children by default is fantastic because, in that culture, children become so confident in that environment. When you see a child of no more than two- or three years old walk up to you, the child will start waving and smiling in the absolute expectation that you are happy to see it and will wave and smile back. So much so that it pre-empts you from waving and smiling at it by waving and smiling at you first.

I've almost never seen this in all my years in the UK. Because children overall, in the UK, do not grow up in an environment where they are treated as if they are important, special, revered and loved. At least not by complete strangers.

I've often wondered what it would be like to run an experiment where children were brought up in an environment of positivity, positive self-talk, reverence and love, to see how they developed at an older age. Unfortunately, most of the experiments which claim to create these environments turn out to be cults, where the children they claim to love are eventually manipulated and abused.

Nonetheless, the Andalusian culture in Spain, at least in the early 2000s, is the closest I've ever seen to this type of experiment. I'm not trying to say that there aren't child abusers. I am saying that, as a culture, Andalusia loves and reveres its children, and it's part of the region's DNA. It's ingrained in the everyday way of doing things, and I'm sure if analysed, the statistics will show the mental and self-esteem benefits of this.

So, if you want the best for your children, start by creating an environment at home where they know that they are important and loved. I know you think you already have, but you probably have not. Your environment probably points to them being loved, yes loved, but… also a draw on your time, an expense, a problem to take to activities, an annoyance at times, a nuisance at others. All these things will be picked up on by the child. Once your home environment has been secured, work on their secondary environments to replicate this security. Even if this means getting rid of negative aunties and uncles or changing their school. All of this will have an overarching effect on how they see themselves and the world, what's possible in the world, their place in it, what they are willing to accept in terms of treatment from others and what they are willing to believe in terms of what they can achieve with their lives.

Ground Zero and Gratitude

Ground zero. I have been unfortunate enough (or fortunate enough, depending on how you look at things) to have hit ground zero a couple of times in my life. By ground zero, I mean rock bottom, physically, financially, or spiritually destitute. This has happened for different reasons, at differing times involving different aspects of my life.

The biggie, obviously, was losing my property portfolio and business, going from being a multi-millionaire property mogul one day to realising that I had only 20 euros to my name and two children under the age of 10 depending on me for their sustenance and survival.

Another example is when I contracted COVID-19 in 2021. My experience with COVID-19 was the complete loss of the ability of my brain to send instructions to my body. At the start, I had fourteen days of the usual symptoms: shortness of breath, fever, and diarrhoea. But when I came out of the fever, I literally could not instruct my body to get out of the chair, wash my hands or walk across a room; I would think it simple instructions for mundane tasks which I had performed thousands of times before, I would tell myself to do them, but my body wasn't responding.

I literally had to start from scratch concerning everything I did, like a child or somebody who had come out of a coma. And then within a year of that, I had a similar experience when I was diagnosed with heart failure. Whereupon, coming out of the hospital, I slept more hours than I was awake, again losing all control of my willpower.

One last example, which wasn't as dramatic as the previous one, was when I had a nasty cough that lasted for a month. Upon hearing me wheeze, somebody unhelpfully suggested that I might have cancer. I went to the doctor, who sent me to the hospital and ran some tests. And while I awaited the results of those tests, I started to think about what I would do if I was given just six months to live. I thought about all the things I had promised myself that I would do and all the things I wanted to get done.

I wouldn't wish ground zero on anybody.

The aim of this is not to give you a rundown of my medical history.

The aim is to make you think about how you view your life, how you use your time and if you are progressing and getting everything done. I always say that everybody should have a medical emergency at least once in a life, preferably once every five years. Because there's nothing like thinking that you are going to die to reframe your priorities, get you to focus and get you out of your head. Genuinely believing that your death is imminent helps you to reassess your priorities from doing all the stuff that everybody else wants you to do, all the stuff that society tells you that you should be doing and forces you to be aware of the stuff that you actually want to do or get done before you die.

Once this has been acknowledged, this death-led focus will help you learn how to prioritise those things and give you an urgency to get them done. You lose the ridiculous arrogant assumption most of us live by, where we take life for granted as if we are going to live forever and have plenty of time to do the important stuff that we should be doing now.

But for me, the concept of gratitude is equally important. You see unless you've had one of the experiences I've previously outlined or something similar, it is easy for your life to lose perspective and think that you have nothing to be grateful for.

You may be having a bad day today, and when I say that, 'You should practise gratitude,' you reply, 'What the hell have I got to be grateful for?' My response would be, 'If you don't know what you should be thankful for, you need to think about your ground zero.'

If you're physically fit and your finances are above subsistence, it's very hard for people to imagine ground zero. Sometimes, I think life or the Universe brings people to ground zero just to remind them of what they have to be grateful for.

You see, when I was making enough money to live on but not achieving the financial success I wanted, I would have easily said, 'I don't have anything to be grateful for.'

But when my living means fell below subsistence, and I had less money than I needed to support my family, I realised just how lucky I had been to be making more than enough for us to survive and making enough money to be comfortable.

If I could have compared the two points, I would have fallen on my knees and cried in gratitude for having enough money to pay all our bills, keep a roof over our heads, keep two cars driving, and have a little bit left over for life's little pleasures.

Because I didn't have enough money to pay our bills, our cars broke down, and we didn't have enough money to fix them; this circumstance led to all kinds of upset and stress: extra travelling, dropping somebody off here, picking someone up here, getting a bus for this, arranging a pickup or a lift for that, promising to pay this, missed direct debit payment for that.

That's when you realise how much you really have to be grateful for, in the same way, that I only realised how much I took my health for granted until after I had lost it. I was in good health in my early 20s, having trained with several UK martial arts champions in the dojo I frequented. Even years after I left full-time martial arts classes, I always tried to keep my health and fitness to a good level.

When I complained to myself about how badly the level of my health had fallen, how much weight I had put on, how unfit I was, how I could no longer do the things like forward somersaults, cartwheel kicks, and box splits that I used to be able to do and stuff like that. I didn't understand how lucky I was; I had no idea how healthy I was because I did not know what ground zero was. That is until I got COVID-19, and rather than not being able to do a forward somersault or a box split, I could not even summon the willpower to get myself out of my bed and walk into the shower. It took me over an hour's worth of willing myself to move until I finally got enough energy and power to get up and move my body from one place to another. I had never experienced anything like it, and at that point, I again would have fallen on my knees, bowed my head, and wept with joy and gratitude for the ability I previously had to just get up, shower, go into a dojo and just do some shadow boxing as the fat, overweight, middle-aged bum fighter that I was when I was complaining about my lack of health.

Understanding ground zero is powerful. I truly suggest you appreciate it (i.e., how bad things could be) and employ it yourself (i.e., appreciate what you have) before the Universe uses it to remind you that you really do have something to be grateful for.

The Universe does not do this out of spite or because it's mean. I think the Universe does it because you're asking it to. You tell the Universe that 'you've got nothing to be grateful for'. It tells you, 'Oh, yes, you do.' You say, 'Fuck you. I don't believe you.' It says, 'Okay, I'll show you.'

Another way of looking at it could be that you tell your subconscious that you have nothing to be grateful for, and it says, 'Instructions accepted. Running the program called nothing to be grateful for now.' Then, as part of this program, it removes everything you could be grateful for from your life.

It's a simple lesson, and the lesson isn't one of power, arrogance, or haughtiness from the Universe. It is not designed to make you fall down before it with gratitude and servility.

The point of the lesson is to teach you that the only way to get more in life is through gratitude for what you already have. This method helps you and directs you to get more of what you want; that is the Universe's job. Its one purpose is for you to have more in life. If you lose the ability to be grateful, you massively reduce your ability to get more. Therefore, it's the Universe's job to teach you how to be grateful so that you can use your gratitude for what you have as the springboard to get more, as the launch pad to access all the wonderful things in life that the Universe wants you to receive.

So, if you lose your ability to be grateful, or through your short-sightedness and arrogance, you are not grateful for what you have. It's really the Universe's job to take it all away so that you have a platform to understand that you should have been more grateful for what you had at the time and through that, springboard yourself to much higher levels of achievement and abundance having more to be grateful for.

I wouldn't wish ground zero on my worst enemy. But at the same time, when people get stuck in a rut of not understanding how to be grateful for everything they already have when they have so much to be grateful for, their lack of acknowledgement of this holds them back. Although I wouldn't wish it on my worst enemy, for you to get the things you want in life, I would always definitely wish it on my best friend. As my university friend Sudashana Sharma once told me, 'We go through troths in life so that we can rise to new peaks.' This is why I believe people hit ground zero, not as a punishment, bad luck or misfortune, but as a part of the process of moving from where they are to where they can appreciate all that they had so that they can have the right attitude and frequency to move to where you want to be.

Love Yourself First

So, here's an important exercise. I want you to think of somebody who you have been in love with. If you have never been in love, think of being in love with somebody. Now, I want you to write down 10 things you did or would do for that person to show them how much you love them.

This isn't an accounting exercise, so if for any reason you can't come up with 10, at least come up with five or six. Now, these are things that you would do for somebody who you are absolutely besotted with—I mean, really, really in love with, crazy about, infatuated with—and whose well-being is of the utmost importance to you.

It is well known that if we love someone, whether platonically or emotionally, we care about them more than ourselves. We care for them more than ourselves, and we wish better things for them than we do for ourselves.

So, write that list. Write a list of what you would do for the person you care for more than yourself. Write about how you would like them to be treated. What would you do if they were mistreated by others? What would you advise them to do if other people mistreated them? How would you treat them on their birthday? What would you do to make them feel appreciated? What would you do to show them that they are special? How would you protect them from people who wanted to mistreat them? What would you do to help them if they were unhealthy?

How would you treat them generally? How would you touch them? How would you hug them? What would you say to them? Would you tell them that you love them regularly? Would you tell them how special they are? Would you tell them how much you care for them?

Now, once you've got that list, whether it's 5 things, ten things or more, take a moment and read that list of all the things you would do for somebody you truly loved.

All done, great because that's the list of things that you now must do for yourself. Do them all to yourself (err except the kissing which might be a bit logistically difficult).

You see, the most bizarre paradox of humanity is that so many of us are brought up to think that we are not worthy or important. So, we project the love we should have for ourselves onto others. Because we're taught that we shouldn't have that love, or we don't deserve that love. In the same way that we are taught not to talk to ourselves (which is a massive mistake), we're taught to project our love to other people. We have so much love inside of us, and we haven't learned to be grateful for our own existence, to appreciate the good that we can do, to appreciate the good that we bring to the world, so we project all of that love to others. Now, I'm not saying you shouldn't love other people or that you should become a narcissist and love only yourself. I'm saying that if anybody else on this planet is worthy of love, you, too, are worthy of love, and you don't have to wait for others to love you.

In fact, you shouldn't wait for others to love you. Your primary source of love should be from yourself. Let me say that again: Your primary source of love should be yourself.

Think about this logically. When you were born, you were helpless, and you needed parents or guardians to take care of you. So, the primary source of love you received came from your parents or guardians. But your parents and guardians are only meant to care for you until a certain point in life. In most Western societies, that is until about 18 years old. In some other societies, it may be as young as 14 or 15, but past that point, they are no longer responsible for your care. You're considered an adult and responsible for your own care. So, once you pass this point, why are you still looking for love outside of yourself?

If your parents were responsible for your care and gave you the love you needed to thrive, be well-adjusted, happy, and confident, then told you that it's time for you to go and take care of yourself. Then, isn't it also your job not only to feed yourself, clothe yourself, and provide for yourself economically but also to provide for yourself spiritually and emotionally?

Well, yes, it is!!

But what so many of us do is we move straight from our parents' emotional support to our friends' emotional support and then from our friends' emotional support to our significant other's emotional support.

There is a joke about guys who never learn how to cook, clean or wash for themselves. They literally leave the home of a mother who cooks, cleans and washes for them and goes straight to their girlfriend or their wife who cooks, cleans and washes for them. I particularly remember working with one gentleman who had never learned how to cook, clean or wash. He went straight from his mother's house to his wife's house. Coming from one person who did his chores for him, he went straight to another.

Of course, these are extreme examples in the modern age because most men and women learn how to do these rudimentary things. Men learn how to cook, clean, and wash. Women learn how to change a tyre or do some DIY, so these stereotypes are no longer realistic.

But emotionally, so many of us go from the love and care of our parents straight into the love and care of somebody else, missing the point that the person who is meant to take over the responsibility for our love and care is us.

The person who is supposed to take over our financial, social, and moral responsibilities from our parents is us.

So, look at that list hard. If something on it sounds corny, then don't do it. But you need to do the things on that list for yourself, primarily before you try to do it to anybody else. If you can't do those things for yourself and you don't do those things for yourself, you will never be able to do them for someone else. Because you, the source of the love you want to give, will be lacking in love.

You'll be projecting the love that you should be giving to yourself to somebody else, meaning that you're lacking in the things that you're giving away, and you'll be going to that person for them to fill you up with those things, and if at any point they fall short, it's going to cause a rupture in your relationship.

Telling Yourself You Love Yourself

I almost guarantee that somewhere on that list will be telling the person that you love them. Being told that you are loved is one of the most important aspects of human conditioning. Yet, in many surveys, many people don't remember being told that they were loved, even by their parents.

Parents tend to tell us they love us when we're very young, too young to do things that cause them annoyance or dissatisfaction. But the moment we're old enough to start doing things they don't like, they tend to drop the term 'I love you' a little bit like they do in their own relationships.

They start to assume that we should know that they love us. After all, they cook for us, clean for us, drive us to school, and buy our school uniforms. Of course, they love us, and we should know that. Plus, they feel corny saying it, and even worse, they feel hurt when they tell us that they love us, and we reject them by not saying it back.

But the time a child starts to have some kind of agency, they have every right not to say 'I love you' back. The parents are the adults, and they should be mature enough to understand that they can say 'I love you' to a child without receiving an 'I love you too' back. They should be mature enough for this to happen and for it not to offend or hurt them. That is the root of unconditional love.

But unfortunately, most parents are themselves, still like children, and once you stop saying 'I love you' back, they stop telling you they love you. They stop giving you the emotional support that you need as a child because they are not getting that back from you. Even though they're adults and as adults, they shouldn't require the reciprocation of that emotional support from you; they should be giving it to themselves. But they are not, so they do.

This is why you need to say, I love you to yourself. If you can do it auditorily, that would be great. If you can only do it mentally, do that until you can bring yourself to speak the words out loud. It's even better to say it out loud like you would with a genuine friend. If you do it with a sincere compliment, for example, think of something about yourself that you're proud of and say, 'Dude, you really did that well, man, I love you for that.' This helps.

When you overcome an obstacle, look in the mirror and say, 'Well done, bro. I love you for that. I can't believe you got through that. Well done. I love the way you handled that situation.'

But most importantly, you should tell yourself you love yourself daily. The same way that you would tell your romantic partner in the honeymoon phase while you're still besotted with them. In this phase, you tell them that you love them, and you never run out of reasons or ways to tell them that you love them.

Sometimes, you look at them and think, 'I love your hair, I love your eyebrows, I love the way you scrunch up your nose when you laugh, I love the way your lips move when you talk, I love the way you hum when you clean.'

There's a great joke about this: somebody lists all the things that they love about a person in the honeymoon phase, and then, years later into the marriage, that same list is the list of things that they hate about them.

But the truth is, you have plenty of things to love about yourself. No matter what you've been told or taught or what society gives you as standards of beauty or behaviour, there are plenty of things about you that are lovable. That's why there's somebody for everybody on this planet. For absolutely everybody on this planet, their traits or behaviours are the things that will make someone else fall in love with them.

The key here is to fall in love with your own traits and then look at yourself in the mirror and tell yourself that you love yourself. Now I suggest doing this every day, 10 times in the morning and 10 times before you go to bed at night. Brushing your teeth is a great time to do this; just do it before or after. Toothbrush in hand, look at yourself in the mirror and tell yourself that you love yourself, ten times, out loud. If, like me, you have a real adverse reaction to staring at yourself in the mirror (people don't often talk about this, but it's a genuine thing), then the eye gazing technique is pretty powerful.

Just gaze at yourself in one eye and tell yourself that you love yourself five times, then change your gaze to the other and tell yourself you love yourself five more times. This is an amazingly interesting technique because if you get scary monsters when you look at yourself in the mirror, you'll discover that they only come from one eye, which is interesting enough. If this is the case, I will wager that the eye is the one above the right temporal lobe where negative thoughts are held.

But the more you practise this technique, the more you will discover that the scary monsters go away because even scary monsters dissipate when told how much they are loved.

So, to recap.

Look at yourself in the mirror daily and tell yourself that you love yourself at least 10 times. That should be the cornerstone of your day. 'I Love you' out loud at least 10 times per day but preferably 20 times a day, 10 in the morning and 10 before you go to bed.

This will start to fill the hole that was left by your parents, who stopped telling you that they loved you because you pretended that you were too old for that stuff now, but it wasn't true. The hole left by your fake friends who said you were friends for life, then stabbed you in the back and dropped you to hang out with other people. The hole left by the person who swore to you that they would love you forever, but they lied.

You probably told your parents to stop telling you that they loved you way too early. You were a child, and this made you feel more adult. As you grew up, you had all the people around you who loved you but thought that you should just know it by the way they behaved. This list now includes your partner, who has probably stopped telling you that they love you for everything that you do.

Remember, just like when you were a child, when you meet someone new, they tell you they love you for every single thing that you do, making you feel as if you are perfect without having to put any effort into it. But as a relationship goes on, that love starts to become dependent on the things you do, and suddenly, you are missing that love.

The reality is love was never meant to be given to you by anybody else. If you believe in God, then you were created in the image of God, in the image of perfection; you were most definitely meant to love yourself. You were never meant to rely on love from any other human being. Love from other human beings is a bonus, and conversely (as most things are), the more you love yourself, which fuels you to go out into the world and do good things for yourself and others, the more others will love you.

The less you love yourself, the more insular you become. The more scarcity you see in the world from not loving yourself, the less love you will have for you to go out and give. And the less love you have to give, the less love you receive back.

Many things in life are counterintuitive in this way. Still, as converse as it seems, it's true. The more you have, the more you can give, and the more you give, the more you get. The less you have, the less you might want to give because of fears of scarcity, and the less you give, the less you get back.

So, love yourself first. Then, use this reservoir of self love to go out and give love. As you give love freely, you will see that you get back more love from more places than you ever thought possible.

Love Yourself, Again

So, look in the mirror and say, 'I Love you.'

Say I love you to counteract other people and their stupid fucking judgments. The way they judge you on what you wear, 'I wouldn't wear that. I wouldn't match those shoes with that shirt. Are you really wearing that dress?'

The way they judge you when you try your best. 'Is that all you can do? Can't you do any better than that?'

The way they judge you for the things you feel. 'Why would anybody want to do that?', 'Can't understand why somebody would want to be with someone of the same sex.', 'How could you agree with that political policy?', 'Do you really believe that thing? You're disgusting.'

Tell yourself you love yourself because you know that you're not perfect. Still, you are most definitely perfectly deserving of love. Faults, warts, and all, you are most definitely deserving of love. Tell yourself that you love yourself because you know that you can change. Even if there's something about you that you are not happy with, it's not set in stone. None of it is. It can change.

An excellent point made by Maxwell Maltz, the author of the book Psycho-Cybernetics, is that he would do plastic surgery operations on people and physically change their appearance. Yet they would still think that they looked the same as before. Your ability to change is based on what you do differently and how you see yourself. Because even if you physically change your body, you can still have body dysmorphia and think that you are overweight or too thin. You need to change and see yourself as changed to get the result. So, you can change; nothing about you has to stay the same. There is no failing, fault, disappointing characteristic, or foible that cannot be repaired.

Many people will find this hard to believe, but I changed my laugh. I am a big fan of the comedian Jimmy Carr. I liked his unique laugh comprising nine notes that rise in an almost melodic pattern. I didn't like mine, so I changed my laugh to reflect his. I did not take all nine notes; I used the last two and embellished them with an Ainsley Harriot kind of Caribbean strain, a bit like the Lenny Henry character Uncle Deakus, now I think of it. Strange right! You might think something as spontaneous and fundamental as the way you laugh would be set in stone, but it isn't. I changed it, and so can you. You can change anything. So, love yourself to improve your current life and your future. With love.

Felix Joseph

PRACTICAL

First Thing in the Morning

What is the first thing that you do when you wake up in the morning? Have a think about that. I truly believe that the first thing you do when you wake up in the morning is massively underrated by most people. It is unfortunate that for most people nowadays, the very first thing that they do when they wake up in the morning is to check their phone. But for other people might be to talk to their partner, or if their partner is anything like mine listen to their partner.

But here's the problem: If what you feed your brain is of such importance—and I'm hoping by now you're starting to appreciate that this is true—then the very first thing that you feed your brain, the first time that your consciousness returns after sleep, must be of some importance.

We all know that if you're woken up out of your sleep by loud banging from the building site across the road, screaming from your annoying neighbours who argue all the time or the incessant ringing of your doorbell by a very early delivery man, these things can immediately set you off down the path of being in a bad mood. I have a very talkative wife, and she used to like to wake up and talk first thing in the morning, which means that the first things in my brain were her priorities, good or bad. If she wanted to talk about someone who annoyed her the day before, then that's the first thing that entered my brain; if she was frustrated or scared about something that was happening, bills we had to pay, or problems we had in life, that was the first thing that entered my brain.

If she was happy, great; at least, that was the first thing that entered my brain. But it was what she was happy about that entered my brain first before I even got a chance to think of what I was happy about. It was only when I took physical steps to change this process and ensure that the first things I thought about were mine that I started to see a change in how my day unfolded.

Similarly, if your first thing in the morning is to turn on the News, again, you're doing yourself a massive disservice. The first thing you'll get is other people's versions of a story, and if the first thing you do is check social media, then the first thing you'll get is other people's lies.

Let's be straight about this. Other people try to promote to you that they're living their best life. They are not telling the truth about their lives, just promoting the life they want you to believe that they are living. And with the News media, you're going to get people telling you the version of the story that they want you to believe based on the facts of whatever actually happened. So, their political allegiance, moral compass, or the whims of their advertisers will dictate the version of the truth you get.

How is any of this going to help you to be happy? How is any of this going to help you to be more successful? How will any of this help you to be more productive, calmer, and have more peace in your life? Aren't these the things you want?

Because if you want more calm, peace, success, and happiness, then I suggest that the first thing you put into your brain, the first thing you allow to enter your consciousness, the first thing that your awareness consumes, is what you choose.

Positive self-talk is excellent for this. If there are some statements or beliefs that you want in your brain, things that you want as the first things that enter your awareness so that you can follow them as principles, mantras, or belief systems throughout the day, then they should be the first thing that enters your brain in the morning.

This is what I do now. Before I speak to anybody, I meditate, feel gratitude, and play some positive self-talk, so the first thing that enters my awareness is what I can do, what I can achieve, what is possible, how good I can be, how wonderful the world can be. The fact that everything is for me, and nothing is against me, the fact that things that may look difficult can actually be overcome.

That's the first thing that enters my brain nowadays—not other people's priorities, beliefs, fears, worries, opinions, stresses, lies, or pretences.

Like most things, you have yet to determine if this morning system will be helpful, so I suggest you try it. If you have a talkative partner or spouse, wake up half an hour before they do and think the things you want to think. Do a gratitude practice, 'segment intend' your day, listen to some positive self-talk, or go to the Good News Channel (positive News, not a religious channel) and only allow yourself to hear good News.

Do whatever suits you, but make sure that you are in control of the first thing that enters your brain in the morning. I'm sure that most of us have had the experience of having one bad thing happen to us in the morning, which seemingly creates a domino effect of bad things that occur throughout the day.

How many of us have had a day which started by being woken up by the noise next door, going half asleep to get a glass of water but dropping a glass and then having to clean that up, and therefore being late for work, and then being frustrated in traffic, beeping at somebody who cut you up so you cursed them and flipping them off, and then arriving at work late to have your boss reprimand you for your time keeping making you even more annoyed, so you are not concentrating on your work and start making mistakes which causes everything to take longer. Hence, you are late to leave for your lunch break, so your favourite meal will be sold out when you get to the food truck. Need I go on.

It could just be something as simple as going to social media and seeing somebody you envy posting that they've just done something extraordinary, something you wish you could do. This post causes you to really believe that their life is much better than yours, making the first thoughts that you have for that day be that you are not good enough, that your life isn't good enough, that you're not successful enough, and that you'll never achieve the things you want. Why does it always happen to you? Why do you never get the things that you want? Why does your life suck so much?

That type of thought pattern as your foundation for the day will not bring you good, happy, positive, and productive results. So, take control of your mornings and pay particular attention to the first things that go into your brain when you wake up.

The First Hours of the Day Should Be Yours.

In addition to making your first thoughts your own, the truth is that the first hour of your day should be yours. Now, before I even continue, let me deal with the objection. I know that this will not be possible for lots of people. I remember when my children were very young. They used to get up at 5:30 in the morning. So, for me to make the first hour of my day totally dedicated to me and my needs, I would have been awake by 4:30 am.

This was never going to fly for somebody who would have to follow this process with a two-hour commute and then work a full eight-hour day.

So, if this isn't possible, I totally understand. I'm not asking you to join the 5 am club or any foolishness like that. But I must also tell you that, in the period of my life, when I got up at 5:30 am, I wasn't so interested in spiritual things, but I was into exercise. So, because my children woke up so early, they went to bed early, as did my wife, meaning I could spend the last hour of my day working out while everyone else was asleep.

You can adjust this to suit your circumstances, but the key is to understand that you really need to have an hour for yourself every single day.

In some ways, this is a silly concept because, obviously, every hour of your life is yours, right! But in the world that we live in, we don't get to dedicate every single hour of our lives to ourselves, not really. We actually spend our whole lives dedicated to other people's priorities.

If you have a young family, as I just described, when you wake up, your first priority will be tending to your children. Your partner may have some things that they want you to do, meaning that you're now dealing with their priorities, not yours. Whether it's fixing things, taking out the trash, ironing clothes, making breakfast, or planning the weekend, this may not strictly be your priority; it may be something you're doing for your partner.

If you work for somebody else, you're working on your boss's or your supervisor's priorities, working towards your company's aims and mission. If you work for yourself, you're working for your clients, priorities, and what they're paying you to do, so you are not spending your day working on your priorities.

Most people are lucky if they get an hour or two to themselves nevertheless for themselves, and by that point, they are usually just exhausted and want to be entertained or rest. But you really need to spend a minimum of an hour on yourself, and if possible, you should spend the first hour of your day on yourself because this will set you up for the rest of the day. This will set you up for how you interact with everybody else's priorities and everything else that's thrown at you throughout the day.

Anthony Robbins calls this his Hour of Power; Vishan Lakhiani also refers to it, as do many other teachers. I've been doing this for as long as I can remember, one way or another, but I agree with the Vishen Lakhiani concept. At the very least, you should make time every single day of your life to exercise, learn and take in some kind of mindfulness practice, whether it be one of the various forms of meditation or something else. Something that centres you and grounds you, that helps you to release the pressure, something other than alcohol, computer games, telenovelas, or porn.

I recommend the first hour of your day because, for me, it's so significant that you start the day with your priorities. Do not start the day by looking at your mobile phone. Make it the last thing you do in the morning. Start your day by making sure you ground yourself and centre yourself, whether it's through meditation or some other process. Do some form of exercise, even if it's just a warm-up or stretching, to get your body ready for what you will ask it to do, which is to carry you throughout the day. And if you can do some learning, that would be preferable. Do some reading, watch a course, or listen to some self-talk, a self-improvement audiobook or Podcast to prepare your mind for the coming day.

If you did this every single day, you would find that as the priorities of other people or unexpected unfortunate things occur, whether they're physical or mentally challenging, you would be perfectly positioned and poised to deal with them in a much better way than if you just got up in the morning, grabbed your phone, started scrolling through social media, and ingesting other people's junk.

Set yourself up to have the best day, every day, by prioritising yourself and your physical and mental health. Give just one hour out of the 24 that you hope to live that day to yourself first, and watch the following 23 hours unfold better than you had ever expected.

Doing Things in a 'Different Way'

Do something in a different way every single day. This idea was popularised by Dr Joe Dispenza, though many other teachers share similar philosophies. The concept is simple: for example, I changed how I showered today. Usually, I start from my head and work my way down, crossing my body in specific patterns. But today, I began by cleaning the entire left side of my body from top to bottom, then worked my way up the right side, ending at the top of my head. This was completely different from my usual routine.

The reason for this change is quite self-evident yet still worth mentioning. As creatures of habit, we are designed to learn how to do things and automate those processes, and we often forget the power of doing something differently. This isn't the same as doing something new—although that is closely linked—but rather approaching a familiar task from a fresh perspective.

Doing something 'differently' is essential not just because it keeps the brain active and helps create new neural pathways, aiding in neuroplasticity, but also because if you're trying to solve a problem and keep approaching it in the same way, you're unlikely to find a new solution. As Einstein famously said, 'Insanity is doing the same thing over and over again and expecting different results.' This concept applies directly to problem-solving.

For example, let's say I have a marketing problem, and I'm trying to get a specific product's marketing strategy to work. Suppose I keep approaching the marketing campaign in the same way with only small variations, whereas, in reality, the whole foundation of that approach is flawed. In that case, I'm much less likely to achieve the breakthrough I seek than if I take a completely different approach. Of course, I'm not suggesting that you throw the baby out with the bathwater and take a new approach whenever you encounter a problem. In marketing, for instance, you're supposed to iterate—make small changes. However, the key concept here is the willingness to change and to do things differently if you want a different result.

This 'change muscle,' like any muscle, grows from habit. By doing 'everyday' things differently, you're not only creating new neural links and pathways' but also developing a habit that will aid you in approaching problems differently. It's much like the idea that your keys are always in the last place you look—but if you always look in the same place or approach the search in the same way, it will take you much longer to find them. If you always assume they're in the house and never consider that you might have dropped them outside near your car, then you'll never find them because you're limiting the way you approach the problem.

Ultimately, this practice is about teaching yourself to expand your neuroplasticity, create new neural pathways, and build the muscle to do things differently. We all know that success is often just an accumulation of failures, so you must try different ways of doing something and accumulate those failures before reaching success. Success on your first attempt can only be the result of two possibilities: you were either lucky—(which is fine, I mean luck is necessary and appreciated)—or you're a natural, which means you have some innate ability that allows you to excel at that task effortlessly. Everyone else must learn from failure, iterate, and eventually succeed. Thus, cultivating the habit of 'doing things differently' is essential.

Focus... It's Not Just a Song by Xzibit

You get what you focus on. I don't think this is really up for debate. For example, if I had two tasks in front of me—one to build a toy car from Lego parts and the other to write an essay—if I focus on building the toy car, it's clear that the car will get built, and the essay won't get written. No surprises here so far, or, as some might say, 'No shit Sherlock.'

When we talk about focus in the so-called world of woo-woo, it's simply an extension of this idea. Focusing on one task over another brings that task to completion first, so it's not a big leap to understand that focusing on a particular outcome is more likely to make that outcome occur. The reason isn't some magical intervention by fairies or angels—though if you're into that, I won't argue. But rather your own personal efforts to bring about the result.

Let's take this further, into an area where people often feel uncomfortable. Say you want to be a successful businessperson. You can focus on everything you're good at and use those strengths to build a belief system that propels you toward running a successful business. Or you can focus on the naysayers—the people who tell you it can't be done, who remind you of others who have failed before you, and who dwell on the negative aspects of business, like how much money you could lose or how much of your life you could waste pursuing it.

The time you spend worrying about what can go wrong is time you're not spending on making things go right. It's as simple as that. If everyone around you talks about what could go wrong, you'll also spend your mental energy thinking about it. Worse yet, you might start spending your physical energy and time building systems or doing work to prevent things from going wrong, which is not the same as putting your time and effort into making things go right.

It's like spending all your time building a dam because there might be a flood instead of building a port with built-in flood prevention that could become a thriving commercial centre if there isn't a flood. Both tasks might occur in the same physical area but are not the same activity. Your choice will depend on your focus, expectations, and beliefs.

I'm not saying you should never plan for potential problems or think about what could go wrong. But if your focus is constantly on the negatives, what might fail or go awry, and you tend to follow through on what you pay attention to. Your efforts will, at best, be focused on mitigating worst-case scenarios. This is very different from putting your efforts into creating a best-case scenario and working toward success.

How to Rewire Failure so That it Leads to Success

God knows I needed to learn this when I was younger, and I'm including it here because I'm sure many other people need to learn it, too.

One of my favourite quotes is that your key is always in the last place you look for it. Well, so is success?

Success is usually the result of several failures. This is true for almost everybody except the rare few lucky people who are phenoms. But once you've ruled out lucky people or naturally gifted people, everybody else who is successful only got there by going through a number of failures and course corrections.

The biggest mistake I made, the biggest mistake that anybody can make, is focusing on failures, to put more emphasis and more emotional attachment to the embarrassment, the shame, the upset, and the disappointment of the failures you inevitably meet on the way to success.

Over the course of my life, I have attached more emotional value to these failures than to the times that I succeeded.

In his book *Psycho Cybernetics*, Dr Maxwell Maltz explains it very clearly. The whole point of this process is to go through the failures, learn from them at the time, use them to 'course correct,' and then try again until you succeed. Not to go through the process, have a failure, not course correct but do the same thing and fail again, or use the failure as an excuse to give up and not try anymore. That's the first big mistake.

The second big mistake, which is probably even more dangerous in the long run, is rather than learning from the failure, wallowing in it, focusing on it, remembering it, emotionalising it, replaying and reusing it over and over again to your own detriment.

Not only to traumatise yourself but as a foundation for a set of beliefs that teach you that you can't succeed in this thing and then as a bigger foundation of a belief that tells you why you can't succeed in other things and ultimately, for some people as a foundation for why you can't succeed in anything.

Failure is part of the mechanism for striving towards success in our goals. The problem is that we were never given a user manual to teach us methods of achievement, so we use it wrongly. Rather than adjusting our guidance system to eventually hit the target, we take the failures as the actual target itself.

We make the mistake of focusing on the failure as if the failure now becomes the target. We focus on the fact that we had a failure, the results of the failure, the feelings of failure, the disappointment of the failure, and the emotions of the failure as if the failure had become the aim itself. And when that becomes the aim, you soon realise that what you are actually focusing on in your life, what you are unwittingly aiming for by sheer virtue of paying attention to it, is failure.

The Athlete Example

I have never been an athlete. I've never been any good at track, gymnastics or any of the field events. But like most people, I'm a huge fan of the Olympics, particularly the 100 meters, which I think has historically been the biggest draw of all Olympic events. In terms of Sport, the only one I have ever excelled in was Martial Arts but as I like athletics, I try to transmute what I know from my discipline to that one.

I previously made an example of how athletes, particularly the 100-meter sprinters, can demonstrate the correct use of the will and how the correct use of the will shows that some of this Hippie Shit is not that impractical at all. In his seminal book, 'The Science of Getting Rich', Wallace D Wattles points out that using the will is not to force anybody or anything else to do your bidding. I know that this statement is quite revolutionary because when we talk of willpower, we usually talk about somebody who creates a result through the sheer force of will.

When I first abandoned using any esoteric concepts such as the law of attraction or anything outside of the realm of pure hardcore business in my life, my business survived and, in some cases, thrived 100% based on my willpower. A mixture of what I could get myself to do, what I could get other people to do, and how I could force situations which were going against the result I wanted into turning around and going back in the opposite direction. I basically brute force attacked problems and situations with nothing but hard work, expertise and a constant, constant barrage of willpower until I moved them in the direction that I wanted them to go. My business survived for over seventeen years based on this massive amount of willpower and effort sprinkled with expertise and good relationships.

This is what most people think of when they think of the will.

If you read any of the alpha male styled business manuals, they all promote the exertion of your will over other people in one way or another. But Wallace D Wattles said this is not the correct use of the will. In fact, he goes as far as to say, if forcing somebody to do something by physical coercion, i.e. slavery, is a crime, then forcing them to do it by mental coercion should also be a crime. Oops, there goes every single alpha male businessman's whole business strategy in one line.

Wallace D Walter says that the will is primarily to teach yourself what to think and force yourself to think it.

Now, that is a fantastic statement because, at first examination, it would seem that the power of will, which is so strong it can bend other people's minds to do your bidding, is underused in this way.

I mean, cult leaders and successful businesspeople can use it to bend crowds and change their opinions. Political leaders, particularly people who have done devastating things on the planet, such as Henry Kissinger, Pol Pot or Hitler, have bent whole nations to their will, to their belief system, to do their bidding, even against the person's own morals or good.

So, it's incredible for him to say it's only there to help you control your thoughts. And this seems like a ridiculously underuse of your willpower. That is, until you try to control what you think, you realise how hard it actually is.

Research has shown that the average two-year-old is told 'no' between 200 and 1000 times, per day. So, the environment, for most people, is one of overwhelming negativity, where the majority of what you're told is what you can't do, what you shouldn't do, what you won't be successful at, and what your limitations are.

Shad Helmstetter says that by the time a child is 18 he would have heard the word 'no' 148,000 times if they were living in a normal well-adjusted household. So, imagine what happens in a less well-adjusted household.

Now a human won't even reach full maturity in terms of brain development until they reach about twenty-four years old. But it is around this time between the age of 18 and 24, potentially earlier, depending on your culture, you're launched into the world and told to make your own way.

You are told to make your own decisions and use willpower to get the desired results. Your willpower is what makes you get up in the morning and exercise. If you want to be fit, your willpower makes you get up and go to the gym. If you want to pass an exam, your willpower makes you pick up the book and study.

If you want to be a musician, it is willpower that makes you go to the studio every single day and record music or sit in your house and write or pick up the guitar and practice every day even when you don't want to play.

The direction of your activities for any point in time is governed by your willpower. Your willpower is the ability to say 'I will' …. and then do what I will myself to do.

Now, using your willpower to control other people is the equivalent of saying, 'You will do what I will you to do.' Now depending on the persons involved it might be easier to get somebody else to do something based on what you will them to do than to get yourself to do what you will yourself to do, because your mental pre-programming puts up a wall of reasons why your subconscious will tell you that you can't do it.

This creates things such as procrastination, active procrastination, self-sabotage, lacklustre performance, or just outright failure. So, in understanding this, I totally know where Wallace D Wattles comes from.

If you have had 18 to 24 years of negative programming, you will need to find a way to overcome the negative pre-programming that you have been given. Find ways to counteract the negativity that you've grown up with, that has already been installed in your brain with new concepts, ideas, beliefs, faith, thoughts and instructions. New ideas which move you towards the achievement of the things that you want to do.

This is a second-by-second, minute-by-minute, hour-by-hour, day-by-day trial. This is why we say get a counter and count every negative thought you have, because once you are aware of them it's the purpose of your will to counteract every single negative thought that you've had programmed into your brain with a positive one. Use your will to contradict negativity and add positivity until less and less negative thoughts arise, and more and more positive ones do. Particularly in the field of what you want to achieve.

So, what has this got to do with athletes?

Well, I was thinking that when an athlete runs a race, if winning was a result of them exerting their will over other people, then the scenario would be one where the athlete exerts their will over the performance of the competitors in the other lanes to try and reduce their performance so that they can win.

Now admittedly, in sports there is definitely a level of psychological warfare and 'psyching people out' which goes on. But at the end of the day, the truth is, when you line up at those starting blocks and that gun goes off, all you have to rely on is the result of what you have willed yourself to do.

If you willed yourself to get up early every morning and train, if you willed yourself to do those two or three extra squats after you screamed,

'I can't do anymore.' If you willed yourself to study the track if you willed yourself to practice getting out of the starting blocks quicker if you willed yourself to hold on at top speed for just a few milliseconds longer than you thought you could.

If, by using your will to control your thoughts and your beliefs, leading to changing your actions and your actions alone, you did those things. Then when that starting gun goes off, and only you are running in your lane, and you have no control over the performance of the others. Then the exertion of your will, over your beliefs, leading to your actions, are the only thing that will make you run faster than the people in the lanes next to you.

Because you can't exert your will over them, but you can exert your will over yourself, and if you have exerted your will over yourself, better than the people in the lane next to you have exerted their wills over themselves, then you can win the race.

Now, life isn't a competition. This is just an example to try and clarify my opinions of the use of your will.

To make it clear yet again, how much negativity has been programmed into you, and to give you the contrast of my experience from launching a brute force attack on everything around me to gain success, as opposed to only exerting my will on myself to create excellence, brilliance, harmony and sending out the right messages at the right frequency to have it received by the things I want.

Well, I've tried both, and I cannot emphasise enough the massive change that adopting the latter has created. Because at the end of the day, there is a belief that what you're looking for is looking for you. If what you're looking for is looking for you. You don't have to brute-force attack anything to get it. You don't have to brute force attack other people to stop them from getting it before you because it is looking for you; their things are looking for them.

This is why Christian scholars love the quote, and I paraphrase, 'What God says is for you; no man can stand in your way.' You might think it's the last piece of gold in the mine, and two men are fighting over it, but why would you fight? If that piece of gold is for you, it's for you. If it isn't for you, don't worry because tomorrow morning, dig a little deeper, and another piece of gold will appear.

Understanding this shows that you don't have to brute force attack and use your will to overcome anybody else. The key is to use your will to overcome yourself, reprogram yourself, and enforce those programs into beliefs, faith, and actions that will bring you to the running of your own race in your own lane.

Let your will improve your performance until you achieve your personal best. And when you've achieved your personal best, people may compare you and decide that you won the race, i.e. beat others. But for you, it won't matter as long as you've achieved what you were trying to achieve, which is your personal best.

The key and using your will to program yourself and arrange yourself to run your own race, in your own lane and do the best you possibly can. That's the process.

The Will vs. the Way

So, how do you achieve anything? For most people, achieving any goal comes in one of two ways. They have a natural predisposition to be good at the task. For example, they're naturally good at football or math or mechanical-type stuff, fixing things, so it's easier for them than other people to achieve any result in that field. We tend to call these people Phenoms or prodigies.

The other option is to master a skill through sheer force of will. People use their willpower to create discipline to train themselves in the skill and practice it so that they can perform the task effectively.

This is what we see in school every day. Most people don't have the proclivity to be good at ten subjects; the probability is that you will only have a natural ability in maybe three or four of the subjects taught, so your ability to pass exams in the rest has to come through the sheer application of your will.

Luckily, some people have a natural ability to study, meaning they can study almost anything and be good at it. I'm one of those people, meaning academia was easier for me than for others. But some kids in my school were brilliant at sports or naturally brilliant at woodwork, and they would excel at those subjects. People who were naturally brilliant at history or geography would excel at those subjects. But when it came to something like math or chemistry, they struggled.

This is everyday life, and although I could, I'm not going to make this chapter about the inadequacies of the school system. Businesspeople and alternative educators are researching these issues and proposing changes that hopefully will be adopted, but that's not what this chapter is about.

I mentioned how we learn because it offers us a template, a blueprint of how we think we should use our will in school. You use your willpower to 'Will' yourself to learn things you are told you have to learn to pass the exams that will enable you to pass the school year.

We carry this concept into business as great businesspeople are often seen as people who use their will and mental force to fight against all obstacles and overcome all challenges to achieve great things. Using their willpower to build huge companies, achieve magnificent growth, beat the competition, gain impressive accolades, and, most importantly, make copious amounts of money.

But is that really the best use of the will? Is that really the best way to achieve those results?

In one of my favourite books, 'The Science of Getting Rich' by Wallace D Wattles, Wattles says that the proper use of will is not to force the achievement of anything. The proper use of the will is to control what you think.

This may seem strange or even a wasted use of the will. I mean, if you could use your willpower to train yourself to run every single morning and improve your technique by 1% every single day until you're one of the fastest runners in your town, then your city, then your country, then the world, is this not the best use of the will?

This would be hard to deny, so I won't say that training yourself to think the correct thoughts should be the only way to use will. Although admittedly, the previous example only partly represents results gained by brute force action because you would have to train how you think to get yourself to do all the actions that achieve those things. You would have to train yourself to think that it is important to get up at six am before everyone else, stretch and run. You would have to train yourself to think you can improve and run faster every day. You would have to train yourself to think that it is worthwhile to continue training when you hit a block, and it seems like you're no longer improving, and then to keep training for six more months before you see an improvement. You would have to train yourself to think that you need to eat properly and get proper nutrition. Train yourself not to go to that party tonight with all your friends because you know you've got to be up at 5:30 in the morning to train.

You would have to train yourself to think that you can't afford the kinds of distractions that your peer group revel in, parties, sexual relationships, drugs, gaming consoles, late nights, junk food and holidays. So even though it seems as if the results came from the action-taking use of the will, they really came from the thinking use of the will.

Wallace D Wattles says that 'training yourself to think is the hardest work humans can do,' and upon trying it, I realise that this is true. Training yourself in what to think and how to think is the hardest work a human being will ever do unless you've been taught how to do it from a very young age, so it was your habitual way of being. But since that's probably not the case for you, and I'm sure you don't believe me, let's have a little experiment.

The first time you do the negative thought clicker experiment (we will explore this experiment again in this book) is a great example. Get a clicker, put it on your phone, and click plus one every time you have a negative thought. Now, try to train yourself not to think negatively. Use your willpower so that every time something happens where you would normally have a negative thought, try to train yourself not to think that way. You'll see how difficult it is.

Now, here's a fun one. Try to train yourself not to get angry no matter what happens to you in your day or week. No matter what happens to you, try with your willpower to train yourself not to get angry about it. If somebody rear-ends your car, your child disobeys a direct order or argues with you when you ask them to fill the dishwasher. When that person at work continues with those microaggressions or pretends that your work was theirs and steals your thunder, vying to take away your opportunity for promotion again. Or it's bonus season, and you're not given a bonus, just some bullshit excuse from your boss, or your lover does that irritating thing yet again, no matter how many times you ask them not to. Use your willpower to avoid getting angry at any of these things or other things that normally push you to anger. Good luck driving on the roads!!

How about using your willpower (and if you're a judgmental prick like me, this will be the one that really teaches you the lesson) to not criticise or judge anybody for a week. When your friend comes to you with the latest gossip about your other friend or the person in the office, don't criticise or judge them. When your neighbour takes their dog out and lets it shit on the path without having a bag to clean it up again, don't criticise or judge them. When your neighbour plays loud music on a weeknight, even though they know you have to get up early to go to work in the morning, don't criticise or judge them. When that lady wears that totally inappropriate dress to work again, coming in as if it's a nightclub and getting all the attention of the guys in the office, don't criticise or judge them.

Then, you can get to the fun stuff like meditation. Sit down, relax your body, close your eyes, and then will yourself to think about nothing. No thoughts, no phrases. Don't remember that in thirty-five minutes' time, you've got to start cooking dinner. Don't think about the person who annoyed you earlier today at lunch. Don't think that you've got to make sure you pay your rent on time and the landlord's given you new account details to pay it into. Don't think about anything; completely silence your brain and sit there in absolute silence without the constant narrative, without the chatter and without any thoughts. Yeah, again, good luck with that.

So, if you try any or all of these, you'll realise you have almost no control over your mind. Very little control over your thoughts. It's bizarre that we don't think about this. We tend to think that our brain is just our brain. But how often do you really think about how much control you have over your thought process? Our brain is like a toddler that's just learned to walk, and he's running all over the place and causing havoc in our lives because we, like the parent, should be running behind it and making sure that it doesn't get into trouble. Ensuring it doesn't touch the hot stove, pick up a sharp knife, or fall off the cliff's edge. But we don't. We don't exercise our willpower over our brain and control it. We let our brains have negative thoughts because we think that negative stimulation in life is a reasonable cause for negative responses. We allow our brain to get angry and only control our anger based on the rules and norms of society, where if our anger spills over into verbal or physical violence, then it is deemed unacceptable or even illegal.

We most definitely allow our brains to criticise people. In fact, we love it. God knows I used to love to get around the water cooler at work and gossip about the other people in the office, pouring all that negativity into the world. And we allow our brain to talk to us constantly, constant chatter, sometimes useful, sometimes utter bullshit, sometimes stuff that makes us feel sad, insecure, or even terrified. We allow it to chat, chat, chat, chat, chat to us nonstop, as if we have no control over it as if we can't tell it, 'Hey, that's not useful,' or 'Okay, shut the fuck up now.'

We do not use willpower to control our brains, at least not most of the time. As I said before, if you're an athlete, you use your willpower to control your brain enough to tell it to do things that you want it or need it to do in terms of instructing yourself to conduct the actions that you need to improve your athleticism and win your next meet. But you don't use your willpower to control yourself, to be less judgmental, get less angry, be less negative, or to just be happy for the sake of happiness, just because you can.

And it gets even worse. Those are just your thoughts. But since there is every possibility that the brain is a transmitting and receiving station, which is picking up the thoughts broadcast by other people around it, or maybe even other people from the other side of the world. Your ability to control your brain and what goes into it, or at least how it responds to the information it picks up as a receiver, should be key.

I mean, have you ever had a truly disgusting thought, and you asked yourself where the hell that came from? Something you know is completely out of your belief or value system, but it popped into your brain, and you were like, why did I think that? Well, as I said before, that is probably because your brain is a transmitting and receiving system, and that thought was outside of your moral compass and your value system because it didn't come from you; it came from somewhere else. Luckily, because it's outside of your morals and values, you probably won't act on it. But it's important to understand that your willpower is what you need to help you with that process. Your willpower controls your brain, thoughts, and how you react to them. Many people whose normal value system would not allow them to punch a person in the face when confronted with somebody who is aggressive might receive a thought from somebody who is a lot more aggressive. And with the buildup of pressure from other things, receive a thought that says, 'You know what, there's no point talking to this guy. You should just punch him in the face.' This is potentially why many people get into situations which leave their friends and relatives to say, 'That was so out of character, they never normally would have done that.'

The 'use of your will' is to control those thoughts so that those thoughts are not the boss of you; you are the master of what goes on in your head. And if you trained yourself to be the boss of those thoughts, you'll find it so much easier to control situations like that.

There's another side to this, and it's super important because, as I started out saying, we truly believe that our willpower is what we use to attain things, solutions and improvements, and I'm not saying that it isn't. But here's another way of thinking about it. Just imagine if we actually didn't have to struggle to get the things we wanted in life. Just for a second, go with me and imagine if the things that you wanted in life, the things that you intended to have, could be achieved, and received without struggle.

For example, let's say that you saw somebody struggle and use their willpower to overcome obstacles and fight their way through until they built a successful business with a turnover of 60 million pounds a year, and you wanted the same result. Imagine if you didn't have to use your willpower to beat the competition, overcome obstacles, fight against problems and put out business fires, work 18-hour days to outwork everybody else, be smarter to outthink everybody else and braver to out-challenge everybody else. Imagine if you didn't have to be quicker, smarter and stronger than everyone else in your field to build a business like that. Imagine if all you had to do was want to build a business like that and go ahead with your work, putting your best efforts forward in the creation of your products, managing of your staff, delivery of your service, and building of your brand and reputation, just working to your best ability in a relaxed manner without brute force.

None of the…must dominate? Rah, rah, rah, entrepreneur shit that you see every day. None of the no sleep, no days off entrepreneurship tropes you see on Instagram. Imagine if all you had to do was put your best efforts forward, and opportunities, along with a bit of serendipity, made the way easy for you.

Wouldn't that be a lot nicer? Wouldn't it be a lot more pleasant? It might feed your ego-less because you wouldn't be able to tell stories of how you had to fight against problems and dominate everything in your environment. But it would certainly be a nicer process.

Well, there is a belief system that suggests this is the truth. That all you need to do is make the intention of the things that you want, and then diligently and wholeheartedly, with happiness and love (because you love what you're doing), work towards them in a normal way, and the doors to their achievement, the serendipity, the good luck, and the ease of how things could possibly happen and occur will be opened up for you.

This concept is based on the idea of frequency. That if you use your willpower not to dominate your competition, fight against obstacles and go to war with other businesses, but to control the way which you think. If you use your willpower to reduce your negative thoughts, fear, worry, the concept of lack, and thoughts of having to dominate the competition and warring with other businesses. If you use your willpower, reduce your necessity to criticise, judge, hate and be angry. Just keep your thoughts in the positive frequencies of positivity, happiness, and love for what you do. Appreciation and care for your customers, infatuation, and joy with the product you're selling, making it the best it possibly can be, and cooperation with other companies when competition is the option.

The frequencies from these positive thoughts are all you would be doing to clear the way for the things you want to come to you. You see, this concept is based on the idea that anything you want actually wants you. That's why they say the word 'desire' when broken down to its etymological roots means from the father. De, Sire. 'Sire' translating to father and De translating to 'of'.

If you want something, you might think that it's you who wants it, and it is either indifferent to you or does not want you, meaning that you have to conquer it, but the term desire tells a different story. If you assume that what the Father means is the infinite intelligence, God, the universe, in the way that Jesus called God the Father, in quotes such as 'Our Father', 'thank you Father', 'Father, why have thou forsaken me'. Then your desires are things that come to you from God, the Infinite Intelligence, the universe, that's where they come from. This means that this higher power wants you to have them because the urge to have them comes from it.

And if it wants you to have them, it won't make you go and fight for them unless overcoming the struggle is part of the result it wants you to have. If you want your child to have something, you will want to clear the way for them to receive it. You'll want to help them get it. You won't make it difficult for them to have it unless you want them to have the experience of overcoming a challenge to get it.

But here's the thing: As a parent or even as a friend, how many times have you wanted somebody to have something only to have their behaviour pattern or belief system set them on a course of actions that stops them from gaining it?

You might have a friend, and you really want them to be able to go out partying and have fun, but because they have painful social anxiety and believe that they're not likeable or they believe that they're uncool, no matter how often you set them up to go to parties, they don't go and enjoy themselves. Or it could be that you want them to have a relationship. You're a really good friend who wants them to have someone to love. You know they like somebody, and you try to set them up with that person. A person who really likes them as well. But again, their insecurities block them from turning up to meet the person or from talking to them while they're with them. Their own insecurity and anger stop them from understanding that this person's actions are those of somebody who likes them, and they misinterpret everything that this person does, which blocks them from their own good. As a business coach, I see this in business all the time, where people's insecurities, anger, negative thoughts, and judgments block them from going forward and making the decisions or taking the actions that would move their business forward.

The point I'm making to you is that if you were to look at your biggest problem, it probably really isn't overcoming your competitors, overcoming obstacles, using your willpower to brute force, or bludgeoning your way through to success. Your biggest problem is probably the lack of control that you have over your own thoughts. The lack of control you can exert over your beliefs, bad habits, and the frequencies they create. The frequency that your persistent thoughts and feelings force you to emit.

This affects you in two ways. There is the practicality that the lack of controlling your bad habits creates: anger, being difficult to work with, negativity, seeing the glass as half empty, thinking things can't be done, not giving your total effort, judgmental and critical of yourself and other people, and not building good relationships. These are the practical aspects of not controlling your thoughts, which stop you from going forward and achieving the things you want.

And then there's the spiritual aspect of it. The frequencies that you emit. These are the frequencies that block all the good that 'your father', the infinite intelligence, the supreme power, is trying to send you because it wants you to have the things you want. It is sending you the things that you want, but you're blocking them with the way you think and the way that these thoughts make you act.

All of this can be counteracted and counterbalanced by the proper use of the will. When used correctly, the will is not used to overcome obstacles; it is used to create a way in which obstacles clear themselves, leaving you a clear path to your goal.

Anger

Here's something I want you to think about. Within the autonomic nervous system lies the sympathetic nervous system, which is designed for fight-or-flight responses in your body. This system was developed over our human evolution so that when we were in danger, our body would spike chemicals in our bodies such as adrenalin and cortisol, strengthening the reaction speeds and the effectiveness of our muscles so that we can fight or flee from imminent danger. Now, in terms of our evolution, imminent danger was represented by things like a Woolly Mammoth or a Sabre-Toothed Tiger, maybe a stampede of Elephants, or a rival tribe coming to ransack our village, steal our women and kill us. So, anger partly existed to kick-start the process, which created the chemical responses needed to give us the physical and mental strength to fight or run when necessary. This is why people tend to get angry before they fight. Anger helps you to kick-start all these chemicals in your body, which you will need for the fight response, and often the same chemicals if, indeed, in losing the fight, you opt for flight.

I want you to think about this and keep this in your mind every time you absolutely lose your shit in anger because somebody takes your parking spot or moves your food in the fridge or smiles at your girlfriend, or makes a sarcastic comment about you at work or reads your WhatsApp text message but doesn't respond immediately.

The point I'm making here is that these activities do not warrant anger responses. They are just not severe enough to be counted amongst the circumstances for which anger was created.

To really put this in perspective you must understand the payoff. To create the chemicals that kick off the physical response for us to have the potential for fight or flight, the state that your body is put in is a non-optimal state. Your optimal state is when you are relaxed and at peace.

This is your parasympathetic nervous system state. Your fight-or-flight state is a state where all your levels are ramped up to the maximum so that your body is ready for any eventuality which is why we cannot stay in this state for any length of time. It is a short-term state designed for emergencies. A state only used to get ourselves out of the rare difficult situations before returning to our usual, peaceful, relaxed demeanour.

But now there are no Woolly Mammoths, rampaging Elephants, or sabre-toothed Tigers, and unless you're an avid football Hooligan or a climate change protestor, there are not many warring tribes going out and fighting either.

Yet we keep putting ourselves in this state repeatedly, all the time, for insufficient reasons that do not warrant this type of reaction. All this unnecessary anger is clearly not good for us. Scientists have marked out very clearly that people who have this as their constant state, who are constantly putting themselves in states of anger and eliciting the fight-or-flight chemical reactions are creating a terrible toll on their bodies. Then they go on Facebook and debate as to why people don't live for 125 years anymore, as the Bible suggests. In fact on social media, we often get into blood boiling arguments with people we will never meet. The answer is obvious: you won't live to 125 because you don't live the way you should. One of the key causes of this is your culture of constantly putting yourself unnecessarily in the angry fight-or-flight state. A state which frankly burns through our human resources for no reason, poisoning our minds and bodies with a constant flood of chemicals which were designed to be used sparingly, putting us in positions of ill health.

Angry Again?

I believe that children are born with everything human beings need, except the one essential thing, which is the ability to take care of themselves sufficiently to survive. Kind of ironic, huh! But anyway, other than that, I truly believe that babies are born with pretty much everything they need.

For example, no one teaches children how to breathe correctly. But aside from the other millions of things that their bodies do without being consciously aware, they breathe in the most efficient way for humans to breathe. I point this out because, as an adult, you are retaught how to breathe if you go to meditation or yoga class. As a Martial Artist, I was taught how to breathe. We were all born breathing correctly, yet we forget and pick up bad habits, so we must be taught what we were born doing naturally. That's the kind of thing I'm talking about.

The other thing that I find so fascinating about children is their happiness. Toddlers usually have happiness, which honestly makes me think that they're closer to God. The bliss you try to experience while you're meditating is something they seem to have without effort unless disturbed. They have a fascination with the world, which we lose and again try to recapture through things like meditation.

But the point I want to make here is that children have a much better way of dealing with anger than adults. When something makes a toddler angry, they have a tantrum. They shout and scream and cry, snot themselves up, and get all that anger out, and then 30 seconds later, all that anger is gone.

As humans, we're taught not to get angry. What we do is suppress and repress all that anger. We suppress and repress it for days, sometimes months or even years, and it stays in us like a poison, like pollution. It seethes in us, ready to burst out at the most inopportune moments against people who have done nothing to deserve that tirade of anger that we've kept seething within us due to something that was done by somebody else years ago.

This is why I'm such a fan of Dr David Hawkins's approach, which he explains in his book 'Letting Go'. When something makes you angry, no, I don't think you should throw your dummy out and drop it on the supermarket floor kicking and screaming. However, it would help if you did something to release that anger as soon as possible. Do something in the moment, at least in the hour. As I said, my favourite way of doing this is to imagine all of the horrible things that I'd like to do to the offender. All of the violent and destructive things I'd love to do to the person, or the situation would express how I really feel about it. I do this until I'm exhausted by those thoughts, until I become drained, or they become so comical that they get rid of all the anger inside me. I do this so that I don't end up carrying anger around with me because I know this is tantamount to poisoning myself. I do it so I don't carry it around, putting me on a low frequency. So I don't end up carrying it around with me like a time bomb ready to explode on somebody totally undeserving of its ferocity.

Self-Defence Is No Offence.

Before anybody gets it twisted by me writing a book called practical hippie shit, allow me to explain to you the reason why the only sport I've ever been involved in is martial arts. I have, to my memory, never attacked anybody. Still, I have defended myself from attacks and created situations where my attacker came off worse than I did.

If you examine nature, you will likely find that every living entity will try to defend its and its family's lives from attack. This is the true cause or reason for the fight-or-flight response, which many of us misuse by getting worked up, frustrated and angry over minimal things. Like all animals, the third most important body part I possess is my thighs because they allow me to run from predators, but in the absence of that option, I also train myself to be able to fight if necessary. So, make no mistake, just in case you want to try it. The practical side of this version of my hippie shit does not say turn the other cheek. Nothing in nature turns the other cheek; it either runs away in self-preservation or stands its ground and fights to the death. Now, you might have heard from a hippie that if you only have 'positive vibes, mannnnn!!!' no bad will ever come your way. As much as there is truth in this, I wouldn't bet the farm on it. It is undoubtedly true that if you don't start trouble or court trouble, you will see less trouble. I also believe that it is true that angry people who want someone to pick on will select their victim based on several characteristics, which means that your frequency and demeanour could make an angry person walk right past you and punch the guy who is next to you in the face.

Dr David Hawkins talks about the levels of consciousness, which include peace and pure love, and these are the states in which this is possible. In these states, you can hug a hungry lion or put your head in the mouth of a crocodile. This is the Christ consciousness that all who aim for enlightenment are trying to achieve. However, in his book 'Power vs Force', Dr David Hawkins suggests that only 1% of the population will have achieved this level, so I would not suggest that you rely on it and learn how to fight. If you do not want to harm others, then the best you can hope is to follow the ancient Indian Martial art of Kalaripayattu, which teaches you to strike your attacker down and then immediately begin healing them. In terms of fighting for survival, I use examples of nature, but for humans, this isn't strictly true. All signs point to the fact that we have a much stronger capacity to communicate with higher powers in the universe than most other species on this planet. So, when confronted with danger, I ask the creator for guidance. Believe it or not, I have found that this diffuses most situations, which could potentially turn violent. I talk to the creator, asking for guidance, and the raging drunk who has been threatening me inexplicably takes a pause and decides that I'm not worth the hassle to fight, curses me and walks away. The potentially violent situation can change by asking for guidance so that no violence will occur. But If, for any reason, diffusion isn't possible, I tend to find the guidance allows me to defend myself to the appropriate level where I don't get injured by the attack, but at the same time, I don't do irreparable damage to my attacker, in terms of hurting them permanently, where I would have to go to prison, or they might die. So remember your connection to the infinite intelligence in all things, ask for guidance in your moments of danger, make sure you know how to defend yourself and treat life like a boxing ring, and 'be prepared to defend yourself at all times.' Because if you are thinking that hippies are soft, well, in terms of staying alive, if you make it a choice between you and me, please be sure to understand that I will do everything in my power to make sure it's you and not me, and the only woo woo we'll be hearing is the woo-woo of the ambulance if you make it that far.

The Two Wolves

It is challenging to understand that the more you worry about something, the more you perpetuate it. This includes problem-solving, which, for a practical guy like me, is the hardest obstacle to overcome. The idea is that when I think about something and constantly try to find a solution to it, I perpetuate it as a problem and prevent the finding of a solution.

This is hugely counterintuitive and actually goes against all forms of common sense. How can you solve a problem without analysing and thinking about it? So, I like to use the two-wolf analogy. There's a wonderful story that supposedly comes from Native American Law, which says that every man has two wolves within him that represent two distinctive personality traits. One of the wolf's personality traits is fear and anger. The other one is positivity and kindness, and the one that grows in power and eventually overtakes his whole personality is the one that he feeds the most. Therefore, if he feeds fear and anger, he becomes more fearful and angrier and does fearful, angry things. If he feeds positivity and kindness, he becomes a more positive and kinder person, so a life of positivity and kindness is the life that he leads. As I said, the key premise here is that the wolf that is the most powerful, the wolf that grows in power and, therefore, dominates his life, is the one he emotionally feeds.

I want to take this analogy and apply it to your problems. Let's say that you had two fires. You built two fires, and they are side by side. One fire is the fire of your problem. Let's say that the problem is that you don't have enough money, and the way you feed this fire (problem of not having enough money), is by putting more wood on this fire. It's already burning, and you put more wood on it by thinking about it constantly. Thinking about the fact you have no money. Being scared about the fact that you have no money. Thinking about all the things that you can't buy. Worrying about the debt payments you're going to miss. Thinking of how embarrassing it will be when you go out with your friends and can't afford to pay for your share of the meal. Thinking about your clothes that are worn and the new clothes that you can't afford. Thinking about the fact that you might miss your rent payment and get kicked out of your house. All these thoughts are fuelling this fire, and it's blazing. It's getting bigger and bigger and bigger. You have no money. You have no money; you have no money. You're making this reality bigger and bigger and bigger. I have no money. I have no money. I have no money. You're making it bigger still. Bigger and bigger.

Now, as the problem-solving practical person you are, your belief is that you're thinking about all aspects of these problems to solve them. You think that the fact that you're running around looking for freelance work, looking for people to borrow money from, or thinking of ways to win money are all solutions. But all they are more fuel for this fire. I have no money. I have no money. I have no money. Until the 'I have no money fire' is blazing out of all proportion. Now, as we said before, the subconscious mind is impersonal. It doesn't hear the part that says, 'I don't want to' have no money. It only hears the part that says, 'have no money', and it believes that you want it to create a reality in which you have no money. And the fact that you put so much effort, thought and emotion into this means that it must be really important. So, it will ensure that this is the reality you get.

Now. Think of the other fire. The other fire says I'm wealthy and abundant. I have everything that I need. Now, I know your practical, realistic brain will abhor this fire because you're not rich. The reality is that you don't have enough money to make all of your bill payments. But as we've just discussed, if you keep putting fuel on this fire, a fire of financial success, then like the fire of lack and scarcity, it too will get bigger and become a bigger and bigger reality for you.

So how about we start finding ways to fuel abundance fire? I mean, surely you are abundant in some things, surely you are abundant in some ways. If you live in the West, you are categorically more abundant than most of the world's population. As a parent once said, his son's response to being asked for a sweet treat by his son was, 'You had breakfast this morning, that's more than fifty percent of the children on the planet had; that was your treat.' Similarly, I once told a friend about my financial problems building my first multi-million-pound property portfolio. 'I'm lucky to have these problems,' I said. 'These are first-world problems; at least I don't have to worry about where my next meal is coming from or if a bomb will fall on my house and kill my family.'

So, understand that you are abundant in so many ways. Surely, there is some level of truth in the idea that you're abundant. You just need to identify your blessings and be grateful for them.

One exercise is to look at the amount of money that you do have and think of all the things that it can buy, or least think I have money rather than I don't which is not actually true. You probably do have money, just not as much as you would like. So as opposed to thinking about all of the things that it can't buy, even if you've only got $1 think of the things you could buy from the dollar store.

I could buy this. I could buy that. I'd buy that for a dollar!

Think of all the things you can do that don't need money. Think, 'If I go and see my cousin, he'll give me some free bagels because he owns the bagel store.' That is abundance.

Or I know that I can get my car serviced by my uncle because he owes me a favour and loves to service my car. That's a $250 car service that I can get for nothing. That is abundance. Think of all the things that you can get for free. Then, once you've moved away from all the practical ways that you do have money and are abundant, we can move on to part two.

Part 2 is programming your brain to fuel the abundance fire. In doing this, just remember that you're only reprogramming your brain. You can tell yourself that you're wealthy as an instruction instead of a reflection of your reality. You can tell yourself you're rich as an instruction instead of a reflection of your reality. Because what you're doing is fuelling the fire that says I'm abundant, I am rich, I have enough money, I'm financially secure, I can pay my bills. It's a program to be followed and executed, not an objective critique of your current reality.

And as you put more fuel into that fire, the fire of your wealth and success, that fire will grow, and the universe will say, Oh, you're abundant, you're rich, you have enough money, you can pay your bills, and you seem to be very confident and putting lots of emotion and effort into this belief, this must be important. Okay, I'll make sure that this is your reality.

So you really need to think about a fire you're fuelling.

Now, I'm not trying to tell people to sit under a tree, forget their problems, and let the woo-woo universe solve them. So, the best way to achieve this process for practical people is a practice commonly known as 'Giving it up to God.' Because in terms of relying on wishful thinking, I know you're probably not there yet. (I'm certainly not.) And let's keep it real. I like my ability to take action.

As Wallace D. Wattle says, 'By your visualisation, the things you want are brought to you, but by your actions, you receive them.'

So, I'm not saying to take no action. Suppose you have a financial problem, and you need to raise some money. In that case, there's nothing wrong with doing research, analysing to solve the problem, looking for the best solution, doing things, and taking action. The problem comes with the way you think about it. If you think about it in terms of, I don't have enough money, I don't have enough money, I don't have enough money, I don't have enough money. The universe will create that for you or at least support the creation of that reality.

Don't try to get slick and change it to, 'I wish I had less money problems. I wish I had less money problems. I wish I had less money problems. I wish I had less money problems,' because the impersonal nature of infinite intelligence, as explained by the book *'The Edinburgh Papers'* by Charles Troward, will simply only hear the 'I have less money, I have less money, I have less money' part and create that as your reality.

What you need is to do your work, whatever it is that you're doing to receive more money, do it with the viewpoint of 'I have enough money', 'I have more than I need', 'I have all the money I need', 'I'm rich', 'I can buy loads of things', 'I can pay all my bills', 'I'm confident about my financial situation'.

It's the way you think and feel about the situation that creates reality. Doing the same work with the thoughts of 'I don't have enough' will make sure you don't have enough. But doing that exact same work with the thoughts of 'I have more than enough' will eventually cause you to have more than enough.

Your Influence

I did a Facebook post yesterday. It got one comment, and because I've worked in digital marketing for some time now, I know not to let that worry me. Plus, it wasn't a post designed to get a lot of engagement. But then, when I looked back at the post, I realised it had 109 plays. It was a piece of music I'd made using AI, and while I was in the shower, this reminded me of this concept in the woo-woo. It is a concept which I think comes from ancient texts and can also be found in the Bible. Either way, the idea is of a book that keeps a record of absolutely everything you've ever done.

Interestingly enough, biological science (and this is not woo-woo at all) believes that they have found the exact part of the brain that remembers absolutely everything we have ever done, seen, and thought. They say that it is all stored, even if we cannot recall it all at will. It's all recorded—a record of absolutely everything that ever happened in our lives. And it's stored in our brains. Curious, right?

So it is pretty interesting in itself, that this concept, which we find in the Bible and other ancient text such as the Egyptian Book of the Dead, this day of judgment, of St Peter standing there with the book of everything that you've ever done in your life ready to tell you if you are able to enter the Kingdom of heaven. It's pretty interesting that we have scientifically found that books exist in our brains. A recording or book of absolutely every single experience, every thought, everything we've heard, everything we've seen, is recorded in a section of our human brains. Everything is there, ready for examination; all our actions are recorded for judgment.

But that's just the first part. The second part, which I find even more interesting about this record of everything you've ever done, is not the existence of the record itself but the idea that a record is being kept of you. The 'Egyptian Book of the Dead' talks about the negative confessions where you die and on the day that you judge yourself, you are asked questions, and I paraphrase, 'Is your heart as light as a feather?'

And the reason this interests me relates to the success or lack thereof of my Facebook post. Because, like many people, I wanted to have a bigger impact on the world. I had hoped that the things I've done and the people I've helped would have a massive impact, well, at least the good stuff. Many people dream of being pop stars and affecting millions or great speakers and inspiring thousands of great inventors, creating new technology that affects the lives of millions, or sharing their talents with the world in some other way where their talents have a massive impact.

Now, I think it would be fair to say, based on statistics, that not everyone in the world can be a George Washington Carver, a Nikola Tesla, a Bill Gates, an Elon Musk, or a Reginald Lewis.

Not everybody can have this kind of massive effect on humanity. We can't all be Gandhi or Mother Teresa. I think the problem with this is that the promotion of people who are so successful in influencing the world and become legendary in their status causes us to demean the effects that we can have in the world and the importance of the things that we do.

Many singers have given up on singing because, after a few years of making music, they realise they will never be as successful and internationally recognised as Beyonce, Taylor Swift, or even Bad Bunny. Due to this, they no longer see the point of making music. They don't think that they can have any real effect, and certainly not the effect that they want to have.

But the beautiful thing about this is that the 'Book of Records' would know, and that's how we come full circle to my Facebook post. You see, when I sent the Facebook post, I saw one comment and assumed that maybe only two or three people had seen it. Only when I saw the one hundred and nine plays did I realise that almost one hundred times more people had engaged in that post than the comments had shown me. That's when I realised the true effect of that post. Of the one hundred and nine people who played it, maybe they didn't want to comment on it, but it still affected them. They are still engaged with it; it still has some kind of effect on their life. It could have been positive, it could have been negative, but the effect was there.

And that's a great analogy—a real analogy, a factual analogy—to understand the effect you can have with your life.

Just because the things you do may seem to only affect a handful of people (because those are the only ones who give you feedback in terms of making you aware that you have affected them), that is possibly only 1% of the people affected by the things you do.

It's akin to the butterfly effect, the idea that a butterfly flaps its wings in Indonesia and creates a Tsunami in London.

For example, The life lessons that you give to your children will affect the things they say to their friends, which will affect the things that their friends do and say to their other friends, and that, in simple terms, is how the butterfly (which is you) flaps your wings in Indonesia (teaching your children), and create a Tsunami of change thirty years later in London (The effects of your influence in your children and their peers).

Imagine, for example, if one of your children's friends was influenced by the beliefs or viewpoints you instilled in them and, as a result, decided to go into the Amazon jungle to start a massive Conservation Project. This could occur just by your third-hand influence; the people you deal with directly can be influenced even more.

So, it's important to be appreciative of the effect you can have, both positively and negatively. Don't underestimate the power that you will bring into this world. In fact, if you take it to the next level of woo-woo and believe there is an overarching power with some kind of control (as I like to think), a supreme being that somehow stitches together this insane patchwork, this crazy jigsaw, this absolutely insane version of mousetrap, where you do one thing, and it hits this thing. That thing drops onto another thing, causing this ball to roll down a slope and knock over that last thing. Then, a whole domino set goes off in another direction, and a snowball starts rolling down a mountain, causing an avalanche.

If you take the leap of faith and believe this, then one little thing you're inspired to do could have amazing results worldwide. The only sad part is you won't get the credit for it. You won't get the thousands of screaming fans or business adulation. You won't be canonised as a Saint or lauded as one of Forbes' most influential people. But it doesn't mean that what you do doesn't have a massive effect on the world.

So, every time you think that what you do doesn't matter, remember that for a simple Facebook post that got only one comment, one acknowledgement that it had been seen, one acknowledgement that it had existed at all. Over one hundred people actually saw it. Nearly one hundred times more. That is the practical reality of the influence that you can exert, the influence that you can create by your words and your deeds. So, make your words inspirational, powerful and true and make your actions just, wise and good.

Shoot Where They Are Going to Be

One of my favourite scenes from the movie Gangster Squad is when the character played by Michael Pena, the youngest member of the squad, is taken under the wing of the older, more established policeman who shows him the ropes. As the old guy is teaching him how to aim and ensure he hits the target, he says, 'Don't shoot where they are; shoot where they're going to be.'

This has always been one of my favourite quotes, but I've recently come to a new understanding of it. My new understanding relates to its value when used to create positive affirmations.

Like many people, I used to struggle with 'I AM' statements that were simply not true. Lots of people talk about the difficulty of running around saying, 'I am a multi-millionaire' when, in actual fact, their mortgage payment has just bounced, their car payment has just bounced, and the utility company is about to cut off their water.

These realities do not gel well with constant thoughts of wealth and success, and no amount of wishful thinking will overcome them. But this is where the concept of 'don't shoot where they are, shoot where they're going to be' comes in.

You see, your reality right now might be a financial lack, but you don't shoot your affirmations or self-talk toward your reality as it is; you shoot your affirmations at where it is going to be.

Shoot them at the things that you're trying to program into your brain and make it believe and act on. Should your affirmations be where you are currently financially, or should they be where you fully, wholeheartedly intend and believe that you are, in the future, going to be?

This concept brings us to the Be Do Have (we will discuss this more later in the book). If you can embody the actions and attitudes of your future self, enact them now, and believe them wholeheartedly, then you can create 'I AM' statements based on where you are mentally now and where you will be physically in the future.

'I am rich. I am successful. I have more than enough,' can be said because you're not shooting at where you are right now. You're shooting at your destiny. You're shooting at where you know without any possibility of failure you are going to be in the future. You know this because it's very clear to you that if you continue your present trajectory with your present beliefs and put in your present energy, ignoring every obstacle and failure and continuing to go forward towards your aims, it is impossible for you to not make progress. And if you continue to make progress, it becomes very unlikely that you won't achieve your aims, at least on some level. To use as line from another of my favourite movies, *Scent of a Woman*, where Al Pacini giving another Oscar worthy performance says, 'I've been around.' I bet you thought I was going to say, 'Whooohaaaa!!!' The reason I like this quote is that I have indeed been around. I've seen people who looked like their dreams were impossible to achieve their most unlikely goals. So, when I say consistent action and belief yield results, I say it from 54 years of observation.

One of the strangest things I've done to myself on multiple occasions is achieve my aims and not even notice it. I was so busy and focused on the process that I never stopped to 'ring the bell' as they say and celebrate that I had achieved what I wanted. I didn't pay any attention to the fact that my wife and I had built a multi-million-pound property portfolio until after we had lost it, and upon telling the story at a seminar, I saw everybody freaking out at our past achievements. I didn't even mention that we had, at one point, actually had a million pounds in the bank. In fact, the first time I meditated regularly, the reason I stopped was because one day, I realised that I had actually achieved all but one of the things that I was meditating for. It scared the shit out of me. I thought to myself that this was something that could be very dangerous in the wrong hands, and I stopped using it immediately. See what I mean about the debilitating effects of fear.

I've also had instances where things that I affirmed or visualised to manifest came into my existence decades later without me having to lift a finger towards their achievement. All I had to do was intend them and apparently forget about them.

What does that mean? It means that if I said I am that thing 'Be' at an earlier stage before I became it, for example, in the past, which we commonly call 'then', I was right. I was right in the future of 'then', my present, which we commonly call 'now'. Do you get it?

If that isn't batshit crazy enough for you, we can add even more woo-woo by adding the idea that time does not exist. Ok, I know I'm stretching it now, but stay with me. Quantum science posits the idea that time is at the very least definitely malleable on many levels and is not the strict pedestrian entity that we assume when we think of time progressing in a linear fashion from morning to afternoon to evening or from day to day to day.

Authors note… I struggled with this chapter and concept and marked it for non-inclusion in this book due to my inability to explain the concept properly. So, I stopped work and went to prepare my lunch, putting on an audiobook to listen to as I always do during mundane tasks. The book was 'Autobiography of a Yogi' by Paramahansa Yogananda; I had reached chapter 30: The Law of Miracles. This audio reminded me that the concept that I was struggling to explain was Einstein's law of general relativity, which espouses that time is not sequential but, in fact, relative. This is the type of non-coincidental coincidence that I am talking about. Anyway, the explanation of the general theory of relativity is beyond the scope of this book, I will leave this as a reference for you to look up and research on your own, but if you need any assistance, I recommend a great book called 'Quantum Theory Cannot Hurt You' by Marcus Chow.

If we add this concept to the mix, then what I am saying is not just some deluded wishful thinking. The difference between what you are today and what you are tomorrow, your level of success or your achievements today and your level of success and achievements in five years' time, is actually non-existent if time is malleable and not the sequential thingy that we assume it is.

Make way for the crazy train. Wooo Wooo!!!!!

So, it's only our concepts of time, reality, and change that make us think that these statements are not actually feasible and make us feel like we're lying to ourselves.

If we change the way that we look at time and change ourselves to a full understanding that at so many points in our life, we have moved ourselves from one thing to another successfully, then 'I AM' as a statement of something that you have not yet achieved is nothing more than shooting at where you're going to be, as opposed to shooting at where you are. Because if you really understand time on a non-pedestrian level, as the older policeman tried to explain in Gangster Squad, shooting where you are is guaranteed to create a scenario where you miss because you have moved on by the time the bullet arrives. But if you shoot where you're going to be, then by the time the bullet gets there, that's where the target will be.

Well, this is the same thing. 'I am successful' doesn't mean that you're successful today. It means that successful is where you are going to be. Success is the reality that's going to be created, and you're going to allow none of the current circumstances or situations, obstacles or problems stop that.

And if that's where 'you're going to be,' you can claim it now. Accept it now, be it now and believe it now, even if you receive it later.

Negative Thoughts

I probably shouldn't be writing this because I literally only started doing this exercise 25 minutes ago, but I think it was either Plato or Socrates who said, 'All learning is remembering,' so I know that this will work. Plus, by the time this book has been released, I will have done this whole exercise and be able to give a full account of its efficacy.

I got this version of this exercise from Sean Haggleson, who can be found on YouTube on the channel 'Finding Fushima', but I had heard of it from other places before, which is why I am including it here. I am using the version he suggests because the way he explained it made all the other explanations of it make more sense. Plus, his explanation is the simplest version I've heard. So, I will take his explanation and meld it with the others to give you the full benefit.

He recommends using a physical counter, but I recommend using your mobile phone because, for most people, your mobile phone is the one item that is always on your person. There are very few times of the day when your mobile phone is not physically on or right by you.

So, get your mobile phone, go to your app store, search for 'Click Counter', and download it. It will have something like a plus and a minus sign, so you can just click the plus every time you want to add to it and the minus every time you want to subtract.

Now, at the start of the week, from the moment you wake up in the morning, do one click to increase the number on the counter every time you have a negative thought. Do this for a week and see how many negative thoughts you have daily. In Sean Haggleson's video, he had about four hundred and thirty-three negative thoughts daily. This is the state of your reality.

After a week, repeat this exercise, but now, once you have acknowledged the negative thought, immediately think of logical, realistic thoughts to counteract it.

Now, you might want me to define negative thoughts. Well, I think you have to do that for yourself. I already have fourteen negative thoughts this morning, and I've only been awake for 25 minutes.

So, how did my day start? Well, it started with me worrying about a phone call I'd been dreading for months. The call concerned a business deal that had gone wrong. By acknowledging that I feared this call and was thinking negatively about it, I could tell myself not to think about it and not to work myself up into a frenzy as I would normally have done many years ago.

I was thinking about all the bad things that could happen on the call, thinking about lots of bad things that probably wouldn't happen on the call, and working myself up into frenzied, negative, fearful, angry, upset emotions.

I was immediately able to stop the fact that I was thinking about that call and say to myself, 'It hasn't happened yet. There's no point worrying about it now. It hasn't even occurred. Whatever happened has happened so let's not dwell on what hasn't happened yet. Let's just think about nice things.'

And that is what I did for the next 20 minutes. I thought about the things I was grateful for. I thought about the things that I found blissful. In fact, I entered one of the best and most enjoyable, blissful states I've had in a long time, and all off at the back of stopping myself from going into a negative frenzy when the first negative thought of my day appeared. Now, I'm only human. So obviously, that fear and resentment of having to make that call soon reappeared, and when it did, I did the same thing again, and I got the same result.

This is why I am sure of the efficacy of this practice because it already removed a mildly traumatic event that I was going to give to myself this morning.

When my alarm clock went off, I got out of bed and was amazed to see how I had collected the following twelve negative thoughts. The first one was when I went to the bathroom to urinate and bumped into my wife as she came into the room. My first thought was negative: 'Why are you here at this exact point in time as me? Why are you in my way?' Yes, I am a moany old man.

I immediately recognised these negative thoughts and told myself that's not the thought I want. Let's have another better thought. Let's have another try. Okay, so what else could I think? How about, 'Oh, this is hilarious that I've just been trying to walk into the bathroom at the same time my wife is walking out of it.' I love my wife. She's great. I'm happy she's here. As I came out of the room, the dog was standing in the doorway. I was quite surprised that even my dog being in my way caused me annoyance, although it didn't annoy me as much as my wife being in my way; read from that what you will. But the fact that he scratched himself and didn't get out of my way gave me negative thoughts three and four. As I said, I'm a moany old man. I caught my negative train of thought, which lasted for maybe 10 seconds, and then I went back to my first thought, 'Isn't our dog cute?'

'Isn't the noise he makes when scratching himself funny?' I followed this thought with the words 'Excuse me, dog,' and he moved out of my way.

Next, I checked my phone, and I saw that there was a notification from an influencer who I didn't like. My initial thoughts were 'This fucking guy, today I'm going to purge my phone and stop all my notifications from people that I don't like. It's not healthy for me to be seeing notifications from people when the first thing I think when I see them is, fuck them!!! I mean, if that's how I feel about them, why are they in my environment? Why am I putting them in a position to give me negative thoughts?'

So, it's twenty-five minutes into my morning, and this is where I am, right now, recording this message as an audio for use in this book when it's eventually finished.

Author's note… I have been using this technique for months now. I no longer need the counter; I just register my negative thoughts and immediately counteract them, and the effects on my overall happiness have been life changing.

Okay, the second thing I must say about this exercise is that I'd heard about it many years ago, but that version involved writing down every negative thought, which, at the time, I really wasn't ready to do. Partly because of the time required to do it, and the reason I wouldn't give it the time was because I didn't really understand its importance. The last Twenty-five minutes have shown me the importance, and therefore, I finally understand how powerful a tool it is and why this version, which doesn't involve the annoyance of stopping, getting a pen and writing every three minutes, is so powerful.

Now, if you have the time or are so inclined, feel free to use the written version and write down each negative thought because you'll be absolutely amazed at the number of negative thoughts you have in a single day.

Although the second version involves writing down every negative thought, it has the added benefit of allowing you to review this at the end of the day to analyse your predominant thoughts and track their improvement. Now, I know that this is laborious, so I suggest you do it with a voice-to-text app on your phone. It only takes seconds because this way, recording the thought literally only takes you as long as it took to have it.

The key to this written version of this exercise is that it gives you a pattern of your thoughts. You can then go back at the end of the day and look at what you've written (or listen to your audio) and see not just how many negative thoughts you had but what they were about. You can see what you're thinking negatively about and what's causing you to think negatively. Just knowing a notification made me think 'fuck you' to that influencer, could help me to discover that my social media feed is causing me to think negatively all day long, and I need to make a change.

If I work in social media, this might be something that I can't avoid. I may just have to change the way I respond to the information that comes in. But if I don't work in media, I may decide that I genuinely don't need those feeds or whatever it is that's causing me to have that reaction. I might decide that I'm going to simply cut them out of my life to give myself fewer things to feel negative about.

Admittedly, there are two ways of looking at this. The first is cutting things out of your life or changing your environment. Some people might see it as running away from your problems, but I don't think this is true. I think you have every right to control your environment. But the second, which is just as effective and you'll have to do anyway (because no one can control their environment 100%), is learning to replace your negative responses with positive ones.

I recommend that you do a mixture of both. You should control the things in your environment, such as notifications from influencers whom I obviously dislike and really shouldn't be getting notifications about. Just unfollow the accounts and cut them out of your life.

The second is to find a way to deal with the things that you cannot get rid of easily or immediately, such as your job, your neighbourhood, and your body.

These are the things you need to work on changing your negative self-talk about. If you walk into your office and think, 'I hate this office,' you need to think of another phrase to tell yourself as you get to work, maybe, 'This is my office. I'm grateful to have this job. It pays all my bills.' Or 'This office comes with my job. I'm going to enjoy it as best as I can.' Maybe this might be an improvement.

If you can stretch it as far as 'I love this office. It's a comfortable place to work. It means I don't have to work out on the streets. I love my view, even though it's only a view of the wall. I find new, interesting things to see in it every day.' Even if this sounds like a Pollyanna version, where you tell yourself you love and appreciate the things you hate, do it. This will be annoying to you at first because you will feel like you're lying to yourself and bullshitting yourself but remember, the key here is your mind is accepting some new programming. That's the key. You have to remember it's not about lying to yourself. It's about putting a new program in your mind. It's about understanding that everything you believe is just a program and the programs you already believe were put in there.

It doesn't mean that they're right, and it doesn't mean that they're true. Once you understand that the programs in your mind are not necessarily the truth, you will be much more comfortable replacing them with any program you want.

It's amazing how we believe that truth is objective, whereas when it comes to the mind, truth is just a program. And we know this as a fact because you can have two people in the exact same situation confronted with the same obstacle. The obstacle is the truth. The way they approach the obstacle that's the program. But for them, the program is the truth and the beliefs that the program creates lead to their actions and the faith in which they take them. Those actions define their realities. A simple example would be of two people walking on a trail who are confronted with a mountain; the truth is, there is now a mountain in front of them.

Their programming will define how they approach it. Mr A, who was brought up with lots of positive programs and has a can-do attitude, decides to scale the mountain because he believes that he can get over it, and he doesn't want to go back. He wants to go forward because he is a positive person. So, he begins to scale a mountain, and his belief leads to this faith that he can scale the mountain and get over it. So, he takes action to scale the mountain, and after much difficulty, gets to the top, gets over the other side and continues on his way.

Mr B was given programs of negativity and failure as a child, so when confronted with the same obstacle, his belief is that he won't be able to overcome this obstacle because he wasn't always able to overcome some of the obstacles in his past. He was always told that he wasn't good at achieving things, that he would be a failure and never do anything good. So, when confronted with the mountain, he decided that this was an obstacle he couldn't overcome, and he would have to go back and not complete the trail.

That's the difference between truth and your belief. Truth is the mountain; the mountain actually exists. The belief that comes from your programming is dependent. So don't worry about telling yourselves lies because the lie you think you're telling yourself is just a computer program you're putting into your brain to tell it how you want it to function. It doesn't change the truth. It just changes the program of how you deal with the truth, and your programming of how you deal with the truth is what creates your reality.

Two Plans

Before you embark on any activity, you need two plans. You need a plan of what you will do if it's successful and a plan for what you will do if it fails. It always amazes me, particularly in the TV industry, when stars are interviewed, and they explain just how surprised they were when the show they were cast in became a massive hit. They often say that they had absolutely no way of dealing with it, and I always think to myself, didn't you think about the possibility of the show becoming a hit, and if it did, what would you do? How would you deal with the pressure of success? How would you deal with fame? Surely, if you're cast in a brand-new pilot for a show, there's the potential it will be successful. Equally, if it didn't become successful, didn't you have a plan for how you would deal with the failure? If you went for the casting and got rejected, didn't you have a plan for dealing with the rejection?

This is just another example of how people bumble their way through their lives. If you go for a job interview, you should have a plan for what you're going to do if it goes well and you're successful, and you should have a plan for what you're going to do if it goes badly and you're not. These don't have to be meticulous plans. Nobody wants to plan their life away, particularly based on results that may or may not happen. A simple, vague scenario will suffice because, in most of your actions, there's a 50/50 probability that the result is either successful or not. Based on that, pre-planning what you will do in each of those scenarios will save you a lot of worry and pain.

If you plan for what you're going to do if your meeting is successful and your proposal is accepted, then you're already one step ahead if it is. You have a plan for what you're going to do. Suppose your meeting is unsuccessful and your proposal is not accepted. In that case, you won't sit around confused and worried, unsure of what to do next because you only have one option. You've already got an idea of a backup plan for a second move. Chess players will understand this very well. And I'm not trying to ruin people's lives by having them strategize every five minutes of it. But I think that there are often only two real probabilities for all of the major things in life. Your plans are either successful or they are not. So, you should have a basic idea of what you've gone to do depending on which one of these two scenarios becomes the reality.

If You Have to Be There, Be There

This is one of those painstakingly obvious 'No shit, Sherlock' comments in this book, but let's be honest, it's something that almost none of us do. We've all been in a situation such as working a job that we didn't want to do but took because we needed the money. Or maybe we know that we will be leaving a particular position soon, so our level of commitment absolutely tanks because we know there is no future in that position. Maybe we're invited out to a party that we don't really want to attend but feel committed to turn up. Worst still, we are in a relationship that we really want out of, and we know it's only a matter of time, but we stay just biding our time for the right circumstances to come along when we can end it.

No matter the circumstance, no matter how you ended up there, since you're already there, be there. What I mean by being there is to be present. Be present. Be aware. Be engaged. Be focused and treat the situation like it matters.

Even though you know that you're leaving that job in four weeks, it doesn't benefit you to treat it with disdain. It doesn't benefit you to treat it as if it's unimportant, and let me tell you why.

Firstly, you should want to help your colleagues, some of whom you like or have respect for. You don't want them to remember you as the guy who treated that job like crap and made their day-to-day life difficult just because you were leaving. Secondly, until you leave, you must spend your time there anyway. So, since you must spend time there, put effort in, be fully engaged, and try your best. Maybe try to help set things up so your colleagues can work well without you. Help put systems in place and organise processes to help with future productivity. They will remember you fondly, and if your company is any good, they will also appreciate this and write it in your reference. But even if none of the above happens, which is very often the truth, at least you will know that you worked as well as you could until you left, which means you didn't violate your own standards. You kept your standards of excellence and positivity right to the end. If you sit there, looking at the clock, trying to do the bare minimum, backing out of work. The real person who suffers is you because you drop your standards. There's no way of doing a poor job without dropping your standards unless you're the kind of guy who delivers poor-quality work when doing their best.

If you think that when you get to your new job, the one you really want and will love so much, the one that you're so excited about, you will do an amazing job. You do yourself no benefits by doing poor work in your current one. The energy you save by not working properly in the job you have or are leaving will not get transferred to your new job. In fact, it's more likely that the attitude you pick up of not doing good work in the job that you currently have or are leaving will be the thing that gets transferred to the new job that you claim you want to have an amazing impact on when you start.

Hold yourself to high standards and always work well under all conditions. Because since you have to be there, be there.

Now, apply this analogy to everything else in your life.

If you're in a relationship, just doing the bare minimum is no point. Because you know it's on its way out. There's nothing wrong with still being engaged and still being the best person you can be. Because, again, it doesn't just benefit the partner you're with; it also benefits you. If you're being a shitty partner, it means you're being a shitty person. If you've been a shitty person to someone else, you're also being a shitty person to yourself. Because while you're being a shitty person to them, you're also there. This is not benefiting you. It's not benefiting the way you see yourself; it's not benefiting what you tell your subconscious about who you are. You can't tell your subconscious that you're a wonderful person while being a shitty person at the same time. Because your subconscious will see your actions and take them over the words. So, if you have to be there, be a good partner, even if you think the relationship is on the way out. Remember, it's practice for the relationship you want to be in.

As for the event, this is probably the easiest scenario for you to appreciate because, surely, you've been at an event that you didn't really want to go to or didn't have great expectations for. But as you turned up and got involved, you had an amazing time. Well, this is why if you have to be there, you should absolutely be there. Since you're at the event, anyway, try to find a way to enjoy it. Try to see what's enjoyable for you at that event. They may have certain activities that you're not interested in. Fine, move away from those and try to find the people or activities that interest you. Find the people or things that you do find interesting and engaging. Like I said at the start, 'No Shit, Sherlock.'

When you find these things, whatever else is going on in the event, even if it's just one person who, like you, thinks that a Cirque du Soleil-themed party is a bit ridiculous and pretentious, that one person who sees the place in the same way as you could be your connection for the evening, your reason to have a great time and maybe even form a great friendship.

Even if there is no one else to relate to, then maybe the problem is you. Maybe even though you think it's all a little bit silly and pretentious if you just threw yourself into it, you'd find out and that you enjoy it, much to your surprise.

Because I repeat, since you're already there, because you had to be there, you might as well be there. Present, attentive, aware and open to enjoying yourself. Because if you can't be those things, then honestly, you were better off declining the offer and not attending in the first place, to all the above.

This simple attitude will bring greater enjoyment to all of your life's activities, and it is what goo-goo Pollyannas mean when they say, 'Be present'. My variation on this is yes, be present, be engaged, be open and willing, give your best, or don't be there at all. If you must be there, don't waste your life moaning about it; get the best out of it. And if you don't have to be there (and let's face it, this is true most of the time), save your energy and life force and don't. Your life force is the one thing we never think about, even though we have definitive proof that we only have so much of it. We know it is limited because we die. So, if you don't have to be there, save your life force and use it for something else you want to do.

Your Perfect Day

I want you to think about your perfect day. Think about a perfect day that you had in the past. If you can't remember a day from your past that was almost perfect, like maybe a wonderful birthday you had, an amazing day which was part of a holiday, a brilliant day with your lover or a love interest that you had. Then, think about what a perfect would look like to have.

Here's the key issue, please pay attention to how much of that day you spent complaining. How many times that day did you say, 'This is shit.'

'This is terrible.' 'Things never work for me.' 'I hate doing this.' 'I'm scared to do this', 'Why do I have to do that'?

I would wager that on your perfect day, or at least the nearest perfect day you can remember, those thoughts, those sentiments, those statements did not arise as part of your day. Maybe you said something like that once or twice throughout the whole 24-hour period, but the majority of your day, your thoughts and comments were more like the following.

'I'm so happy I get to do this.' 'Isn't this fun?' 'I can get this done.' or, 'Wow, I can't believe I achieved that.' 'Well done, Me.' Your perfect day would be filled with these types of comments.

I use this example to counteract the concept that positive thinking is Pollyanna's thinking. I mean, let's face it, when you have your perfect day, whether it's your birthday, a day on a luxury holiday, Christmas day or whatever. Some part of you thinks, 'Wouldn't it be great if life was always like this'? And that's probably usually answered by yourself responding with, 'Oh yeah, that would be grand, but in reality, it can't be.'

But the fact that the major thought on our best days is wishing life our life was always like that should tell you that the way you think and relate to life on your best days is how you really want to relate to your whole life.

The reason you don't is that you've told yourself that living this way is unrealistic, that you can't relate to life in that way, act in that way, hold those beliefs and have those experiences.

And guess what? The people who do live like this, you hate them because they're the Jesus creeper-wearing, long-haired, googly-glazed-eyed hippie shit people, and they are as annoying as fuck. But just remember this, you're the hypocrite, not them. You are the one who has fantastic days, and you wish that your life could be just like those days all the time, but you don't do anything about it.

You don't take the steps in terms of controlling your own thought processes to eliminate the negative self-talk, negative belief systems, and negative paradigms and replace them with positive which would swiftly give you more days that feel like your perfect day, every day.

Days where your vocabulary doesn't include: 'This is shit.' 'Why does it always happen?' 'Why does it always happen to me?' 'I'm no good at that.' 'I'm so embarrassed.' 'Oh my god. I'm so scared. I bet this goes wrong.'

When you take the time to eliminate these phrases from your vocabulary, you eliminate the thought processes and beliefs that create them. You will soon see that more of the days of your week, month and life resemble your perfect day, and perfect day after perfect day can only lead to one thing, a near-perfect life.

So start to look closer and closer to those few perfect days you have had. Think about your thoughts, feelings, language, and vocabulary on those rare occasions and replicate them. Don't wait for the correct circumstances to replicate them; replicate them to create more of the correct circumstances.

Hug It Out

30 years ago, when I was in university, my good friend Jasvinar introduced me to the concept of hugging. I remember she told me the scientific reasons why hugging was so good for you and that you should hug your family, friends and anyone who would let you hug them. She was my first friend, and she would hug me regularly. She introduced me to hugging, and I never stopped. Multiple proofs exist that hugging is good for you. I believe it comes from the fact that, as children, most of us would have been hugged by our mothers. Our parents would have carried us in a hugging motion as babies. We would go to our parents when we were upset or hurt, who would cuddle us until we felt better.

Personally, I hug everybody. I give my male friends a manly hug (as Riley in The Boondocks would say, 'No Homo.') Just joking, folks. Please don't cancel me!! I hug them to show my appreciation for their support and brotherhood. I give my female friends a 'No, I am not hitting on you' hug. An appreciative hug to show them how much I care about them and that I'm there to support them. I have a hug for business associates and a different one for people I'm truly in love with. I want to show them how deeply I appreciate their existence and the important place they hold in my life. Hugging people kick starts those feel-good chemicals that stimulate your well-being. Of course, you must get people's consent before hugging them. There's nothing worse than being hugged by somebody you don't want to hug you, and nothing more awkward than trying to hug somebody who doesn't want to be hugged. But if you build the right relationships, although they don't seem as cool as a really cool DAP or a funky handshake, a hug is better for the well-being of yourself and the person you're hugging, and most definitely communicates more support, appreciation and affection than any gesture done at arm's length.

Breathing

As a young adult, whilst going through my first journey through what I would eventually name hippie shit, I remember writing one day, 'It took me 23 years to learn how to breathe.'

This is obviously not true because if I had not been breathing, the leading cause of all death, namely lack of oxygen to the brain, would have ensured that I most certainly would not have made it to 23 years of age. But at the time, I was learning different types of breathing for different situations and results. I couldn't believe that I had finished both schooling and university. Yet, neither had taught me anything as basic as the most effective breathing methods.

But in the world of Hippie shit, so much is said of breathing. You may wonder why so many of these hippie shit practices focus on breathing. Whether it's yoga, meditation, martial arts or other activities, all of them have associated and different breathing practices.

My view is because, as I just said, the leading cause of all death to every single human who has ever lived ever is lack of oxygen to the brain. This means that breathing is not only important but actually the most fundamental thing we do in our lives to stay alive.

It seems that although we are born breathing perfectly from the stomach, into the diaphragm, up into the chest. In most instances we forget this and adopt bad breathing practices based on what we're doing or how we now live.

So, we should be taught to understand the importance of breathing. This would make absolute common sense. Just like it would make common sense to know how important the nutrition we put into our bodies is and how to find good nutrition because that's what keeps us alive. Since breathing is the most fundamental aspect of our existence, it would make sense, basic common sense, for us to investigate ways to breathe more effectively.

So that we can get oxygen to our brain in the most effective way and not only stay alive but thrive through this essential oxygen. Many people, including Winston Churchill, were claimed to have used oxygen tanks to boost their productivity and focus.

I could really talk about this for ages. There are different types of breathing for different purposes. But I hope the point I made explaining how fundamental breathing is to your being alive will inspire you to investigate this further. So, I will leave it there for now and allow you to explore the different breathing methods for your health, sports recovery, and bliss.

If you don't investigate different breathing methods, just be aware that since the leading cause of all death is lack of oxygen to the brain, learning to breathe effectively should be your number one priority. If you want to keep that oxygen going into the brain and stay alive.

Food

Food, other than the undeniable fact that the nutrition we put into our body has an almost complete effect on how well our body functions. I am completely non-plussed in terms of giving you dietary advice. I've been a vegetarian for 23 years. Shit worked for me, but I also appreciate some of the other diets. For example, the caveman idea of only eating meat maybe once a month, in the same way our earlier ancestors would when meat was scarce. I see how this would give you a good balance. My simple suggestion is to find an expert in this area, such as Dr Mahdi Brown, who has studied health sciences, applied his brilliance to it, and can walk you through a healthy Food and Nutrition process based on your needs.

Sleep

Sleep is another thing on the long list that scientists still need to fully understand.

Dr Deepak Chopra says that you should sleep until your body wakes. Yep, that's right. No alarm clocks. I would have never understood this concept as a young and working man. I had no idea that this was possible until I started my own business and had control over my time and schedule. The whole idea of sleeping until my body was ready to wake up without being forced out of my sleep by the alarm of a clock to make some appointment that was set based on somebody else's schedule, not mine, was unthinkable.

The change is quite miraculous. Here's a simple reason. I tend to find that when I haven't had enough sleep, and I'm tired, I'm far more susceptible to fear, anxiety, worry and stress. It's as simple as that: if I haven't slept enough, it's hard to meditate and get into a peaceful place. Worrisome thoughts, anxieties, and thinking about problems flood my mind far more than when I'm well-rested, and these negatives continue throughout the day. I am much more likely to make mistakes doing things I usually do without any problem. I'm much more likely to spill the sugar, drop the milk, or bump the rear of my car whilst backing out of my parking space. Sleep is essential, right up there with food and breath. Even if we don't quite know how and why we need it, it's evident that we need at least eight hours every night, and it is most definitely better if we sleep according to our circadian rhythms. Still, we should also give our bodies as much sleep as needed, meaning that you go to sleep when you're tired and only wake up when you're not.

Exercise

If you are not aware by now that you really need to exercise your body, preferably every day, but at the very least two or three times a week, you really haven't been paying attention. I explained that my favourite form of exercise over the years has been martial arts because it perfectly balances physical muscle and stretching workouts. I also went through many years of doing what we call Hard and Soft days, where I would train martial arts on a Monday and Wednesday and then do yoga on a Tuesday and Thursday. That way, I alternate my body between 'hard', rigorous exercises and 'softer' stretching-based exercises. But that's just me. You really need to find an exercise routine that suits you. My recommendation for the best exercise is to find a sport that you absolutely love and do it. This will remove the pain, the mental pain, the annoyance, the oh my god, do I have to do this from your exercise routine. Most people don't go to the gym simply because they don't want to go to the gym. They don't enjoy going to the gym, and it's not an enjoyable experience. It's a 'have to', not a 'get to' experience. You need to turn your exercise into a 'get to' experience, something that you're so excited that you have the opportunity to do, not something that you're so frustrated that you have to find the time to do because somebody tells you it's good for you. So go and find yourself a sport you like. My favourite sport was martial arts. I've enjoyed learning and getting better at the techniques; it was my 'get to' exercise. I was so excited to go to class, work off my stress, learn something new, and improve what I had already learned. That's why I stuck with it for over 30 years. If martial arts isn't your thing, that's absolutely fine. Even if you don't know your thing, it's not a problem. Start trying stuff out. Join a tennis club. If you don't like tennis, go to the courts and start playing basketball with the guys. If you don't like basketball, try kicking the football around in a park. Football is not your thing; borrow a bike, go for a ride, and see if you enjoy that. That's not your thing; go to the local ice skating rink, Put on some skates and try ice skating, join a dance class, go hiking or swim.

The options are endless. There are literally hundreds of sports. Surely one of them is going to be the thing that you enjoy. And enjoyment is the key. Don't worry about how good you are at it. A few years ago, I used to play at the basketball courts. Sometimes, other guys would come and play one-on-one with me and utterly thrash me because they was so much better at it than me. It made absolutely no difference to me. I just enjoyed playing. One of my greatest feats was a guy who came once, who used to be a semi-professional and beat me in a one-on-one game. He came back a year and a half later, and I had played so much just out of enjoyment that I beat him; that said, you don't have to have a target.

Your target is enjoyment, and the enjoyment will lead you to your greater target, which is better physical health.

Scratch the Record

Later in this book, we discuss how worrying is like praying for what you don't want. Yet, if you're anything like me, you probably think you can't visualise. It's so difficult to bring up images and pictures in your mind's eye of the things you want, things that would empower you. Yet somehow, when you're worried about something that hasn't happened and probably will never happen, you have no problems bringing together vivid images and feelings of exactly what that would be like.

So, this is an embellishment of a technique I originally heard from Anthony Robbins, but Jose Silva, Vishan Lakhiani, and other teachers have something similar. I love it and have found it to be very, very powerful. Since worry is usually thinking about something that has not happened (because if it had happened, you wouldn't be worrying about it; you would be dealing with it), the key to this technique is to destroy the image you are worrying about, debunk it and take away its power. And the way you do this is by mocking it and showing it for its stupidity. Then, whilst you are already in a state of effective visualisation, bring the scenario back to a real-life scene reflecting the reality you want.

So, here's an example. Let's say that you are scared that your presentation tomorrow will absolutely bomb. You're thinking about how you will feel when it all goes wrong. You're thinking that the horrible person in your office who always looks down on you will laugh, and your Boss will frown. Well, the key here is to catch yourself in the middle of that visualisation, in the middle of that feeling, and then to mock it.

First, try to brighten the images in this visualisation and then distort them. You can distort them in any way that suits you and your personality. Maybe turn them into black and white. Turn the whole scene into a Charlie Chaplin or a Keystone Cops movie where all the characters who were putting you down start to fall over clumsy, making them look stupid. Change their features so that they look unattractive, dumb and ridiculous. Then, something stupid is thrown into the image, like a golden elephant flying through the office. Anything that makes the whole scene absurd. The aim is to take the negative visualisation and ruin it. One minute, it's a very real scene of a painful trauma that you're thinking is going to happen to you in real life. The next minute, it's an absurd farce that could never happen in a million years. I mean, how could it happen; a Golden elephant is not going to fly through your office tomorrow morning. Right!!!

This is a super powerful tool. I have used it very effectively for destroying traumatising memories from my past, which were extremely painful every time that I replayed them in my mind. I used this tool to distort them and destroy them. Again, how you distort and destroy them is down to you. Use any visual effect that suits you. I like the Keystone Cops film effect, but I've also used other things I enjoy, such as anime. I take an image, such as a vision of my failure, and turn the whole thing into an anime film. Then, I change the characters into exaggerated animated characters. Once I animate the characters, I can jump up, destroy them and stop them from doing the things that humiliated me. I can become that powerful person I always wanted to be; I can be as powerful as I want to be; I no longer suffer embarrassment and mistreatment; I am treated with respect and deference.

The purpose of this exercise is not to change you into a narcissist or sociopath; the aim is to change your visions from somebody who is put upon, treated badly and put down into somebody who is respected and treated well. After all, it's your imagination dude, visualise life as you want it, or at least think things that make you feel better.

So, remember, you're in control of it. It doesn't have to be reasonable. I repeat. I don't advise you to become a narcissistic lunatic, but at least you can take the power to balance out the negative and self-deprecating feelings that you might be having. Feelings are where you get put down, and you feel less than others. Change those images to pictures of you being powerful and strong.

Why is this a powerful way of doing things? The power lies in the real key to this process, the fact that it requires no additional effort. If I were to tell you to sit down in the morning and visualise good shit happening,

I know there's probably less than a 30% chance that you're actually going to do that. It's going to feel Hokey; it's going to feel corny; it's going to feel silly. Plus, you will tell yourself that you don't have the time to dedicate a whole five minutes to this practice.

But hijacking the thoughts that you're having anyway is so powerful because you're already having them. You don't have to set aside time to put yourself down to worry, panic, or think about all the things that can go wrong. You're already doing it! So, all we're doing is taking the time you're already using to do something that you're already doing, which is visualising possibilities and having feelings about them and then changing them. Changing the negative possibilities into comical absurdities so they no longer seem like a reality. And then by changing those into wonderful possibilities where, rather than horrible things happening or absurdity occurring, that scene changes into something positive, beneficial and uplifting for you and your life.

HIPPIE SHIT

Why Do It? Why Not?

The number one point of all this practical hippie shit is simple: What have you really got to lose by at least trying to apply some of these principles? Most of these practices take only a few minutes a day. While some gurus or leaders might suggest spending hours on this stuff, most people, including myself, will tell you that just ten to fifteen minutes a day of trying these practices is enough for the results to be at least beneficial.

We're talking about a small portion of your day, maybe half an hour less of listening to music, watching Netflix or playing video games, in exchange for trying out a few principles that could potentially improve your life. So, what do you really have to lose? It doesn't take much time, and the only thing you might lose is some of your old beliefs.

These beliefs might make you feel superior, thinking that all these people teaching hippie shit are just a bunch of idiots and that you're smarter because you live in the real world and deal with cold, hard facts. But as we've pointed out in the science section, the vast majority of what we consider proven, knowledgeable science is limited, constantly evolving and still can't be definitively proven.

So, aside from your feeling of superiority in dismissing 'woo-woo' ideas, what else is there to lose? Very little. It might take 15 minutes of your life, time you'd most likely spend doing something unproductive anyway.

You don't have to lose any part of your personality. I'm not a big fan of the 'you must believe' mentality. You can and potentially should apply some of these principles with scepticism. So, start with a healthy dose of doubt. Once you see and experience the benefits, you can explore practices requiring more belief.

I don't think you should dive into practices that demand significant belief right away. That approach might feel forced and inauthentic. Instead, start with something you can believe in, see if it brings you any benefits, and then use those positive outcomes as a foundation for exploring practices that require more faith.

So, what do you have to gain? As I mentioned earlier, when you ask people why they do anything, the root cause usually boils down to a desire for happiness. Many people find that, even if they don't achieve the material goals they've set, like the perfect partner, becoming a millionaire, or obtaining a status symbol, these 'hippie shit' practices can help them feel calmer in life, even in difficult situations and generally more contented and happier.

These practices can help shift perspectives, cultivate gratitude, and appreciate the things and people around you, increasing happiness. They can also help manage stress, reduce your time in anger, and improve your outlook, benefiting your mental and physical health.

The root of these practices is the potential for the happiness you think material things will bring you, with or without them. Maybe your manifestation practices will lead to those things arriving; maybe they won't. But regardless, your overall level of happiness and well-being will likely increase, and that's what you were after in the first place, isn't it?

Even if you don't get the perfect partner or achieve your ultimate goal, you'll probably experience better relationships with everyone around you. And you might discover that the relationship you thought you wanted isn't what you truly needed after all.

In short, there's very little to be lost in trying these practices, but a potential lifetime of huge benefits is to be gained.

That's why I took the time to write this, and I hope you take the time to use anything in the book that resonates with you, try it out and reap its benefits.

Manifestation, the Reticular Activated System and Segment Intending

So, your friendly neighbourhood hippie will happily tell you that if you visualise something, it will be brought into your life by either the universe, the law of attraction or potentially any number of other hippie shit mechanisms. Now I totally understand why practical people call bullshit on this.

However, there is a more practical way of looking at this concept, which I absolutely love. It is the concept of the reticular-activated system, aka the RAS. The reticular-activated system is not just something that the woo-woo crystal-gazing hippies believe, but a scientifically proven part of the brain's functionality.

I asked the font of all knowledge ChatGPT to explain it, and the answer is below.

The Reticular Activating System (RAS) is a network of neurons located in the brainstem that plays a crucial role in regulating wakefulness, attention, and arousal. It filters sensory input, prioritising stimuli that are important for survival or align with our focus while ignoring irrelevant background noise. By controlling the brain's state of alertness, the RAS helps maintain consciousness and allows for a smooth transition between sleep and wakefulness. Additionally, it contributes to selective attention by determining which external stimuli reach higher brain regions for further processing.

But I didn't understand that, to be honest, so I asked it to explain it again so that a thirteen-year-old could understand, and I got the following.

The Reticular Activating System (RAS) is a part of the brain that helps you stay awake, pay attention, and be alert. It acts like a filter, deciding which sounds, sights, or feelings are important enough for you to notice and which can be ignored. For example, it helps you focus on your teacher's voice in a noisy classroom. It also plays a role in waking you up in the morning and helps keep you alert during the day. Basically, it helps your brain decide what to pay attention to and when to wake up.

Phew, Ok, that's better.

So, this gives rise to a phenomenon that I know you will have personally experienced. Let's say that you want to buy a new car. You go to a car dealer, and you see an unusual coloured car, for example, a turquoise-coloured Toyota Yaris, and you say to yourself, 'That's really unusual. I've never seen one of those in that colour before. They couldn't have made many of those.' You then leave the showroom, and on the way home, all of a sudden, what do you start noticing? Turquoise-coloured Toyota Yaris cars. Cars that you had never seen before but are now apparently everywhere.

You say to yourself, 'Jesus, I would have never believed that there were so many turquoise-coloured cars in my area,' but the reality is that they've always been there. You never noticed them before because your brain is a deletion machine. As a deletion machine, for you to function, particularly in this attention-grabbing world, you need to ignore the vast majority of things in your environment, a function which your brain does on autopilot.

We simply couldn't function very well if we had to pay so much attention to our morning routine that we had to relearn how to brush our teeth, wash ourselves like we did when we were children, and eat our breakfast without spilling the food all over the place.

We basically automate so many of these things, and an additional aspect of that is that our brains delete most of the things that we don't need to pay attention to in order to focus on the ones that we do. So, for example, if your wife drives a red Honda, then you probably have in your mind to pay attention to the red Honda, especially sneaking a cheeky pint at the pub because it could be your wife driving past you. If your dream car were a white Ford pickup truck, then a white Ford truck would get your attention. But while you're busy paying attention to the white Fords, red Honda, and all the other things you have to pay attention to whilst walking up and down, such as stop signs, other pedestrians, and dog crap on the sidewalk, your brain has to delete lots of other things that are not as important so as not to be overwhelmed.

This is the basic premise of the science behind the RAS, explained albeit in layman's terms. If you don't believe it, then don't argue with me; argue with the scientists.

So, if we accept the premise that you have a reticular-activated system that tells your brain what to pay attention to, how does this work in terms of manifestation?

Well, in explanation, let's continue the example of the turquoise car, as I think many of you will have experienced this scenario. A scenario where there's something that you didn't know existed or that you've never paid attention to, which you suddenly realise is absolutely everywhere.

Well, if you agree with me regarding this experience, you will see that until turquoise cars were brought to your attention, you barely noticed them at all. Then you will see quite clearly that you can miss things other than just cars.

You might miss whole TV series, sporting events, and many other things you weren't paying attention to. You might miss fashion trends or clothing lines, the kind of clothes that you never paid attention to, so you only realised they existed once you looked for one and you realised they were everywhere.

Well, could this possibly also be true of business opportunities? You see, the reality is that sometimes the things you want, such as business opportunities, potential romantic partners, investment or funding, and ways to lose weight, are right under your nose. They are right in front of you, but because you've programmed your reticular activated system in such a way as to not notice them or, to be more specific, you never programmed your reticular activated system to look for them, you don't see them. Other people who have their reticular activating system programmed to search effectively for these things will indeed see them and take advantage of them, but because you do not understand this, you call those people lucky. Your viewpoint is that those people are lucky because these opportunities come to them without paying attention to the fact that, in reality, these opportunities were there and available for everybody; they may, in fact, have been offered to you first. But you had programmed your brain to look past them.

Now, this concept works very keenly in tune with things like belief. For example, if you have a belief system that rich people are all crooks and are not to be trusted, then you will have programmed your reticular activated system not to pay attention to rich people or, even worse, to look for rich people in order to avoid them. Programmed not to pay attention to opportunities offered by rich people means that you will literally walk right by these opportunities. When somebody else who's programmed their brain differently sees that person and has access to that opportunity, you will call them lucky. Or, based on your belief system, where you have programmed your RAC to look for successful people and how their success could be interpreted as luck, or if you are so minded, you might even say that they're probably crooks.

So, this manifestation thing isn't only about sitting down and conjuring shit out of the ether by closing your eyes and visualising them or waving your hands in the air until they appear out of nothing.

It is actually about seeing the things that already exist, picking up on the opportunities that are already in front of you, and having a belief system and structure that allows you to see them and take advantage of them. That is also part of how you manifest your reality.

You don't do it just by the law of attraction conjuring things out of thin air (although there is truth in this, too). You also do it by having your brain programmed by setting goals, targets, intentions and beliefs so that you can see the things right in front of you and take the actions required to receive them.

Repetition

I think it's well worth restating this point, just in case it hasn't come across clearly in any other chapter, that repetition is the key to programming your brain.

When we talk about your brain indeed being programmed, the key to this is repetition. In the same way that we discussed that going to the gym once would not make you physically fit, your parents didn't say to you that you were a loser once and caused that to be programmed into your brain.

They probably told you that they did not think you were successful in a variety of ways over the years. Over and over again, subtly and blatantly. Maybe it was reinforced by your so-called friends, who weren't genuinely good friends. They were just insecure people themselves who wanted to make themselves feel a little bit better, a little bit more important and a little bit more special. And they achieve this by putting you down rather than exalting you for what you're good at, which is what true friends do, while you do the same for them.

Far too many of us as children have friends who like to keep us around for their own purposes. I'm not saying they don't like us, but they definitely don't want us to rise above them or to rise out of their friend group. So, they see no benefit in helping us see what we're good at; they get much more out of the relationship by holding us in our place. In Australia, they call this the tall poppy syndrome; in order to keep all of the poppies at one level, they cut off the head of the one that stands tall. Just so they would all be at the same level, and they wouldn't have to bask in the shade your elevated height creates.

So, the programming that you received didn't come from one or two instances. It came from the constant repetition and from many sources. Most of what you heard in the first 18 years of your life would have been overwhelmingly negative, hence the negative programming of almost everybody in the world. And hence the positivity and the success rate of the handful of people who started their life with a combination of positive programming and maybe the odd million-pound Trust Fund, just to get started on any ideas that that positivity sprang forth.

So, keep it in mind that it's repetition that does the programming in the first place. This is why listening to self-talk works, repetition.

So, although you're now an adult, nothing has changed from when you were a child; the programming of your brain still works by repetition.

The only difference is that now, as an adult, you are aware of the repetition. It annoys you. It sounds corny, it sounds hokey, it sounds untrue, and it challenges your concept of reality. Unfortunately, the only way to rewrite those programs and all those years of parental, familial and environmental negativity is more repetition.

That's it. Apparently, even hypnosis can't do it because hypnosis activates a different part of the brain, and hypnosis, in most instances, is temporary because your mental programming is coming from the hypnotist, not from yourself.

If you want to be reprogrammed, you will have to go through the same process that created your original programming, which is repetition.

And let me repeat. It's going to feel painful because the first time it happened, you were too young to be aware of what was going on. You didn't think that your brain was being programmed. It was just life. You were just spending another day with your negative mother, another day with your mean bullying brother or sister, another weekend with your father who is dismissive and hard to satisfy or your so-called Friends who never seem to give you your due praise for the things that you could achieve. All of that information created a repetition in your brain that gave you the paradigm and beliefs that you have right now.

If you want to overwrite this now as an adult, you are going to be aware of every single time the program is run to institute the new belief system and change the paradigm.

So be prepared to get uncomfortable because you were programmed repeatedly. But you didn't realise it the first time around. And now, to overwrite these programs, you're going to have to do it whilst fully aware of what is happening, and it's going to be quite annoying. You'll feel like Winston in the George Orwell Novel '1984' being brainwashed with doublespeak, but it's the only way to get it done, and I promise you it will be worth it.

Affirmations & Self-Talk

Here is something that took me literally decades to learn, fully understand, and internalise. I am talking about the concept of self-talk, you know, the things that you say to yourself in your head. That constant narration (if you need more clarification on it, there is a great TV show from the early 2000s called Peep Show, which uses this as its central theme). Well, if you do not have a constant narration going on in your head, do not be concerned; apparently, only 50% of the world's population does, but if you don't, you probably have something similar, just that it's a visual or a feeling rather than a voice.

I guess that I really struggled with understanding and accepting the importance of self-talk. Although I was aware of it for decades, it wasn't until I was in my 50s that I finally felt as if I understood the concept that the language you use to yourself has an enormous effect on the results you get in your life.

The language you use when talking to yourself has an absolute effect on the results you get in your life. So, I know we've already discussed how your environment, what your parents and peers say to you, affect how you see the world and your paradigm, which informs what you think is possible.

But I want to take it one step further. Learning not to speak to yourself in negative language or terms has a massive effect on your well-being. I'm going to give you one example that I hope you will be able to relate to, which will help you to really understand.

Have you ever had pain, such as bumping your leg or banging your toe, which really hurts? Now you're walking around with this pain in your toe because you bumped it recently, but at some point later, maybe in a few hours, the pain subsides. If this happened, have you ever had the experience where you thought to yourself, 'Oh, I banged my toe earlier, and it was hurting? I wonder where that pain went,' and immediately the pain returned. What you have done with your language is to give yourself the reverse of the Placebo effect. Rather than removing pain with the pretence of pain-soothing medication, you are giving yourself pain where none exists.

If you have chronic pain such as back pain or knee pain (both of which I've suffered with), you expect that pain to be there daily. If, for any reason, you wake up or are going about your day and you realise that the pain isn't there, and you think to yourself, 'Hey, that's great. My back pain isn't here.' (which is quite normal to do), I almost guarantee that the pain will return. You are telling your subconscious, 'Hey, there should be a pain in my back,' and upon your instruction, it will return.

As I write these words, I realise that I could possibly create pain in my back today just by writing this. Once you understand this power, it does two things.

Firstly, it should start to make it real to you that what you say to yourself, your self-talk, and by interpolation of that, your affirmations, incantations, all the stuff we use, be it words or visualisations, have a power that is very real. They have a real effect. If you can bring pain into your body that wasn't there or your body wasn't feeling at the time just by mentioning it and without planning to call it into action, this is proof of words having a real tangible physical effect.

To me, this is quite miraculous. It not only shows that your words have power and can bring things into your reality, but it also shows the impersonal nature of your subconscious mind. That you didn't say, 'I want pain.' What you said was, 'Where's the pain?' And it gave you pain. This, unfortunately, also works for 'I don't want pain.' Your subconscious mind will ignore the filler words and just go to the keyword 'pain'. It'll ignore the part where you say, 'I don't want' and just go to the part where you say 'pain', and then whatever part of the body you suggested, toe, hip, neck, it will deliver the pain to.

If you imagine it with a personality, it would say, 'Oh, you said pain, neck. Okay, here you go.'

If you've ever experienced this, then it is your absolute proof that this hippie shit works. Because you've done the hippie shit, just in reverse. You've done it by affirming something you didn't want and delivering it.

So, although I was aware of this for decades. It was only after these decades had passed that I really began to understand it. Because it sounds so stupid.

Plus, one of the reasons the positive affirmations didn't work was because of the way hippie shit people introduced them to me. I mean, when someone says to me, 'There are no problems, there are only challenges,' and I've got a real fucking problem, such as not being able to pay my rent this month, I immediately go to a mental place called, 'Fuck off. That's not a challenge. It's a fucking problem.'

So, the way these things are pitched, at least for me, brought up so much resistance and resentment it delayed my ability to penetrate them because whether it's from Anthony Robbins or from some gooey-eyed spotty post-teen who hung out all day playing bad reggae on their guitar. It always seemed to be such bullshit.

But now I am trying to practicalise it because I want you to understand it. I want you to understand it because it's so important. It's so important that you understand that if you don't want pain, you can't say 'I don't want pain,' because your subconscious mind will only hear 'pain' and give you pain.

FYI, I'm still terrified as I write these words at the potential of the pain that I might be bringing into my body today.

You have to say, 'Wouldn't it be wonderful if my body functioned perfectly today?' 'Wouldn't it be wonderful if my shoulder had full motion and could function in every way that I wanted to?' or even more directly, 'I am fit and healthy today. My body is healthy and vibrant today, and able to perform every function I ask it to do with ease.'

I only started doing it this year, but the results are amazing. I do it in the shower. As I wash the different parts of my body, I affirm their health, strength, flexibility, and vitality.

The difference between if I say to myself, 'Wouldn't it be great if I didn't have back pain today,' which would cause my back to immediately start to hurt, and if I say to myself, 'Wouldn't it be wonderful if my body was fit and vibrant today,' which causes my body to function with no pain.

'Wouldn't it be wonderful if my back was strong and healthy today?' 'Wouldn't it be wonderful if my knee joints were flexible and strong today?' 'My shoulder has a perfect range of motion and movement today.' 'My hips are flexible and strong today.'

This is how you have to talk to yourself, particularly if you're feeling discomfort. One of the best things I ever heard was someone mention that you should go as far as redefining pain and calling it discomfort. I know this sounds super cynical, but it's also very powerful. Because when you're diagnosed with something, once you name it, you give it power.

So, when I was feeling the symptoms of my heart disease, I would feel something uncomfortable in my heart and say to myself, 'Oh, my God, that's my heart disease.' 'Oh shit, that's the arrhythmia.' 'Goddam it, That's the over dilation of my heart giving me stabbing pains; I wonder if I'm going to have a heart attack and die?' And what was I telling my subconscious mind while thinking those things? I want arrhythmia. I want the dilation of my heart. I want a disease in my heart. So, as an extension of the principle outlined above, I now say, 'Oh, I can feel a sensation in my heart.' Or an even better version would be, 'Oh, the sensation that I am feeling in my heart is my heart repairing itself,' which is invariably true because human beings are constantly and without stopping at any point in their breathing life, trying to achieve homeostasis. So, these statements are actively true. You are only feeling sensations in your body, and whatever feelings you have result from the body trying to repair itself. The things that you feel as pains, and you call disease, are just your body trying to achieve homeostasis. Your body is constantly trying to repair itself. You're the one dictating that your body has an illness and what it is called and the fact that the sensations you feel are a result of the illness or the illness getting worse. Your body is simply trying to repair itself and improve itself to perfection all the time. So, language and health are uniquely important; perhaps this is why two people with similar health histories can get the same medical issue, and one makes a full recovery whilst the other worsens. That is how powerful your self-talk is and why it is important.

Now, obviously, if self-talk can affect your life in the negative, it can most definitely affect your life in the positive. So please don't be like me.

Don't allow some googly-eyed hippie or on-stage guru to frustrate you into missing the real point. There's nothing woo, woo or bullshit about this.

Your language will actually immediately affect your body. Don't believe me. Keep on telling a certain part of your body to have pain, I almost guarantee you it will start hurting, or something will happen to hurt it.

Now, if this power works both ways, why can't I affirm that I have the body of a bodybuilder and have it happen right away. Well, it's a sad, sad fact that we can bring negative things into our lives much more quickly than positive ones. This is because we've programmed our brains, not just ourselves, but our environment, parents, teachers, and the world, to expect negativity, making it easier to believe in. Plus, negativity feeds into our survival instinct, meaning that we have every aspect of our senses looking for and pointing towards the negative things in our environment as a means to keep us alive. The upshot of this is that we can bring negative things into our lives much quicker.

As such, we have to fight and reprogram our brains and our whole environment as much as possible in order to bring positivity into our lives. As things stand, we can only bring negative things into our lives so quickly because we have already prepared the environment for them to grow.

Don't believe me, give it a try. See how quickly you can get a part of your body to hurt, and once you do, once you are feeling pain and you see that it's true, see how long it takes you to get it to stop. Understand 100% that you can do the reverse and get a part of your body to be more healthy, more fit, more vibrant but it will take a lot longer than it took to make it hurt. Then, once you have this full understanding, realise that with effort, you can replicate this with any other aspect of your life.

Author's note: I was suffering from pain in three parts of my body. My lower back, Knee and shoulder. I decided to adopt the practice of telling myself that my body was fit and strong every morning in the shower. Every morning as I shower and clean different parts of my body, I give thanks for them and say isn't it wonderful how fit and strong 'that part' of my body is. Isn't it wonderful how fit and healthy I am in general? Please note that I never used the word pain or referred to the pain that I had previously been suffering in that area. I just focused on the thought of the area being fit and healthy. It has been months now, and I have barely had a twinge of discomfort in any of the areas. Try it; I think you will find the results amazing.

How to Listen to Self-Talk

If you agree with me, or at least will entertain the idea of the importance of self-talk, I want to give you some hints on how I recommend you listen to it. Firstly, I'll say there's absolutely nothing wrong with putting on self-talk audio, particularly for something like an 'I AM' set of affirmations in the positive while lying down on your bed and just 'blissing out' to it.

I would also like to mention the power of falling asleep to this audio type. Falling asleep to self-talk or affirmations is particularly powerful because the words will penetrate your alpha and theta brain wave states. Scientists suggest that your brain waves change from beta, aka your fully awakened state, to alpha and then theta as you go deeper into sleep. These are the most effective brainwave states to be in when communicating with and instructing your subconscious mind.

But there's also a way to use self-talk, which I think is equally powerful, and this stems from Dr Shad Helmstetter's concept, which was my turning point in understanding the power and importance of self-talk. In his book 'What to Say When You Talk to Yourself', he mentions that children learn language not by sitting down and studying it but by the language being spoken all around them. They learn it by picking it up from the people around them speaking the language, not just by people talking directly to them but also by people that they hear in the background speaking the language. I saw this when I moved my children to Spain when they were three and six years old. With very little formal Spanish language training, I watched them blossom into having Spanish as their first language and English as their second. I didn't have such an easy journey. I did many courses, but most definitely realised my biggest jump in language understanding and speaking really came from a form of osmosis where I knew enough words and sentences to understand things, and then without paying attention, just being in Spanish environments, realised that I'd started to piece together the language to a much higher degree than I ever could if I'd sat down learning specific sentences in a classroom. In language learning, they call this the emersion effect.

This concept really resonated with me, and that's when I really understood the power of self-talk. I'd always understood the power of environment and parenting, the power of being around people with high expectations and for whom success was normal. But I didn't fully understand this in terms of language until it dawned on me that we learn language by picking it up just from being in the right environment, just from people talking about it in our immediate vicinity.

In understanding that, it became so clear to me that this environment, this positivity or success mentality that I'd been so interested in, particularly around children who were born and grew up in wealth, was at the very least aided by the fact that people who expect success, live success and encounter success, always talk success. They talk in successful terms, talk in positive terms, talk in expectant terms, talk in can-do terms. Talk about money as something always available, always coming, never going to be a problem, never an obstacle, and this helps to shape the mentality of the children who come out of these environments by giving them that way of thinking.

So, there is nothing wrong with sitting down and listening to self-talk, but listening to it intently, particularly when starting out, is very difficult because we've become accustomed to ridiculing this type of speech and this type of person. Your brain will reject it, and you will think, 'Jesus, this shit is so hokey; somebody talking all this blue-sky positivity makes me want to puke.'

But if you leave the self-talk playing in a room, maybe somewhere central in your house, as if you had friends visiting, and you were coming in and out of earshot of the conversation, this is far more effective. For example, I have an en-suite bedroom, and I leave the self-talk playing in my bedroom as I get up and go around to the other side of the room to do my exercise. I leave the self-talk playing, consciously ignoring it while stretching, doing my morning warmups and starting my exercises. Then I'll go into the bathroom. I don't actually move my phone. I leave it playing in the bedroom while I'm brushing my teeth, then take a shower. I can barely hear it, but It's audible. I'll come out of the bathroom and leave it playing while I get dressed. If I'm going to get my breakfast, then I'll pick it up, and I'll take it with me, and I might put it in the kitchen, or I might put it in the living room, where it's playing, and I can still hear it while I'm making my breakfast. Again, I position the audio device so it's not so intrusive as if it were playing in my earphones or right by me; it's just playing in the background in the same way that a conversation between your parents or your parent and uncle would be when you were a child. This way, you get to pick it up like children pick up language, attitudes, or opinions because it's just in the background. So, while it's playing in the living room, I'll have made my breakfast, and then I'll come into the living room where it's playing, but it won't be playing on my dining table. It'll be playing on a table in a corner. So again, it's like a conversation being had by somebody else while I'm sat down eating. This is the key to the way I use self-talk. I place the phone in strategic places around the house, so it sounds like a background conversation, as opposed to something that I'm forcefully trying to ram down my own throat or plug into my brain. This is a very effective and unobtrusive way of using self-talk and is much more in line with the concept Dr Shad Helmstetter taught. This is that self-talk, like language, is picked up by being in the background, something that you overhear, as opposed to something you purposefully try to listen to and focus on every word of it.

Self-Talk Addendum

So, if someone overhears you listening to self talk, they are guaranteed to laugh at you. As I said, it sounds really hokey. I can imagine what they'll be saying: 'My God, isn't it weird that you're listening to this person telling you how wonderful you are? Telling you how capable you are, how strong and fit you are, that you are a nice person and that you should love yourself?'

Well, so you should. You've got qualities that you don't even know that you have.

But here's the thing: if you have to listen to somebody say anything about you, isn't it better to hear somebody say good things about you than to hear people say horrible, derogatory, and demeaning things about you? People like that exact person who's taking the piss out of you for listening to self-talk in the first place.

They don't want you listening to self-talk but what do they say to you that is positive? How often do they say to you, 'You're a great person. You're a nice person. I really appreciate you. I admire your qualities.' How often do they say those things to you? Probably never. They'll never tell you even if they think of them; they just expect you to know.

They are more likely to only point out your faults. What they probably say to you is, 'You're full of yourself', 'you're so stupid', 'you're really shit at that'. 'You never get it right', 'Can't you put the thingy back where I left it?', 'Can't you load the dishwasher properly?', 'Bloody hell, that was a near miss', 'You're not a very good driver, are you?', 'You know, you're not the kind of person who can achieve those kinds of things', 'You've never been a good dancer', 'C'mon, you know you're not good at math', 'What makes you think you could run a business when you can't even take care of the family accounts?'

Those are the kinds of things they're saying to you all the time, yet they want to laugh and scoff at you when you listen to somebody or something that talks to you positively. It doesn't matter if it's a prerecorded message; at least it tells you how great you are. So, before you let them embarrass you into stopping. Think about that and as Eddie Murphy, in his 'Delirious' comedy routine, claims that the great Richard Pryor said, 'Tell them to have a Coke and a smile and shut the fuck up.'

Self-Talk Exercise

So here is a self-talk exercise. It has been said that the more of your senses you can get involved in learning anything, the greater its impact on you. I am an auditory learner, so audiobooks are all I listen to. When I read, I read slowly, and reading has less impact on me. My wife and kids are speed readers; they can read a whole book and get the full impact of the information within days. I'm not the same, and as I've said before, understanding how you learn is key to your ability to absorb information and benefit from it.

So, although I recommend that you use audio self-talk, as Dr Shad Helmstetter said in his seminal book 'What to Say When You Talk to Yourself', 75% of our learning is auditory. Plus, auditory learning is our first learning type. Children learn their primary language not by going to school to learn it by rote but by listening to it being spoken in the background by their parents, brothers and sisters, cousins, people in the shops, etc.

Although this is the primary way learning can be achieved, it might not be your primary learning method. You might, for example, be an avid writer. Writing is also a very powerful tool because we learn to write in school, and it's often said that there's a specific relationship between writing things down by hand and the ability to wire them into the brain. So, my advice is, if writing is your preferred modus operandi, then listen to the audio, and if you have the time, write out the statements in the audio to aid the learning.

Unlike me, who has all my audiobooks playing at two times speed, put the audio maybe on half speed so it's spoken at a slow enough pace for you to follow it and write it down. Do this until you've memorised it, and then you can just wake up every single day and write your self-talk.

This approach may work for the many people who wake up every morning and write down their goals, as it's a way of hardwiring them into their brains and wiring their mental computers to move forward and look for opportunities to achieve them.

With Kinaesthetic learning, aka experience, being tactile or physical learning, it can be a little bit more difficult, but going out and putting yourself in situations where the achievement of your goal is recognisable would be the key.

Examples include going to a car showroom and sitting in your dream car, going to the yacht club and spending time with the yacht owners, or going to the country club and spending time in the luxurious gardens whilst meeting people of means, spending time with the people who live the life that you want. This is another way of wiring these things into your brain. As long as you don't go there with a bad attitude, looking down on these people as bloodsuckers of the poor, criminals, or Tim, nice but dim types, living a life of luxury on their parent's trust fund money, which will have the opposite effect to the one you want. If you were to look at these people as people who you respect and people who are not that different from you, people who you can emulate, then this will be another way of learning.

Also, if there's anything in the self-talk statement that you can do, then do it. For example, if the self-talk is about being fit and healthy and talks about exercise, then maybe exercise while you listen to it. If it's about your work and you're working in an environment where it's possible, then do your work while you listen to it. If it's about being a successful property investor, then play it in the background while you're scouring the local newspapers for property deals or in the car while you're driving around neighbourhoods looking for property deals.

The mixture of learning methodologies is said to massively increase their efficacy. So, if you can mix them, then do just that. Play self-talk audio because it's the least invasive, and listening is the way that we learn most things without having to put any focus on them. But as I said, if tactile, aka hands-on, is your learning style, or if you're somebody who likes to write or read, then do that as well.

Use your mobile phone voice-to-text app to make a readable copy of the audio self-talk and read it while you listen. Or sit down with a pen and paper, listen to it and write it out while you listen to it. Or, as I said, engage in some activity that infuses and excites you while you're listening to it. This mixture will help the words wire themselves into neural pathways and help you with the neural plasticity needed to embed these new concepts, your new habitual thoughts, replacing your old habitually negative and failure-based thoughts, which are the ones that have been holding you back.

Belief In Your Statement

Just one more note on positive self-talk, yes, another, it is that important.

When you were originally programmed by your environment, for most of us, some people said words to the effect that you were a loser, and you believed them and internalised this belief without any crucial thought.

They said that you were a loser before you had actually shown any proof of what you were really capable of. So, if, like me, someone told you as a teenager that you were a loser, You at the time probably thought this was a prescription for your life, as opposed to talking about you at that moment, but were they really?

What did they even really know about you to make that assumption? What did they know about what you were or would get good at later?

Did they have any idea of the arc of the trajectory of your whole life and what you would achieve before you died? No, but they said you were a loser, which is a definitive statement as to what you were, all of you, your ability, your current status, and your future success. And what's worse, you accepted it. You accepted their assessment of you, not just then, but what you were destined to be.

Isn't it strange how we can accept negative assessments of our whole lives in one statement? You're a loser, a slacker, an idiot, not very smart, you will never be successful, a criminal, you're just not good with girls, you're not mechanical.

We take all these statements as fact, even though they're said at a particular point in your life by someone who has no idea, not only of the arc that your life will take, where the path of your life will go, what circumstances will bring to you, what skills will be revealed to you due to circumstance? Basically, they have no idea what you will achieve before you die.

They had no idea of what you were capable of when they put you down. They probably only knew about 10% of your true potential (if that) at that time. Yet they make these definitive statements about what you were, and you accepted them.

Now think about this: When asked to accept a statement such as, 'I'm a millionaire,' 'I'm a success,' 'I am brilliant,' or 'I am rich,' we struggle to accept these statements because they're not true. Reality doesn't bear them out. Yet we are happy to accept negative statements about ourselves, which reality does not bear out either.

So again, I'm going to tell you, I don't care how you do it. Everybody will have a different mechanism because we are all as unique as the stars in the sky. But you need to find a way that works for you to believe the things that you say to yourself. Once you do, focus on stopping every single negative statement that you make and replacing it with a positive one.

If you have the ability to replace it with your end goal, such as being a top scientist, and believe that, even at the moment, then do it. If you're still struggling with what we like to call 'reality,' even after I remind you that we're quite happy to believe all of the unproven negative things said about ourselves that don't align with reality. If, after understanding that, you still have trouble saying positive things that don't exactly align with your current reality, no problem. Just find a statement you can believe and use to reprogram what's already in your brain until you find a way to get comfortable believing bigger and more powerful things.

Bear in mind that the positive things you do believe will set the foundation and the bedrock upon which bigger, more powerful and more beneficial beliefs can be installed.

Lastly, I want to reach a point I made with my business partner many years ago. His name was Kevin, and we had a business called Kevin's Felin. It was a mentoring business. I was the business mentor, and Kevin was the lifestyle mentor. I kept saying to him that I was absolutely fascinated with certain famous personality types.

I gave him names like Boris Johnson, Bill Gates or Elon Musk. By the way, I have absolutely no admiration for any of these people, but I was fascinated by them, and this fascination is best exemplified in something said in a Podcast Interview I heard given by the property investor Mark Homer.

In this interview, he spoke about being from a family of modest means, who sent him to an Eton-type private school, and how all the children at that school had an expectation of success.

These children grew up around luxury cars, yachts, mansions, luxury holidays, and staff to help them prepare for things. Successful parents or uncles with successful businesses and, in this environment, just expected success. None of them expected to have to work hard to be successful. Success was their expectation because success was their normality.

As I said before, I think that part of the normality of success these kids experienced was that they were lucky enough to be surrounded by the language of success. You see if you're surrounded by successful people, they don't talk about making ends meet or how unfair the world is, about how hard it is to succeed, how hard it is to get ahead, or how often they expect to fail.

They talk about success, their last success, their plans for their next success, what their successful business partner is doing, what their successful associates are doing, and how they can beat their super-successful competitor, who has just increased their market share.

This is the 'language' they talk in daily, the language of success. These are their conversations. As a child, listening to this and being around it, it's not just the money but the mindset that trickles down. So, in the same way, the child of a criminal will hear the opportunities of how to be a criminal because that would be the predominant conversation amongst their family and friends. That's what they will overhear while playing or talking to their older cousin or being advised by their uncle. They will think being arrested is normal because they'll see their family members, friends and other relatives arrested.

They will probably grow up with a hatred of the police because that will be the mentality of most of the people around them. They will think that life is unfair and that you have to steal to balance the scales in your favour because that will be the prevailing mentality amongst their peers.

This doesn't definitively mean that they are going to become criminals, but it does definitively mean that criminality is going to be the predominant influence that they grow up around, and they will have to have very strong willpower to move against it and be the complete opposite.

Well, in the same way, children who grow up around successful, rich parents, however they made their money, whether they made their money honestly or are just very rich crooks, will grow up around the 'Language of Success'. Expectations of luxury, finery, betterment, and wealth. And again, they would have to have very strong willpower to move against this and opt for poverty. We do occasionally see this when we see the children of Oil barons, etc., decide they want to become environmentalists, hippies or societal dropouts, but this requires very strong willpower to go against all of the training and programming of their environment and, in most cases, is only a phase that doesn't last for long.

But for most people from either of these environments, their belief systems, paradigms, blueprints, world views, and views about life and people will be created by the environments they grow up in.

This is why the rich get rich and breed progeny who become rich themselves. Even if they don't inherit their parents' money, they inherit the mentality of the environment in which they grew up.

This is one of the reasons why the poor stay poor. Even if they were to win the lottery, the fact that they inherited the mental environment in which they grew up, one of poverty, means they will lose that money quickly. Brief research into past Lottery winners will overwhelmingly prove this point to be true, as estimates show that approximately 70% of big lottery winners go broke within a few years. No expectation of wealth, no feelings of worthiness and no financial management ability (all things that children who grow up in a rich environment have), are my guess as to why this is the case.

So, reprogram your brain and find a way to believe in it. Decide what you want to program your brain with, begin your reprogramming practice, and find a mechanism to make yourself believe it.

Imagination

Most, if not all, children are born with very active imaginations. Obviously, children need to be cared for, fed, and protected until they reach a certain age. Still, in many other ways, as previously mentioned, children are born with everything they need.

They simply need a carer or guardian to help them reach an age where they care for themselves. But the carer does not regulate their Ph level, does not tell their heart to beat or circulate blood throughout the body, the carer does not sit there telling the child to breathe every 2-3 seconds or help them with their cell regeneration and repair. The child's automatic functions passed down by millennia of evolution, or God or the universe, whichever you prefer, does that. Still, whatever or whoever created or controls this pre-installed human system, the parental guardian certainly does not. I truly believe that the imagination is part of this pre-installed system. It's an essential part of what we were born with, in the same way, that our cells, heart, liver and kidneys all function without us having to think about their functioning; I think imagination is a key part of our functioning if only we learned how to use it.

A child's imagination has unlimited potential. I mean, just give a child a box, come back in five minutes, and ask him what he's doing or what that box is, and you get a sense of the enormity of a child's imagination. Most parents indulge their children's imagination when they are young, but the problem, in Western society at least, is that we see a child's imagination as part of their childish, immature, and, therefore, non-adult framework.

The parents indulge in it and even see it as a funny, cute or endearing side of a child's personality. But as the child gets older, parents start to impinge on it, and they start to intrude on the child's imagination by telling them that the things they're imagining are unrealistic. They start to impinge on their imagination by telling them to not imagine the bigger goals but to imagine smaller goals that they are more likely to achieve. Basically, imagine goals that are already within their levels of attainment. They are told to imagine things that they already know they can do, as opposed to imagining things that stretch goals or accomplishments beyond the scope of their currently known abilities.

But here's what's interesting.

Over the last 30 or 40 years, we have started to see that incredibly successful businesses such as Google are using a strategy that is the complete opposite. They're using stretch goals in their meetings and projections, saying that they want 50% of their goals to be unattainable in an attempt to see how far they can stretch their teams.

Concepts like OKRs are being discussed and incorporated into business practices. SMART goals are out; OKRs are in.

Why? Well, the reality is that absolutely everything you see in the world that wasn't created by nature, everything that was created with the help of a human, was first created in someone's imagination. A tree, a bush, a river, the sea, a rock formation. These were not created by human imagination. But that house you live in, the chair you sit in, the training shoes that you put on your feet to go for your daily run, the car you drive to work, the computer you use to do your work on, the plane you sat on to take the trip and the roller coaster you went on to entertain your children, even the pen you use to sign the work contract that allowed you to earn the money to pay for the house, car, training shoes, plane tickets and holiday entertainment. We're all created from imagination. Meaning that imagination is surely not a childish thing. It is probably the most powerful thing that human beings possess outside of opposing thumbs, the reason why we can be arrogant and call ourselves the top species on the planet.

Now, if we were to consider the list of things in the above paragraph, without a doubt, a lot of them probably still came from an imagination curtailed to limitations. Maybe the guy who imagined and designed the running shoes you put on this morning to go for your jog actually wanted to build bridges. Perhaps he had always loved engineering and bridge design and had an idea of an alternative to the Golden Gate bridge, a massive structure with a fantastic design, but he was talked out of it by his parents, his peers, his teachers, his colleagues, as they all told him that bridge design would be way too complicated to get into. So, he went into clothing design instead, ending up in a shoe factory and designing shoes on your feet. That is the truth for most people and the reality of most things we use that come from imagination.

However, some people who have the strength will go through a process of self-improvement and self-realisation, deprogramming the limitations others put on them. Those are the people who create the big jumps in our reality.

It is quite funny how we talk about being practical and realistic. Yet the world we live in is defined and moulded by people who are impractical or unrealistic. The people whose imaginations create massive structures like the aforementioned Golden Gate Bridge, world-changing inventions like the aeroplane or computer, scientific structures like the Hydron collider, or other world-changing innovations such as the car production line, which dropped the cost of cars dramatically so that everybody could have one. The imagination of these people who set themselves tasks such as allowing everybody to own a car, a computer in every home or a way to connect all of humankind's information via all the computers in the world to sharing information, or even the creation of large language models which allow technology to provide us with knowledge instantaneously.

They are the ones who change the zeitgeist and the world, so much so that within a few decades, the world is unrecognisable from the world it was before their invention before their imagination and hard work came to fruition.

And I truly believe that everybody has this ability. If we weren't put off from our true vocations, and we weren't told that the machinations of our own individual imaginations were stupid. If we all worked towards stretch goals, if we all worked towards things that we had no idea how we would achieve, we just really wanted to reach them because we saw them in our imagination. If this were the case, human civilization would be pushed much further than it is today.

So just remember, when your friendly neighbourhood woo-woo hippie tells you to visualise and use your imagination, they're not talking about some nonsensical crystal healing childlike 'think of it and it will appear' practice that has no relevance to the real world.

They're talking about a fundamental and realistic principle by which absolutely everything you touch, use, hold, enjoy or depend on for your survival, from medical equipment, right through to the bed you sleep on at night, from the car you drive to the toothbrush you use to clean your teeth. Everything you have in your life that wasn't created by nature was created by the human imagination. It was imagined by somebody; it was somebody's dream, and then it was created by somebody. And that is why you shouldn't curtail your imagination to only the things that you think are possible or just fantasies for enjoyment, as your parents encouraged you to do.

Your imagination is here to help you contribute to the world. It's not here just for flights of fancy or daydreams about something that will never happen. It's there to guide you to what you can really do to contribute to the world, and there's nothing woo-woo about that.

Imagination pt 2

Before we finish our discussion on imagination, as a business consultant, I find it essential to mention that in business, the word vision is always bandied about. Businesspeople need to sell investors on their vision, and a good CEO needs to sell his staff on the vision for his company. These are very, very practical business terms. People like Steve Jobs, Bill Gates, or going back in history, Henry Ford, Rockefeller, or Carnegie are all called visionaries for the way that they saw what was possible long before it had been achieved, how their industries could disrupt and change the way that we all live our lives.

So, vision is a standard business term, and it's associated with brilliance, not nonsense, irrelevance, impractical dreaming or childish imagination. Vision in business is associated with creativity, being ahead of your time, being bold, being brave and changing the paradigm in which we all live. You often find that many of the greatest disruptors in business and industry are partnerships. You have the visionary like Steve Jobs, and then you have the 'details guy' who creates the systems to bring that vision to life like Steve Wozniak; the same can be said of Warren Buffett and his business partner Charlie Munger, Bill Gates and his business partner Paul Allen, and the list goes on.

So, you start to understand the power of vision and its relationship to being brought into reality. Everybody plays a role. We should all collaborate. Things go from the imagination, big and small, into existence in the real world. Once they exist in the real world, they move from practical people (like you), saying that's nonsensical, that could never happen, that's impossible to do, that guy's a dreamer, what a dumb idea or what a waste of time into being something that you use in your daily life. Something that improves your life's efficiency or enjoyment daily.

This is where the rubber meets the road in terms of imagination and reality. As a realist, you need to acknowledge the effect of imagination, particularly in terms of people with stretch goals, goals that even they have no idea how they will achieve. Still, they feel inside them that they really want to pursue.

Because of those outlandish and unachievable dreams, goals and imaginations wind up being your motorcar, home computer, internet access and AI tools you're probably currently using. Some wind up being small inventions such as Post-it notes and other grandiose ones such as the International Space Station or Hubble telescope giving us the ability to look at through space until we can almost see the dawn of time.

Fuck It Til You Make It!

One of my favourite phrases is 'Fake it till you make it.' I first encountered this while studying with the Russ Whitney program when I started my property investment journey. I loved the idea of faking it till you make it. There have been many versions of this concept since then. 'Fake it till you make it' started as a way of pretending to be something until you actually became that thing. The idea was about convincing others that you were what you were pretending to be so they'd take you seriously.

I know this may have negative connotations regarding being seen as a fraud or acting like one. But this concept is so effective because if you walk into an environment and admit, 'This is my first deal, I've never done anything like this, I don't know what the hell I'm doing,' people have every reason not to trust you.

So many people, often the wrong people, are successful because, despite having zero experience and no real knowledge, they carry themselves with abundant confidence. For example, when I worked in IT, I climbed the promotional scale to Senior Technical Engineer. One of the managers brought in to manage me, a nice guy I'll call Tim, once told me a story he thought was hilarious. The first time he was asked to roll out Windows NT, he walked into the office. He confidently told the company, 'Absolutely no problem, I'm a Windows expert. I can roll out Windows NT perfectly across all 100 branches of your company, integrating the servers and DNS seamlessly.' But as soon as the manager walked out of the office, he turned to one of the other people and asked, 'What the hell is Windows NT?'

This is why so many of the wrong people get jobs; they have confidence even if they lack the skills. And worst of all, they are confident they can acquire the skill. Sometimes, they do, and things go well, feeding into their narrative, so they continue to work this way. Sometimes, they don't, and they create absolute disasters, which they usually brush off, only remembering their successes and moving on with the same bluster to the next opportunity. They remain confident they'll learn whatever is necessary to complete it. 'Fake it till you make it' is one way to apply this mindset.

But it goes deeper than that. By faking it, you're not just convincing the outside world that you can achieve something; you're convincing your subconscious mind, which is the most powerful director of your actions and outcomes. Suppose you tell yourself you're nervous, unsure, and don't think you can do it. In that case, you're setting yourself up for poor performance, insecure actions, and bad decisions. But if you tell yourself (while faking it) that you have the knowledge to do it, you'll somehow figure it out. You'll bolster yourself with examples of your past successes, even if they're in different areas. All of this will go into your psyche and subconscious, allowing you to make better decisions, study whatever is necessary, take bolder actions, and increase your chances of success.

But you may have noticed that this chapter isn't titled 'Fake it till you make it.' That's because I was hoping you could take this one step further. The truth is fear is what's holding you back. Doubt in your abilities is what's holding you back. And let's be honest, doubt in your ability to do things you actually know how to do is what's holding you back from going forward and achieving those things.

So, you don't need to worry about doubting your abilities when facing a new challenge. Your own limiting beliefs, past experiences, and negativity from others have already put you in a situation where you can't even acknowledge that you can do things you have 100% proof you can do. Based on that reality, you don't need a 'fake it' mentality, you need a 'fuck it' mentality.

You must train yourself to look at opportunities and ask, 'What's the worst that can happen?' Consider the absolute worst-case scenario of any given opportunity. If it doesn't involve someone dying or completely destroying someone's business or livelihood (and most opportunities aren't that severe), then you need to say, 'fuck it' and jump in with both feet. Once you've acknowledged and accepted that you can handle the worst-case scenario if things go wrong, you can say 'fuck it' and throw your best energy into making sure things go right. This gives you the best chance at success, with confidence that far surpasses the 'fake it till you make it' mindset.

Dohavebebedohavehavebedo?

I hope that title confused you. The aim of the title was to sound like the song 'Zooby Doo' by Tigermonkey. The other aim was to make it reminiscent of Ho'oponopono, which is Hawaiian for (and again, I paraphrase) to make right, forgiveness or put into balance.

I always think that when I hear people who I know are not from the Polynesian background quote Ho'oponopono, it is usually either somebody using the original terminology as a form of respect to other people's culture (although admittedly, if you're speaking in a different language like English, you would be better to translate it), than just to use the word, assuming people know what it means. Or the fact that you're using the word when you know that most people don't speak Polynesian and don't know what it means is everything that's wrong with the hippie shit culture.

It's a kind of superiority. A way of making a pretentious, facetious fool of yourself, that comes with so many people who practise hippie shit. I mean, hippie shit is very much seen as people walking around with Jesus beards, Jesus creepers, eco clothing, which is totally unsuitable for the weather or their environment, with hope candles and incense sticks. Saying things that nobody understands, like Ho'oponopono, whilst refusing to translate it or boasting about their Ayahuasca ceremonies is the kind of pretentious stuff that comes with many practitioners of hippie shit, so I thought I'd have some fun with the concept because this book is meant to be the opposite of that.

'Dohavebe, BeDoHave, HaveBeDo' refers to the three ways of seeing how you achieve anything. Let me explain.

The traditional way that we're all taught to believe we can achieve a goal is through the DO Have Be process.

That means you 'Do' something to 'have' something, and when you have the thing, you can 'be' something. A typical example is you need to 'Do' athletic training before the Olympics to 'have' a gold medal win at an Olympic game. Then you can 'be' an Olympic gold medallist.

Then, I was introduced to the concept of be, do, and have.

This is where the hippie shit comes in. The idea is that before you can actually have anything you have to 'be' the kind of person who can have it. It's almost a mental preliminary to doing the thing. I understand this is debatable, but it's worthwhile to consider. Let's use the following example to demonstrate. Suppose you want to be a multimillionaire; before you can 'do' what you need to do to become a multimillionaire, you must have the mindset of a multimillionaire. You must be a millionaire regarding your outlook, beliefs, and thought processes. You won't be a physical multimillionaire in terms of the money in your bank until you have multiple millions of pounds or more in your bank account. Still, in this example, this is the last stage. Before you have the money, you can be somebody who acts like a multimillionaire. What I mean by this is that if you think small, you make small decisions. Make business decisions based on thoughts of never having enough money to grow. You will never be a multimillionaire. But you will find that many people who achieved multimillionaire status had a multimillionaire mentality even when they were poor. We repeatedly hear stories where the protagonist says, 'Even when I was poor and had nothing, I truly believed. I thought of myself as a multimillionaire. Not just when I finally achieved multimillionaire status, but long before that, I always saw myself as a multimillionaire.'

Same thing with boxers. You often hear them say, 'Even when I was just training, and people were saying to me I would lose, or I'd never make it. I always thought of myself as a world champion.' Other people talk about them in interviews, and they agree, saying, 'He always acted like he was already the World Champion' or 'She walked up and down the place like she was the world champion even when she was just a sparring partner, the lowest rung on the ladder'.

This is the concept of 'Be do have'. You need to 'Be' the thing, and then the fact that you already believe you are the thing will change how you 'do' your daily, weekly, and monthly actions. If you really think you're the best, you will behave like the best, you'll make decisions like the best, and you'll expect the best. You'll demand nothing less than the best, and that change in the way you do things will allow you to have the thing. This is technically the concept of a self-fulfilling prophecy, and that's the second way of approaching it.

Once you can 'be' the person who can achieve those things, you will be perfectly positioned to 'do' the things at the level of complexity, discipline, veracity, intelligence, effort, or intricacy. Whatever needs to be done in order to come full circle will bring you back to actually 'having' that thing as a reality as opposed to just as a feeling.

The last one, explained to me by the very brilliant Dr Mahdi Brown, is a concept that I think may be unique to him. He says that the accurate process is 'have be do.' This is probably the most far-reaching and hippie-shit version of this possible. Some might say that it is technically the law of resonance. Still, Dr Mahdi Brown backs up and explains it brilliantly, so although I don't have his brilliance, I will do my best to explain the concept.

The concept of have be do works basically like this. It's an extension of the Be DO Have, and the best example that I can use comes from the words of Wallace D Wattles, who is genuinely one of my favourite authors. In the 'Science of Being Rich', he says that when you visualise the things you want, you have to live as if you already have them in the now. Now this is hippie shit in this first extreme, and I will totally understand if you struggle with the concept; even I still struggle with the idea of walking around as if you already have something that you do not yet physically possess. But there are examples.

Anthony Robbins tells the story of a couple who set a goal to win the lottery and started walking around and telling people they'd already won. Now, they did not have the lottery money, and that's why I'll say that in this example, it's a dramatic extension of the be-do have. They acted as if they had already won the lottery and in doing so, were 'being' people who had won the lottery. They would live in and pretend as if they had won the lottery, literally doing the things that they would have done if they won the lottery, and as the story goes, in a short space of time, yes, you guessed it, they won the lottery.

More accurately, Wallace D. Wattles tells the story of one of his students who wanted to improve his home, so he began living in his dream house in his imagination. Imagine walking around your home as if it's the house you dream of owning, an idea of your perfect home. Then, you should live in that mental house and walk around your current home as if it's that.

If your dream is a new job and you want to be the CEO of the business, walk around as if you're the CEO of the business. Now I accept this is kind of way out there. I totally get it, but the point I want to make about this is that the aim is to create the feeling.

In my opinion, it's not about having; it's about having the feeling.

So, let's break this down. Everything that you experience comes down to a feeling, how that thing makes you feel. Your interaction with this dimension is all about how the things that happen to you make you feel. If somebody is rude to you, you feel a certain way, which engenders certain emotions. If somebody is kind towards you, you feel something physical, and again, you engender certain emotions. So, everything that you experience is about the way you feel.

So, if you said you have a million dollars, that would mean nothing other than the fact that there is a million dollars in your bank account. But the way it makes you feel would be affected. You would feel different if you had a million dollars in your bank account than if you had just $10.

Similarly, if you had a gold medal for sprinting other than a piece of string and the little medallion made of gold in your closet, you would feel different, having done the work to achieve that medal and beaten the best from all the different countries to achieve that accolade. The key is that you would feel a certain way by having achieved it.

So, my interpretation of 'Have be do' is that the key to this is creating the feeling that you will experience when you 'have' achieved the thing you want. Because if you can replicate the feeling you will experience when you 'have' achieved the thing, then you will be in a position to 'have it' because there's no difference between actually having it and having the feeling that you do. Research shows that the brain cannot actually tell the difference.

The result will be that you feel as if you actually have it. Once you feel that you have it—as I said, you may not physically have it, but you have the same feeling that you will have when you do—that allows you to be the person who can achieve those things because you've already got the feeling of being the person who has that thing.

Another way of looking at this would be to claim it in the future. If you 100% believe that you will get it, then you can believe that you have it already. This line of thought is closer to the ideas espoused in the Edinburgh papers by Thomas Troward. He suggests that once you imprint a desire into the universe, it will already exist in the ethereal world. This means that your desire exists, and you have it, just in the ethereal world and not this one, because time is required for this world to mirror the ethereal one.

So, DohavebeBeDoHaveHaveBeDo. Three ways to manifest what you want, so choose one.

And while you're making up your mind, maybe I'll call Tiger Monkey and see if they'll use this title to make a 'Zoobie Doo' sequel.

Manifestation

So, this is the big one, the most woo-woo hippie shit of them all, manifestation. The best way to practically think of manifestation without feeling as if you've been transported into the middle of some hippie commune with stoners saying, 'Talk into the universe, man!!!' is to look at manifestation as a way of planning.

Manifestations should be considered advanced planning. Most manifestation techniques fall into two or three categories. They either involve visualisation, affirmations, or kinaesthetic activities, which relate to our primary sensory inputs, aka visual, auditory, and touch (including the sense of smell).

As I said, when dealing with basic visualisation or affirmation, you should just look at this like you're planning. When you plan to drive from one town to another, you set your route, and the sat nav tells you all of the turns you have to make along the way. Manifestation isn't really much different from that.

If you're using affirmations, you're simply repeatedly reminding yourself of the route or particularly where you're trying to get to. So, no matter what comes up in the day, what wrong turns you take, what traffic you hit, what closed bridges you meet, if your car breaks down or anything else that gets in your way. No matter what confronts you, the purpose of your affirmation is to remind you of where you're trying to go, remind you not to get distracted, to keep on track, and, what's more, why you're trying to get there.

Equally, visualisation is like a sitemap. This is like having a sitemap, and you're following the instructions visually, on paper or on your screen, as opposed to listening to them auditorily. For example, when you just follow the blue line on a Sat Nav, you may have turned the sound off, maybe you are listening to music, but when the arrow indicates to turn left onto Road N110, you're following the visual of where you want to go, so take the correct turn.

Another way to look at this would be to go back to the days before we had satellite navigation systems. Back then, I used to literally drive with an A-to-Z map in my lap. But at some point, the map would run its course, and I would get lost and have to ask somebody where I was and where to go.

The person asked would give me visual directions. They would say something like, 'Drive up to the church with the steep brown tower, turn left, and follow that road down to the bottom. Then, when you see the red houses, turn right at the red houses and follow that road until you reach a roundabout. Go across the roundabout, and at the very end of that road, you'll see the docks on your left, and the building you're looking for is on the right.'

In this scenario, you look while you are driving. You visualise certain buildings or landmarks and follow them to your destination.

If you had been there before we would use the term following your nose meaning that you're looking for things that you remember from the last time you went to the location, all of this is similar to visualisation.

So, how does this apply to manifesting? Well, in using these techniques, visualisation, affirmation or sensory, you're basically telling your mind what you're looking for. You're telling your mind what success or the correct result looks like, so you recognise it when it arrives. That's all you're doing. It's not as woo-woo as you might think. It's not really all the way out there 'I can make magic happen' hippie shit.

Although many people will tell you that these things are magic, I prefer the definition that magic is simply science that we don't understand yet.

Manifesting is a science that we currently don't understand because we have divorced science from what is now called spirituality. But the concepts and principles of taking vocal instructions or using a visual map are the same and therefore very sound.

If you want to know where to go, you will need directions and a picture of the place in your mind so that you know what it looks like when you get there.

If you're trying to find a relationship, you should have a picture in your mind, if not of the exact person you want, then at least the kind of person you want. You know what I mean, if you want them to be tall or if you prefer them to be short. If you would like them to be blonde or brunette, if you would like them to have swimmers' masculine shoulders or would prefer them to be portly and cuddly.

This is a visualisation based on what your dream or ideal would be, and it will be based on all the different types of people you've met or seen. All your experience, personal and remote, will help you to build a picture in your mind of what you want. Your perfect partner could be, and usually is, based on an individual you found attractive in the past or maybe a film star who made you say to yourself I wish I had a partner who looked just like them. I mean, let's face it, I don't think anybody has ever passed their teenage years without doing that kind of visualisation. Visualising somebody, either a pop star or a film star who they were madly attracted to, or somebody else in their class at school, church or community whom they would love to see. And even if you couldn't date them, you would date the next person in your environment who reminds you of them.

It's all visualisation. And maybe on occasion, you might have even found somebody who, much to your surprise, really reminded you of some of the characteristics and traits of that movie or pop star. You know, the one who you were absolutely crazy about and then one day, someone who really reminds you of them came into your life, and you thought, what a coincidence. Maybe it was, or maybe you just put your reticular activated system into looking for that kind of person, and because it knew what it was looking for, you found them.

I think that's the most practical way of thinking about manifestation: as an auditory or visual map. A map where you use your feelings to direct you to knowing what you're looking for. Knowing what you're trying to find clearly, knowing that you found it when you come across it, or knowing that this isn't it when you come across something that isn't quite right.

And if you continually follow these maps, just like if it was a physical map, you'll eventually find what you are looking for or at least something close enough. Something that you will be satisfied with. But lastly, most impressively, most wonderfully. If you pay attention and pay attention to coincidence when it happens, sometimes your map leads you to something much better than you had ever imagined.

Be Unrealistic

Roxie Nafousi, author of 'Manifest' discusses practical advice in a way that challenges conventional thinking. She offers a poignant insight: 'Any time you decide to settle in your life, it's a guarantee that you won't achieve your manifestation. Settling for "good enough" comes from a place of low self-esteem and a lack of belief that you can actually have what you desire.'

And yes, I know that this is in direct contradiction to what I told you I had done in my personal life, but that is the point of this book, to present you with the alternatives so that you can decide on your level of practicality vs hippie shit and then adjust your actions accordingly.

I have included this concept because this is an important addition to practical hippie wisdom, as this is where hippie shit becomes challenging. It's the point where, as they say, the 'rubber meets the road.' You can blend hippie ideals with practicality, but if you approach your dreams from a purely practical mindset, you may end up settling. Settling for what's practical limits your ability to manifest your desires because you're essentially broadcasting that you don't truly believe what you want is possible or that you're worthy of it.

This book serves as a starter's guide. I want to begin your journey with practicality, to ease you into the realm of what might seem like 'hippie shit.' I am not trying to turn you into a stereotypical long-haired, spaced-out-looking, sign-waving, Pollyanna person who might be out of place in polite company?

However, I'd love for you to start this journey grounded in practicality and gradually become less realistic in your desires and beliefs. The goal is to move beyond limiting yourself to what's 'good enough' and embrace the idea that more is possible in your life than you ever dreamed.

If you feel more comfortable settling in the beginning, that's okay. If it seems good enough at first, then accept what comes your way. But don't let settling become a permanent lifestyle. See it as part of the process and plan to move beyond it when appropriate. Eventually, you'll reach a point where you no longer settle and instead hold out for what you truly want, confident from the past experience of successful manifestations that your process has the power to bring those desires to life.

Different Types of What and How

So, here's another thing that I totally, totally missed when I was younger. Believe me, if I can help you avoid this problem, I know that my time spent writing this book would have been well spent.

I started my journey into 'hippie shit' in my early twenties and could have been at a much more advanced stage than I currently am, but I fell from the path. I got discouraged and disappointed and rejected the exercises and practices, which led me into the spiritual wilderness for about 10 years until that fateful meeting with my business mentor.

But why did I 'fall off' and go into the wilderness? Why did I reject it for so long? It really came down to one thing I was taught, which I now believe was wrong for me at least. I was following teachers with practices who taught me that if I wanted to manifest something, I would have to be very clear as to what I wanted, visualise it, or do affirmations or pretend and live as if I had it already, all of which I still agree with. Still, the one nuance they absolutely demanded was that I had to set an exact date for the arrival of my manifestation.

Now, I'm not saying that these teachers were con artists, but in exactly the same way that many business gurus give you instructions on how to achieve a goal but give you absolutely no instruction on what to do If their process fails. You know, the ones who put all their focus and effort on how wonderful things are going to be when you get what you want, how their system works and what you have to do to get it, but absolutely no focus and effort on explaining what do if for any reason it doesn't work. Oh, well, off to the next Guru, I suppose.

That's what the manifesting teachers did to me. I would have something I wanted to manifest. They would give me some ways of doing that. Looking back on it, some were really very sketchy and half-baked ways (Because they didn't take control of the real issues that I would face when trying to achieve these manifestations), and when these sketchy half-baked, manifesting techniques didn't work, and I'd miss my manifestation deadlines, I would become upset, frustrated, hurt and even angry spiralling into a toddler tantrum, thinking I'm wasting my time with all this stuff, it doesn't work and eventually giving up not just on that process but the whole concept.

If the Gurus had added just one postscript, just a simple line to their teachings, all of this could have been avoided. All they had to say was, 'And if it doesn't arrive by the deadline you set, don't worry, just set a new deadline and go again.' Now, admittedly, this would have created a level of cognitive dissonance because after months of telling yourself that 'It' will occur by January 1st, just brushing yourself off on January 2nd and saying, 'Oh, well, it will be here by March 3rd' smacks of what a Doomsday Cult would say the day after the date they predicted the world would end. But at least it would be something. But no, that simple message would have affected their brand. Nobody wants to buy 'it might take a bit longer than you want', so they kept plugging that you should put an exact date on it, and I am sure that I am not the only person who was damaged by this.

This is why the first time I heard somebody say that this approach was all bullshit and that you should never put a date on your manifestation, my head popped up like a gazelle in the Savannah. I mean, I perked right up because I realised that this was the truth that had been eluding me for so long. For everybody who says put an absolute date on a manifestation, they are not using what Roxie Nafousi calls 'Universal Time'. I actually worked this out myself once I started to manifest things by accident, but I did not accept its validity because it flew in the face of what so many of the gurus taught.

As I said, I'm an absolute warrior for looking back and realising when things I set in motion years ago came to fruition. And at one point in my life, I had set in motion the slightest dream of building an organisation.

Then, one day, after many years had passed, and I had totally forgotten my initial wish, I realised that this visualisation had come true. I simply woke up and realised that it was there. Years after absolutely forgetting that I had requested and wanted it, I realised I had it.

I thought back and remembered setting the intention and being absolutely blown away by the fact that it wasn't even a serious intention. It wasn't even something that I really wanted. It wasn't something that I spent hours visualising or meditating on or affirmed regularly. It was just something that I one day thought, 'Wouldn't it be nice if this happened'? And then, many years later, I realised I had it. My family lineage is from the Caribbean, and the official delivery date in the Caribbean is 'soon come soon come,' i.e., everything comes late. I used to joke that my Guardian angel is Caribbean, so unlike Europeans who can set exact dates on their manifestations, all of my manifestations were late, and that's the reason why my manifestations never came in time or at least on time. But time has taught me that this is not the reason. The real reasons vary, but I will outline the important ones below.

It could be that I'm blocking my own manifestations. That's the most likely source of the delay. I'm asking for something and, in doing so, putting one foot on the gas to have it, but at the same time, holding beliefs or a lack of faith which are in complete contrast to what I'm asking for, and as such, putting my other foot on the brake at the same time. I'm burning a lot of rubber, making a lot of noise and a big stink, but not getting very far and certainly not moving at the speed to get my manifestation to arrive at any particular date.

But there's more. My request could be overruled. It could be that the thing I want is wrong for me and that maybe a higher power, or maybe my higher self, knows that this request isn't what I really want and overrules it.

Or maybe it isn't what I really want, so it doesn't arrive at that time in order to give me an opportunity to think it through and request something better, which will arrive a bit later. This has happened to me on many occasions.

There are multiple reasons why the manifestation might not turn up at that time.

It could be that it takes a little bit longer for the universe to put all the pieces of the jigsaw that will create the circumstances to give me that manifestation in place. This might take longer than the arbitrary date I set for myself.

This is one of the reasons I've learned that every time something looks like it's going to happen, but does not, rather than being disappointed, upset or frustrated and broadcasting on that frequency. I have tried to teach myself to be happy, elated, and excited because the mere fact that I had a near miss is proof that my broadcast is being received and that attempts to make the delivery are being made.

Everyone says there's no reward for coming second, but they're wrong. The award for coming second is coming first next time, and never could anything be truer than in manifestation. If you wanted it and saw the opportunity but just missed it, that means it's working. It means that you're moving in the right direction. Ask any athlete; they don't start off by getting a gold medal. They start off by qualifying and then getting the bronze, then a silver, then maybe going back to a bronze, then maybe having an injury and not qualifying at all. Then coming back and getting a bronze again, and then maybe finally skipping silver and going straight to gold. That's the real manifestation journey. Putting an arbitrary date on something isn't the key. I hope this has been useful to you so far because guess what? None of this is even the point of this chapter.

The point of this chapter is that, in the same way, everybody learns differently. Studies show that some people learn auditorily, some visually and others kinaesthetically. In the same way, everybody learns differently. Everybody manifests differently. This means that affirmations will work better for some people, visualisations will work better for others, and practices, such as using gemstones, may work for another group. Whatever the practice is, everybody manifests differently. Some people might manifest better with exact dates; others may manifest better when giving the universe the freedom to supply the request whenever it is most convenient. So, just remember I was only referring to myself previously;

it might be totally different for you. If you're somebody for whom manifestation on exact dates works. Don't stop putting dates on stuff because of me. Do what works for you.

Exact dates don't work well for people like me, which is also fine. We will continue to manifest, leaving the delivery date up to the organiser, aware that there are many combinations to be arranged and things that we can't see.

How do you know what works for you? The best plan is to try all modes of manifestation and different exercises and see which ones resonate most with you or use a mixture of elements. So, try something; if you find it valuable, use it as long as it works. If not, then switch to a different process if possible. Find the thing that works for you. Do affirmations work for you, or is visualisation better. If, for example, staring in the mirror freaks you out (as it did to me for decades) but closing your eyes and saying thank you to God makes you happy, then I suggest you do the latter. Do you have difficulty making mental pictures and visualising (again, if this is true, then you are in good company)? It might be better for you to imagine how things will make you feel when you have them?

Admittedly, most people tell you that some mixture of all of these is the best, but I personally believe that just as you have a predominant type for learning, you have a predominant type for manifesting, too. All you have to do is experiment until you find it and then use it to get what you want.

So, the key is finding what resonates with you as a human. Every single human is 100% Unique; therefore, every human will benefit from a slightly different manifesting practice. Yes, you have to try them all unless you are that super lucky guy or girl who can try something just once and hit the jackpot. But for the rest of us, we will just have to use trial and error.

The key is to practise with as many different styles and methods as possible. Once you've gone through as many different styles as possible, seeing the ones that seem to give you the results that you want, you can start using that as your dedicated practice.

God's Delays Are Not His Denials, aka, I Planted the Seed Yesterday; Where the Hell Is My Tree?

So, you've been doing all these practices intending to manifest a result, and it has yet to arrive.

Now this is about the time that you say to yourself, 'I knew that this was all bullshit; I knew this Hoogy Paloogi, woo-woo, unscientific, un-fact-based bullshit was utter nonsense.'

How could meditating, visualising, talking positively to myself, or any of these things change my reality?

But that is not the right question. The correct question is, how long does any activity take to yield a result? This is important because, the truth is, none of us know.

I know that in the real world, the practical world, the world of anti-woo-woo, the world of facts, if you are unfit, whether underweight or overweight, and you want to get to your perfect weight, you may change your eating habits and probably start going to the gym. As the age-old adage goes, if you want to lose weight, the formula is simple, eat less and move more. So, how long does that take? How long will it take for you to either bulk up or slim down? I, for one, don't know. I'm not a personal trainer or fitness expert. It might take six months in, but it might take six years. It depends on numerous factors, your commitment to the process being one of them.

Now imagine if you started exercising for two or three weeks, or even worse, two or three days, and then gave up because you did not see any results. Well, in the real world, in the factual world, in the practical, realistic, scientific-based world of non-woo-woo, people would call you an idiot.

Of course, you can't just exercise for two or three weeks and expect to see massive changes in your body. Of course, if you want to lose 50 pounds or gain 50 pounds, it won't happen after three or four weeks of training. The reality is you will have to dedicate yourself to consistent exercises and healthy eating practices to get those results. This is the true cause of the term, learn to love the process. Because if you learn to love the process, if you learn to love the activities. If you learn to love the making of new food, the eating of new food, and the avoidance of bad things that you shouldn't eat, If you learn to find a way to enjoy that process and you learn to find a way to enjoy going to the gym two or three times a week or playing that new sport that you've just started. If you enjoy it, then like everything else that you enjoy in life, you won't notice how long it takes. As they say, time flies when you're having fun, and your enjoyment of the process will distract you from the time it takes to get the results you crave.

Well, unfortunately for you, the world of manifesting is no different. Now, you'll often hear the woo-woo tell you that the things you want to manifest can come into your existence immediately. I'm not saying this isn't true, but I am saying this really isn't helpful. This isn't helpful because it adds to the expectation that, unlike anything else in the world, manifestation can be done with unrealistic expectations.

You see in the real world, if you want to build a house, if you want to learn carpentry, if you want to pass a master's degree or if you want to raise a child, all of these things take varying periods. Still, none of them could be defined as quick, and absolutely none would be expected to occur instantaneously. Yet the moment you start talking about manifestation, visualisation or self-talking, people start working on the expectation of instantaneous results.

Now, there are reasons for this. The first one is because these practices are not scientifically proven. They are not universally or even socially accepted, and you feel stupid enough that you're doing them in the first place, so the last thing you want to do is find out that you have been tricked or conned into some stupid practice that just doesn't work.

But I don't know why you're so worried about that because, let's face it, you've been tricked and conned into all other kinds of stupid practices and processes that didn't work all throughout your life. That is life. None of us are perfect. None of us have perfect reasoning. We don't always make perfect choices, and at some point, most of us, if not all of us, will be tricked into something that is, frankly, untrue.

You could be tricked into a business enterprise that's utter nonsense. Some adverts you see on Instagram or Facebook about an amazing business that will make you millions in a short time, but they don't. Or a special cream that promises to reduce wrinkles but doesn't work. Or you could be tricked by a romantic partner who pretends to really like you but doesn't; they were just using you for their own nefarious means.

Most of us have been tricked at some point by a diet where we are told to just do this, and we will lose weight without having to do anything else. We buy the products, take them, and wait to lose weight, but nothing happens; in fact, we probably put more weight on.

We've all been tricked by stuff; in fact, there is an online scam in the UK every seven seconds. Yes, every seven seconds someone in the UK loses money to a scam. In 2022, the approximate amount of money lost to scams was £570 million, and that only counts those reported.

So I suggest you take the possibility of being misled and wasting your time or trying something that doesn't work for you as a part of everyday reality. The real key to this reality is that if you don't try stuff, how will you ever know what works for you? You can never succeed at anything if you don't try it out, and a part of trying stuff is trying stuff that doesn't work. Whether you're tricked into something that's just bullshit, or you try stuff that works for other people, but for whatever reason, it doesn't work for you.

So the embarrassment of trying something a bit woo-woo is pointless, but I understand why you have it. I've had it because none of us like to be tricked. We feel very aggrieved when somebody tricks us, cons us and wastes our time. Not only do we feel bad about the time and the money we've wasted, but we also feel very aggrieved to have been made to feel so stupid. But I will repeat, that's life; get used to it, and get over yourself. If you're not trying things, you're not even really living. You may as well lock yourself up in a room and have your food delivered and hope that the food that you order, which is the same food every single day, because you don't ever try new stuff, never has a problem with it because you'll still feel tricked if you ordered the wedges and you get French fries instead.

So, I hope I've laid a foundation for why you need to try new stuff and not be afraid of it not working. Now, with all of that said, let's dig into the speed at which things affirmed for or visualised are delivered.

Now, I'm convinced that whatever power is bringing your manifestation to you could do it instantly, but there are probably a couple of reasons why it doesn't.

The one that I agree with the most is the fact that if we, as the protagonist in movies like Aladdin, were to gain the power to instantaneously get anything that we wished for, the rate at which we change our minds regarding what we wanted would create utter chaos. I mean, this really is common sense. I know people who can't even order a meal from a menu in a restaurant without changing their mind five or six times. Imagine if every single time they said what they wanted, it appeared. That one person would have six or seven meals on the table before they finally decided what they wanted. You can test yourself on this, see how often you want something and how quickly you change your mind as to exactly what you want. This is true especially of the big things.

I worked in real estate for many years. I would have customers come out on viewing trips, where we drive them around the area where they say they want to buy the property and look at the houses they said they want to buy. They would arrive telling me they wanted a two-bed penthouse in a certain area. I would drive into that area and half of them would decide they didn't like that area anymore, and we'd have to find another area. Some would decide they didn't like the area, but they still wanted a penthouse. Somebody decided they still liked the area, but no longer wanted the penthouse. After driving around a few penthouses, they would decide that penthouses in any area were not only wrong for them, but they didn't want a two-bed; they actually wanted a three-bed. Oh, and they no longer wanted a sea view but a view of the golf course. Or they wanted to be physically near the sea or no longer wanted a wraparound terrace, but they now wanted a Juliet balcony. This is what you want the infinite Intelligence to provide for you instantaneously? Based on the people I toured the property, if we were using instantaneous manifestation techniques in a three-day viewing trip, most couples would have manifested about fifteen different houses as they changed their minds so often.

Based on my experience with human vacillation, it makes perfect sense that there is a delay before your manifestation is delivered to ensure that your request is consistent and represents what you want. To do that, you must broadcast a clear, consistent picture or affirmation of the desired thing. And once you broadcast a clear, consistent picture, not a two-bed penthouse on one day, a three-bed townhouse on another day, a house by the beach the next day, and a house in the mountains the following day. Once you can know what you want, represented by the ability to ask for it via a clear picture, you're now sending something that can be responded to.

The second idea, which I agree with, is that Infinite Intelligence, unlike the movies, doesn't materialise things for you out of thin air. We've all wished for that power, whether we're watching Aladin or Doctor Strange. Where we can hold our hands up in the air, mutter 'Alakazam' or some other mumbo jumbo, and a brand-new sports car just zap into existence in front of us in our living room.

But nobody ever said that manifestation does that; even the most woo-woo of the woo-woo would not tell you that they can manifest things out of thin air. Wallace D Wattles explains this best; manifestation comes through the process of organised production. I will paraphrase his book 'The Science of Getting Rich' again. 'If you want to manifest a brand-new car, what will happen is that a car will be produced in a country and sold through the normal economic commercial means to the country in which you live (such as being exported through a dealer). The dealer would have the car with the colour and spec you desire and, through normal business and commerce circumstances, will have that car available for you at the price that you want it for or can afford.'

So, for example, if you need it at a certain price, there might be a reason which benefits his own business to cut his prices such as a last-minute sale to meet months end or stock taking. So, when you go to that dealership (the one your inner voice or manifestation sent you to), and only that dealership, he has that car in that model, in that colour, at the price that you can afford, even though normally you could never afford that car. That's how manifestations are fulfilled.

And that process takes time. If you only have a certain budget, it might take time to arrange all the circumstances in somebody's business where it makes sense for them to drop the price on that model. Again, its instantaneous aspect is illogical. This is one of the reasons why I personally don't think putting a date on your manifestations is helpful. Now I understand the logical reason you should give everything a date. As they say, a goal without a date for its completion is just a wish. But I also understand that you have absolutely no idea of the complexity of the mechanisms being put in place to bring you the things you're asking for.

One of the reasons I stopped employing these techniques, I called them techniques because they have delivered me amazing results consistently, yet I stopped using them because I was taught by many, many teachers that you should always put a deadline on your manifestation. Every time I put a deadline on my manifestation, and it didn't arrive by that allotted date, I felt cheated; I thought the process was unreal. I thought that the technique didn't work. I said, in effect, 'Oyt, I planted a seed yesterday; where's my motherfucking tree?'

In fact, putting the deadline on a manifestation gives you positive proof that manifestation doesn't work because if it hasn't arrived by that deadline, then you've proved to yourself the process is bullshit. But what if it wasn't bullshit? What if it was just late? What if it was halfway to you but was delayed, and because it did not arrive at your allotted date, you stopped asking for it, so it stopped its journey towards you, turned around, and went elsewhere?

It is with this thought that we move to the next key. What is the reason why your manifestation might be delayed? And again, this, to me, is super important.

The other reason your manifestation might be delayed is because of you. Now, this is what I used to do to myself. I would go through a process to manifest something into my life, yet I did not believe it was going to happen.

This whole process rests on belief. The whole process works through faith. It doesn't work through anything else. It doesn't work through building pretty pictures in your mind of something you think you'll never have. It doesn't work through saying words repeatedly that you do not believe. It doesn't work by writing down a situation or an outcome over and over again that you don't think is possible or will happen.

It works through faith. It works through belief.

This is why it's so important to reprogram your brain, change your beliefs, which change your paradigm, and give you faith before you embark on any process to enact a manifestation. Without those things as a foundation, you're just building pretty pictures in your mind, repeating strings of words and phrases, writing down pleasant statements and pointless wish lists, visiting expensive houses and cars, and trying on jewellery, which you know you'll never, ever possess.

So if you haven't got the faith, (and I didn't), these things will never manifest. And the reason I didn't have faith is that I was terrified. I was trying to manifest my rent, but while I was asking for the money to pay my rent, the moment I stopped whatever practice I was doing, I would sit there worrying about how terrible it was going to be when I couldn't pay my rent.

I was trying to manifest being a pop star. But the moment I stopped manifesting, I would look at all the other pop stars and go through all the reasons why I could never be as successful as them. They were on a big record label because they had more money, better looking, and better production teams; whatever it was, I ran through every single reason why the system was rigged and why I would never be successful. Then, I would go back, sit down, and try to manifest my success as a musician. One foot on the accelerator, the other foot on the brakes.

I would sit there and manifest how much I wanted a relationship with a particular woman, and then the moment I stopped the practice, I would start thinking about all the reasons why she would never date me or the reasons why it would never work even if she did.

So, these are the reasons why your manifestation isn't working, but I'm going to give you just one last more, and this to me, is the most beautiful. You may have heard the phrase, 'God's delays are not God's denials.' But sometimes God will deny you, but if he does deny you, he denies you to give you something better.

The best example I have ever had was a relationship that I wanted. I was in college, so as a young hormone-driven man, it was so all-encompassing. I was so infatuated that I was dangerously addicted to this person, and it was so all-encompassing that I quite literally forgot all the other things that I wanted. I only wanted one thing. I only thought about one thing and tried to manifest one thing, which was this relationship.

And after many, many months, probably a year of having this obsession, nothing happened.

Well, that's not strictly true; the relationship kind of manifested, but then I did something to sabotage it again. This of course coming back down to my belief structure and paradigm, but even outside of that, I still wonder to myself, why I sabotaged it. I thought it was the universe's job to make that thing happen; even with my self-sabotage, it still should have occurred. It was not until I'd gone through the pain of not having that relationship manifest and thinking that manifestation was utter bullshit. Only after all of this and once the fog had cleared did I realise just how devastating it would have been if we had ever got together. I'm not saying that because she was a bad person; I'm saying that we two together would have been an absolute, unmitigated disaster.

And after many years of experiencing that painful experience and being able to look back on it more objectively, I realised two things. Not only was I saved from an unmitigated disaster for myself and everybody else, but that person was replaced by someone else. Someone else who looked absolutely nothing like them and acted absolutely nothing like them, yet, and this is the key, had all of the personality traits fulfilling all of the things that I wanted from that person. Put simply, they were better than that person for me as a partner in every way.

So, the delay in getting the relationship I wanted was no denial. The delay was the delay my lack of belief made. The person I wanted a relationship with was denied, but I was not denied the relationship. I wasn't denied the things I wanted from the relationship. I wasn't denied the feelings, the happiness, the comfort. All the things I wanted out of that relationship were not denied. I was just redirected to the person who would really give them to me, as opposed to the person I thought could fulfil those needs but would not.

I want to give another example of this as well.

I was trying to manifest a new car, and I had been visualising a particular make of car, an exact make and model of car. Now would be a good time to mention that, like the exact date scenario, this precision didn't work for me either.

This is why, although many teachers say that you must manifest something exact, I think some of the manifestation teachers need to ease up on trying to convince you that you are going to get the exact thing you ask for. I've heard so many examples of people saying that they did not get exactly what they asked for, so manifestation doesn't work for them. Yes, it's important to visualise or affirm something specific, but I really want you to understand that in exactly the same way that when you are manifesting, the focus should be on your feelings, you might get something that matches those feelings, which might differ slightly from the exact item you ask for.

So, remember that the technique is not just the visualisation or kinaesthetic experience of the thing. It should include how you will feel when you get these things? For example, if you want more money, what do you want the money for? How will it make you feel? Maybe what you want to feel is financial security. You want to stop having to worry about money. Well, if that is the feeling that you want, you might be able to get that without winning the lottery and getting a million pounds in your bank. You might get that because you win a competition that pays you 10,000 pounds a month. You're still getting that security feeling around money without having that specific amount dumped into your bank. You might get that by getting another job where you earn a lot more money and are more financially stable. However, you still haven't gotten a million-pound windfall or set up a business to make a million pounds. You might get that feeling through buying shares which give you a certain dividend or annuity. Again, you have regular money coming in, but you didn't win the lottery or own a business.

So, I think it's not always helpful to rely on your manifestation being exact. I think the key to manifestation is understanding that you're going to get the principles of what you want, if not the exact thing, by the exact date. In my experience, this is the key.

Now, manifestation always works through the root of least resistance. So, to finish this analogy, let me tell you how I manifested my favourite car. Over the course of a few years, I tried to manifest three cars. For now, let's call them Car A, Car B, and Car C.

I wanted a red car, which was a Southeast Asian make, let's call this car C. But a few years before, I had visualised a very popular brand of German car, let's call this car A. And then years later, a different Korean car, which we shall call car B. So, what eventually happened? Here's the joke: eventually, I got a mixture of all three cars. I had wanted three different cars over the course of a few years, and what actually occurred was I manifested car B in the colour of car C, but later, I found out that the engine was the exact same model as the engine in car A. I mean, you couldn't make it up. Looking back now, I realise that my belief was not strong enough when I was trying to manifest Car A, B or C, so once I had worked on myself and strengthened my belief, I got the power to clear the blockages, releasing the messages I had been sending in the past resulting in me receiving a mixture of the things I had asked for.

Now here's the thing: if I had decided to reject that car, the mixture of A, B, and C, and continue, I have absolutely no doubt that I would have gotten car C, eventually. But here's what I find important. The car I bought, the mixture of the three, is much better than I ever thought. It is, in fact, my favourite car I've ever owned. It's a mixture of A, B, and C, and this tells me that even though I wanted car C, the higher power understood that the things I wanted from cars A, B and C, not the make and model of the car but the things that I wanted to experience from these the cars. And these things were all in Car B. Plus, based on the fact that the universe works through the path of least resistance, car B was the quickest car that it could get to me under terms that I could afford. So, it presented it to me. It literally said, 'Hey, you want these things. How about this? It's not the exact make and model you specified, but it is the closest thing to the experiences you want to have; want to try it?' 'And I can get it to you quicker than it would take for me to arrange the exact model you requested, which is really expensive in your country, so it would take a long time to come through to you.'

If I refused it, it would have gone away and tried to arrange things through the normal process of commerce, somebody sending something, somebody buying something, somebody needing to make their monthly target, somebody needing to make a quick sale, for some other benefit, whatever the process would be, it would continue to shuffle the jigsaw pieces around until it made a Jigsaw which delivered to me Car C. But because it always works through the quickest route, the path of least resistance, it gave me everything I wanted in car B.

Once again, I am not a Guru, so these opinions come solely from my limited experiences, but I think people need to consider and understand this new way of looking at manifestation.

Now, I'm not trying to tell people to settle. I know that some of the great manifestation teachers say that you shouldn't settle until you get exactly what you ask for, but that is like setting an exact date for its arrival. I think the point they miss is that when you ask for a manifestation in the same way, I want to say this again: you should focus on the feelings the thing will give you. Feelings which are not the thing, they are the feelings it will give you. Then the great power that brings you, the manifestation, will give you something that will give you those feelings, and that thing might not be the exact item that you were asking for. Maybe the exact item you were asking for would not bring you the feeling you want, so the infinite knowing the feeling you want to experience provided you with something else that would.

So, you contradict yourself when you ask for something specific because of the feelings it will give you. Then, if that specific thing doesn't come, reject everything else that comes, even if those alternative things would give you the feelings that you wanted anyway. That's my personal interpretation of this. Be flexible and understand that your manifestations, even if not exact in terms of any particular item, will be exact in terms of the experience or feeling they deliver and might be even better in giving you that experience than the thing you requested.

So, those are some reasons why God's delays are not his denials, and even when they are his denials, they are not really his denials.

This is probably at the far end of woo-woo because some of you will never try manifestation anyway. But if it's something that you want to try or practice, I just wanted you to know what I believe are some of the most misunderstood key issues.

It isn't a process of magic where you materialise something out of thin air. It must come from consistently focusing on the same thing and putting in the work with whatever practice you're doing, whether it's affirmation, visualisation, writing, or kinaesthetic. You have to put the work into it on a regular basis, just like you would when trying to get anything else in the normal way in your world. In the normal world, you have to do a certain amount of work consistently to get anything, and this is no different.

Once you begin, look out for options that are very similar to what you're looking for, because one of those things might be what you actually really want. And understand that it's probably going to take time. Not because the universe necessarily needs it but no matter how desperate you are for the thing, you probably do.

And there's one last point that is really important for me to throw in here. I think you really need to pay attention to missed opportunities. Many, many times on my manifestation journey, I've had something similar to what I want, or the exact thing I want, appear in a way that I can't obtain it.

Maybe it's a girl with the character and personality that you want, but for whatever reason, she's dating somebody else. Oh, I've had it where there's been a car which is the exact make and model I want, and I try to buy it but by the time I call it's already sold. I even had it once when we saw the perfect house, but it had already sold. Here is the massively important point,

How you react to that failure, to missing the opportunity, will massively affect your manifestation. I'm here to tell you that missed opportunities should be celebrated. They should strengthen your belief and cause you to redouble your efforts.

Because they are here to tell you that it's working. A little bit like studying for an exam and taking the test. You might fail that test, but when you look at your grade, you see that you were only a few points off a passing mark. In this instance, should you give up or study and sit for the exam again? Any sensible tutor will tell you that failing by only a few points off the passing mark means that you just need to increase your efforts, improve here, here and here, and the next time you sit the exam you're going to pass.

The same thing would happen if you're a striker on a football team and you're shooting for a goal but miss three or four shots. A good trainer won't kick you off the team. He'll say, you've got so much of this, right? Your speed and ball control are good, and you're getting into the right positions. All you need to do is just go and practice your finishing, make it more clinical, and you're going to be the best striker we've ever had.

So, these missed opportunities, these failures, these things come into your life when the result is almost in your grasp. You can't get them yet, but don't be discouraged. Don't think that manifestation doesn't work, and don't think it's just pissing around with you or teasing you and encouraging you only to give you defeat. That's not what's happening. It's doing two things. Part of it is testing your resolve. Do you really deserve this? Do you really want it? Back to the fifteen things that you would order from a menu before you finally decide what you want; remember that. So, do you really want this? Let's see. Let's put it in front of you. And if you go for it and you don't get it, do you change your mind, or do you want it so much that you continue trying to get it? That's the first part, testing your resolve.

And the second part is that it's showing you that it's possible. It's saying look how close you came to getting it. All you have to do is pursue. All you have to do is persist, and you'll get it next time.

And once you understand that the thing doesn't have to be exactly the item you requested, the thing can actually be something that gives you the feeling, the experience, the joy, the happiness that you expect to get from the item. Then you understand, particularly if you want an exact person in their life, that you may be delivered what you need, not what you want. You don't want a relationship with Peter Wilkinson or with Sasha Mulwani; you want a relationship with somebody who makes you feel the way they make you feel. Somebody who has a similar look, a similar sense of humour, a similar outlook on life, similar physicality, and similar interests. Those things that this person possesses that you want because if that person didn't possess those things, you wouldn't want that person. Well, there are seven billion people on the planet, so you can be pretty damn sure that somebody else is very similar or even has those traits, but in a better form that's more suited to you. And in understanding this, when you miss an opportunity at a relationship with that one person, or you miss getting that exact car you specified, you will understand that it's not an excuse for you to think that this thing doesn't work; it should be an encouragement to remind you that it does. Take that attitude and go on dutifully with your practice and, most importantly, with your faith and belief that this will happen. You will end up with the thing that you want in terms of feeling, experience and joy.

Inspiration from Meditation

One of the most practical aspects of 'hippie shit' is cultivating inspiration through intuition. Most people have experienced moments of inspiration. You might have faced a problem you've been trying to solve, and then, out of nowhere, the solution just pops into your head, perhaps in the shower, while gardening, or during a long walk. In this sense, inspiration refers to finding a solution to a problem without knowing where it comes from. It doesn't come from diligently working on the problem; rather, it comes after you've hit a wall with no idea how to fix it. The problem ruminates in the back of your mind. Then, at some point during the day or even in the middle of the night, you have that eureka moment where you suddenly see how to solve the problem. That's the kind of inspiration I'm talking about.

One of the practical things that can be cultivated through 'hippie shit' is the ability to inspire yourself. Finding ways to access inspiration on demand is incredibly valuable. The whole point of inspiration is that you don't know where it comes from; it doesn't result from methodical work or calculating until you have the answer. Instead, it appears when you've exhausted all other options and have hit a mental block.

Because inspiration is unpredictable, it can be hard to replicate. But follow certain 'hippie shit' practices, particularly meditation, and do them diligently. You'll find that inspiration becomes more predictable. You'll find that you get more inspired when solving your problems. There are many ways to achieve this, including the popular practice of giving your problem to your subconscious mind before you sleep.

My favourite method is meditating, just going into 'the silence', closing off your mind, and seeing if you receive any thoughts that seem to come from outside yourself. There are two popular theories about where these thoughts come from. One is that they are messages from some higher intelligence; the other is that they are thoughts floating around in the ether (based on the concept of the brain as both a broadcasting and receiving station). Perhaps you pick up these thoughts from someone else's brain on an ESP level, but either way, it doesn't really matter.

What matters is whether the thought you receive solves your problem. That's the key. You can only achieve this by quieting your mind. You have to turn off the chatter in your brain and stop broadcasting to receive the message from somewhere else. This is a practical aspect of 'hippie shit'; this is inspiration via intuition. Tuning yourself in and conditioning yourself to be more consistent in picking up inspirational thoughts, solutions, and ideas can move you forward in whatever you're trying to achieve.

Whether you're searching for the perfect relationship, creating a happy, functioning family, building a business, growing an existing business, or creating something artistic like a painting, play, piece of music, novel, or screenplay, closing your mind off and opening yourself up to inspiration will benefit all of these pursuits. Training yourself to receive inspiration will also positively impact other aspects of your life, including your health and well-being.

Three Types of Meditation

Meditation is a topic on which books the size of War and Peace have been written, and it is for that reason that I am going to skim over it in this one. All I am going to do is introduce you to the three types of meditation practices that I have used and found beneficial.

So, here are three types of meditation that I personally appreciate.

The first one is most often missed, but it is one of my favourite types. It's often missed because it's not actually a form of meditation at all, but it could possibly be seen as a form of mindfulness and is definitely a way to get inspiration.

Either way, I find it extremely beneficial and am often extremely surprised and enlightened by the insights it's given me. The practice I'm talking about is simply to sit in a quiet room, get comfortable, close your eyes and just think. Just think; let your mind wander and roam. Don't try to quiet the mind; in fact, do the opposite. Talk to yourself in your head with your eyes and your mouth closed. Just embrace the darkness, embrace your thoughts, and allow your chatterbox and your ego to just talk to you and talk to itself.

There are a few things that I find really useful about this. One of them is that I find the sensory deprivation of having your eyes closed extremely powerful in terms of helping you to focus, move away from distraction and really concentrate on whatever you are thinking about. Secondly, although we spend all day with ourselves, we don't really spend time with ourselves. This world is so full of distractions that we spend most of our time being here but not really being here. You know what I mean?

Like when you're talking to your partner, but they're on their phone, so they're talking to you, but they're not really paying attention, because actually, their focus is somewhere else, dancing cats, synchronised swimming, crazy free runner jumping off of a bridge and somersaulting then landing on the grass embankment, funky dance routine by a celebrity to hot trending song, all while you're trying to convey some information to them. Well, that's actually the relationship that we have with ourselves.

So, it's amazing to sit down with yourself in sensory deprivation (eyes closed, no sounds, smells or touch to distract you), and happily just talk to yourself in your head. See what comes up. See where your thoughts go. See what you realise. See what you work out. See what you resolve. Just see what happens.

I have found the solution to many problems while in this state. In full-on meditation practice, it feels to me like solutions come from another source, like my intuition or my higher self. But in this version, as I'm actually just there talking to myself, I'm pretty sure the solution comes from me. The solution comes from the fact that I've detached myself from all the distractions around me so I can actually really think, talk to myself and work through the problems, analyse them in silence and peace, feel the tranquillity and focus and get the best answers that I myself, my ego can provide.

So, this is the first type of mediation (or non-meditation, if you want to be specific) I use. It is probably one of my favourite types as it brings a great connection to your ego self, the 'you' that identifies as 'you' instead of the 'you' that identifies with 'your higher self' or the infinite power. Yet I find that the mere act of closing your eyes and talking to yourself is a great first step into the practice of doing just that.

The next one is what's most commonly known as meditation. This is harder. I find it frustrating as hell, and often, I have to remind myself that meditation is 'a practice', so keep practising. Expect to fail, and when you do, keep practising. There are too many versions to mention, but the version I am talking about here is where I try to clear my mind and think absolutely nothing. Some practitioners say just let your thoughts float by and don't attach to them. That doesn't really work for me. I am like a bird dog when it comes to catching on to a thought and following it to its logical conclusions; I go all in. So rather than floating by in singular form, one thought tends to lead to one hundred. So, unfortunately for me, the better version of this is to find ways to stop or stunt my thoughts. To stop them from arising or stop them as or after they arise.

I have used the very popular methods of repeating the universal first sound or AUM. Sometimes, I achieve this by echoing the thoughts as they come to my mind to remind me to stop having new ones. I've tried everything, but when I break through to silence and eventually stop the constant chatter of my mind, I experience the exact opposite of the first meditation process, and it is a wonderful feeling. As pointed out in the book, 'Dollar's Flow to Me' by Richard Dotts, when I get it right, I do feel that sense of universal good, that feeling of beneficence, of bliss; I just get a glimpse of it, far from a sadhu walking around in constant contact with the universal bliss who is hardly at any point being fully engaged with the physical material world. I'm the exact opposite. I'm fully engaged with the physical material world, but every once in a while, if I can silence my mind for long enough to just feel the rising inside me of a slight fleeting contact with a feeling that is actually impossible to describe but the term universal bliss is as good a description as any.

Also, this is a state where I know, for sure, that any messages that come to me are not from myself but from some form of higher intuition or power. This has happened to me many a time. I've gone into this meditation, silenced my mind, and the thought pops into my brain, or I hear words or short sentences. The thought of writing this book, the one you are reading right now, came to me from this meditative state. I am not claiming that these thoughts or voices I hear come from God, but as I know myself intimately from my times doing the first type of meditation, all I can say is that I am pretty sure that they don't come from me.

Then, there's the last meditation type: guided meditation. There are so many options from so many different schools and belief systems created by so many different practitioners that if asked for a suggestion, I honestly wouldn't know where to start.

A brief list of some of the guided meditations that have worked for me is as follows:

Deepak Chopra

Dr Joey Dispenza

Ra Un Nefer Amen

Jose Silva

Burt Goldman

Visham Lakhani

But what worked for me might be the opposite of what will work for you. So, research, recommendation and then trial and error are what I would suggest. Because let's face it, how the hell would I know which one of these guided meditations will work for you? There are so many factors. What are you trying to achieve? Where are you in your life? What has happened to you in the past? What styles of communication do you like? Do you want one with or without music? Which music styles do you like, and which do you find annoying? The options are limitless.

So, the best thing to do is to think about what you would like to help with and look for a guided meditation that deals with that. Try to find a practitioner you think will resonate with you and do guided meditations. If you don't get the result that you're looking for, change the practitioner, change the meditation, change the style and keep on going. Like anything else, finding the versions that work for you will take a while. But when you do find something that works for you, then you as a person are going to change, and having changed as a person, it may stop working, so you'll need to find something else.

But if you do have an issue that you want to work on, these guided meditations can be very helpful in bringing your mind and potentially even your soul to the right place to deal with it.

How to Use Technique 3 to Achieve 2

One last point on meditation is how to use it to gain inspiration.

In his famous book, 'The Hitchhikers Guide to the Galaxy or 'Life, universe and Everything', anyway in one of these books Douglas Adams says that the trick to learning how to fly is to perfect the art of throwing yourself at the floor and missing. In the same way, to gain inspiration and intuitive ideas from yourself and then from your subconscious mind or higher self, is to close your eyes, tell yourself you're going to meditate, tell yourself not to think about anything and then pay attention to all the ideas that come up as you fail.

When you close your eyes, the first thing that will happen is that loads of thoughts will come into your mind. I appreciate that some of these thoughts might be negative, superfluous, or ridiculous, but if you have any projects, plans, or problems to resolve, this is very powerful. I tend to find that amidst the useless thoughts are lots of ideas for my business, ways to solve problems, ways to resolve issues, ways to improve things, ways to make things more efficient, new products, new brands, ways to do logos, ways to do marketing, all sorts to things come into my mind as my ego fights to survive and prove its relevance. These things flood my brain when I close my eyes and tell myself not to think about anything. This is my ego fighting not to be quietened. I get some of my best ideas from this process. I immediately break my meditation to write down or record with a voice recorder and then return to my meditation.

Now, obviously, there are times when you actually want to meditate. These are the points when you tell yourself not to think about anything. Then, you follow through and do whatever practice works to stop the chatter in your brain from doing exactly this. But this is a method of trying to quieten your mind and allowing yourself to fail is a very effective way to get great ideas from yourself. As meditation goes, it sits somewhere between the first and second versions I gave you, but this works specifically to get intuition and inspiration to flood from you and through you to help you solve your pending issues.

Meditation Addendum

When you meditate, do it for enjoyment; do not have a target. If you're meditating with the intent to try to achieve union with the infinite, you'll find it much harder. Just meditate to enjoy the experience. If you can't get into a state where you quiet the chat in your mind, then just meditate to enjoy limiting your internal chatter and seeing how much inspiration you get. See how many wonderful ideas you can get from your limited internal chat that wouldn't normally come to you. When your higher self speaks and tells you something intuitive and deep, or you have the kind of realisations or thoughts you wouldn't normally have. Enjoy that. As you limit your internal chatter, you'll start to get intuitions that feel as if they come from outside of you. When that happens, enjoy it as you quiet your internal chatter enough to start feeling more and hearing yourself less. Then, enjoy it in your meditation journey.

On your meditation journey, you may feel sensations in your body. You may feel yourself getting warm or cold. You may get goosebumps. Your body may rise up as if an electrical charge was going through you. You may find yourself convulsing. You may find your body shaking or shuddering uncontrollably. You may find your head is being thrown back as if you're looking up towards the skies, or you're rolling your eyes into the back of your head as if you were about to faint. Your body may shake. Parts of your body may move without your explicit instruction. You may have out-of-body experiences on occasion. All of this is perfectly normal, so don't be alarmed. All of these things are a perfectly natural part of the experience as you go deeper into your meditation. Just enjoy the different experiences the meditation takes you through and patiently allow it to guide you from your current to the day-to-day experience of a different life in the same world. The aim is to get to that place of happiness, joy, bliss, and security that can only come from being connected with the good that created you.

Positive Thinking Again

Let's dive into positive thinking again. The woo-woo version of positive thinking goes like this: You think positive things, and the woo-woo angels will bring positive results. While that may be true in some sense, it's not a practical way of explaining it. Here's a more practical approach: If you think positively, it has been scientifically shown that this will influence your demeanour.

For example, thinking positively affects your demeanour in a way that makes you happier. People who are constantly terrified of things going wrong tend to be more unhappy, which influences how they interact with others. The saying goes, 'Whether you believe you can or you can't, you're right.' Suppose you're thinking negatively, believing that a situation is hopeless or that you won't be able to accomplish something. In that case, you're actually distancing yourself from your ability to achieve it.

Let me give you an example. You know that you can tie your laces, and you know that you can spell the word 'cat.' So, if for any reason you're trying to write the word and you accidentally misspell it, you'll probably laugh it off because you know that you have the ability to spell it correctly. Even if it takes you two or three attempts because you're tired, hungover, or whatever the circumstance, you'll keep trying because you know that you know how to do it.

On the other hand, if it's something you've never done before, and someone convinces you that you can't do it, you're much more likely to give up after a few attempts. Not only have you never done it before, but now you don't believe you can achieve it, which makes it easy to think you're wasting your time even trying.

When you believe you can't do something, you try less and put less effort into each attempt. However, when it's something like tying your laces or writing a three-letter word, you'll keep putting in enough effort, if not your best, because you know you can do it. This highlights how much of a difference belief can make regarding the effort you're willing to put forward. Imagine how far you could go if you believed you could do everything you wanted.

Here's the bottom line: There are very few things that some people can do that others can't at least attempt. As my friend used to say, 'Everybody can learn to sing, but not everybody can become a diva.' So, while you may not be able to play football as well as Messi or sing like Mariah Carey, you can most definitely learn to play football to a competent level and can certainly learn to sing in tune.

These are the starting points for moving forward and seeing how far you can take any practice. The mindset of 'I can't sing,' 'I can't play football,' or 'I can't do this' is what disconnects you from your ability to learn the basics. From the basics comes competence, then greater skill, advanced skill, mastery, and eventually genius.

Rewiring Worry

Why worry? Rewiring your thinking around worry is the best thing you can do. We shouldn't worry because everything in life has a place and purpose. The problem is, in our modern world, we've distorted some of these things so much that they no longer serve their original purpose. We blow them completely out of proportion; we lose all perspective or give our energy to things that are unlikely to happen. What we need to do is rewire our reasoning about why we worry.

The first step to rewiring worry is to learn to worry in reverse. Whenever something worries you, ask yourself, 'How likely is this to happen? Or are we just getting carried away with the possibilities?' Most of the time, we start with the slightest inkling of a possibility and let our minds turn this little snowball into an avalanche of potentially catastrophic outcomes, most of which will never happen. As we dwell on these thoughts, emotionalise them, and visualise the worst-case scenarios, we change our physical state into genuine panic. I'm not criticising; I've done this myself over things as trivial as giving speeches to things as ridiculous as alien abductions. The probability of intergalactic beings travelling from the other end of the universe to our little blue planet and being interested in insignificant little old me is minuscule. Yet, after watching a couple of TV shows about UFOs and alien abductions, I took a walk at night and allowed myself to fall into a state of abject panic over the possibility of being abducted. So, the first way to rewire worry is to look at it objectively, calmly and rationally, and talk to yourself about how likely it is that what you're worried about will actually happen. Once you rationalise the worry, you'll find that in most scenarios, the probability is zero or next to zero.

The second way to rewire worry is to rewire the process. Understand that life is full of possibilities and probabilities, both positive and negative. So, if you are worried about a bad thing happening, play out the opposite scenario. While the opposite scenario, something good happening, might not have as much power (negative emotions and thoughts are stronger than positive ones because they're tied to our survival instinct), it's still worth considering.

Negative thoughts are there to keep us alive, while positive thoughts are there to improve our lives and bring us joy. Even if life gives us experiences of disappointment, sadness, or pain, at least we're alive to experience them. That's why negative thoughts are stronger; they're a survival mechanism and will always be the strongest force operating on us. But nothing is stopping you from rewiring the possibilities. If you're worried about failing your driving test, for example, and you start to imagine everything that could go wrong. A terrible driver in front of you, running a red light, or stalling the car- just remember that those aren't the only possible outcomes; other possibilities are available. Now, consider the possibilities of things going right. You could avoid stalling, meet only courteous drivers, and pass the test smoothly. This is a reactionary way of rewiring.

Let's face it, until any of these things actually happen, each possibility is as likely. Lastly, the final way to rewire worry is to accept and commit to the idea that no matter what happens in your life, even if the worst-case scenario comes to pass, you will be able to handle it. You will be fine. This is often met with the most objection, so let me remind you of something practical: If you're reading or listening to this, then you're still alive. Allow me to paraphrase one of my favourite Facebook posts, which reminds us that we've survived every single one of our bad days up until now; that's a 100% survival rate. Pretty good, huh? You've survived every disaster in your life and every situation where you thought, 'If that happens, I'll just die.' or 'If any of these things have happened, I'd never live it down.' Well, sorry to disappoint you, but you've survived every single one. You're still here, and you still have the opportunity to move forward and improve your circumstances.

Now, I understand that if you've been left disabled, physically hurt, violated, or financially bankrupt, this might sound like bullshit. But all I can tell you is that someone else has been in your position and found a way out to the other side. They found a way to regain a joyful, productive, and fulfilling life, regardless of what's been done to them in the past. So, I'm not belittling your experiences and difficulties. I'm letting you know that you don't have to stay there. There's 100% proof that someone else has come from where you are and reached a better place. The key is knowing that you will find a way to handle it, whatever it is.

Don't get me wrong, there are plenty of things we don't want to handle. We wake up every day and thank whatever we believe in that those things haven't happened to us. We behave sensibly and cautiously to avoid situations where those things could happen. But the point is, whatever happens to you, you have to believe and know that you will find a way to survive. You will find a way to deal with it. And although, when it happens, you might just be in survival mode, maintenance mode, or perhaps even an oblivious state of grief, whether it's grief for your finances, your innocence, or whatever else, at some point, you have the potential to move from survival or maintenance mode into improvement and thriving mode.

So, those are your three ways to rewire worry: rewire it with common sense, rewire it with the opposite possibilities, and rewire it with the understanding that even if the worst-case scenario plays out, in time, you'll be just fine. Rewire it any way you want, but just make sure you rewire it so that your imagination, thoughts, visualisations and feelings work for you and not against you.

Gratitude Questions

Are you grateful to be alive?

Are you grateful that all of your limbs work?

Are you grateful that you can use your hands?

Are you grateful that you can use your legs?

Are you grateful that your brain is functioning correctly?

Are you grateful for the people in your life that you love?

If you are, then go through the people you love and name them. It's OK; I'll wait.

Are you grateful for your daughter?

Are you grateful for your son?

Are you grateful for your husband, wife or significant other?

Are you grateful for your friends?

Think about them. Name them one after the other.

Think about what you're grateful to your friends for?

Are you grateful for your job?

I didn't ask if you like your job. I asked if I was grateful for it.

What would your life be like without it?

Are you grateful for the money it provides you with?

Are you grateful for the ability it provides you to have a home?

OK then, would you prefer to be homeless on the street?

If you don't have a home but you live in your car?

Why are you grateful for your car?

Are you grateful that you don't have a debilitating disease?

Are you grateful you haven't been diagnosed with just five weeks to live?

Gratitude is the frequency that brings us closest to the Supreme Being, the infinite intelligence, the universe, God, whatever you want to call it. Well, I bet that many things are happening in your life, some great and some horrible. But regardless of what is happening, I'm sure you can make up your own list of all the things for which you can be grateful.

Even if some of the things on the above list aren't true for you, whatever on this list is true for you, be grateful for it, and whatever on the list is not true for you, find something else you can't be grateful for. I'm pretty sure that if you really take the time to think about it, there's something else that you can think of that you really can be grateful for.

For me, the key to this kind of gratitude is to think of what life would be like if these statements weren't true,

Imagine if your legs didn't work properly,

Imagine if you couldn't use your arms,

Imagine if you didn't have a job and couldn't pay your rent,

Imagine if your children were unhealthy,

or if you had just broken up with the partner who annoyed you so much and you had nobody to love in your life.

Imagine Losing all your friends and having nobody to confide in or talk to.

What would your life be like?

How much more difficult would your life be every day?

Think of how lonely you would be,

Or how much more stressed you would be.

Think of how much more unhappy you would be.

I doubt all of these things have happened to you at the same time, which means that you have a lot of things for which you can still be grateful.

Still not convinced? OK, think of all the things you do on a daily basis that you take for granted, which could become a chore only performed with great difficulty.

Maybe even think back to a time when something like this happened.

A time when you sprained your ankle and had to use crutches.

Or fell over playing sports and broke your arm.

Or fell out with your best friend and felt lonely,

Or broke up with your lover and felt lost and sad.

Use this to teach yourself how to be grateful for all the things that could be happening to you right now but are not.

And then feel the gratitude for the things that you have.

The problem is because our brain is a deletion machine. We don't practice gratitude for these things every day. Just like we learn how to brush our teeth and have a shower without having to concentrate on it, we do these tasks a few times, internalise them, and then become accustomed to them. In the same way, we learn that we have a functioning body, a functioning brain, wonderful children, and a job that gives us enough money to pay for our housing and lifestyle. We internalise it and become accustomed to it and then we take it all for granted, just like brushing our teeth.

But we shouldn't. We mustn't. Because gratitude is the frequency that brings us closest to the Supreme Being. The teachers say that if we broadcast on that frequency of gratitude, we are broadcasting on the frequency closest to God, and if you really were grateful, if we really are grateful, if you really were grateful for something, wouldn't you want to thank the person who gave it to you.

So many of the things that we have are out of our power, so if you were grateful for them, you'd want to thank the infinite intelligence, the universe, and God for them, and the frequency that you can thank it on is the frequency of gratitude.

So don't take these things for granted. Be grateful for them every day. Choose something to be grateful for every day, or better yet, run a list like the one above every day and feel that gratitude. Feel the gratitude, don't just say the gratitude. Think about the thing. Think about how grateful you are for it. Think about how horrible your life would be if you didn't have it and how wonderful it is that you do have it. Even the mundane things broadcast out on that frequency so that you can connect with the infinite intelligence because that is the frequency that not only gives you those things but, if you build a communication channel with it, will give you all the other things that you wish for, you want, you desire, you visualise, you affirm and you pray for.

OK, that was a bit woo-woo, right? Well, let's wind it back in a bit. The practical attributes of gratitude have been studied over and over again and the results remain consistent. Gratitude is good for your health, it's part of the process of feeling happy. It relieves stress. It reduces unhappiness; it fosters the building of better relationships with platonic and non-platonic partners. It increases your productivity at work and increases overall well-being.

So even if you think all of this broadcasting on the frequency of the divine is just woo-woo stuff, the medical benefits of gratitude outweigh any (if there were any) benefits of its opposite. So, as with most of this stuff, you have everything to gain (namely all of the medically suggested benefits above, along with the possibility of all the broadcasting on God's frequency) and nothing but sadness, irritability, stress, frustration, anger and annoyance to lose.

Nature

There's a report by some scientists somewhere about 'grounding' (and no, I don't have a reference; google it or ask ChatGPT), which suggests that being out in nature significantly improves people's health. In fact, this report specifically noted that health outcomes improve when people take off their shoes and walk barefoot on the grass. What's the reason behind this? Honestly, I'm not entirely sure, but it is based on the science that human bodies work by electromagnetism. So, like all circuits, we need to be grounded. Something like that anyway, but here's my take: because of humanity's incredible achievements and our ability to create, change, and shape the world around us, it's easy to forget that we, as a species, are part of nature.

Everything on this planet we didn't create was made by something else. Whether you attribute it to the Big Bang, an accident, or a divine force like God, whatever you believe is responsible for the universe, planets, trees, mountains, seas, rivers, animals, or even dinosaur fossils, it's impossible to separate us from that same creation. We may procreate to create new human beings, but we definitely didn't design our procreation process ourselves or put ourselves here. Whether you believe in evolution, a seven-day creation, Aliens mutating humans from Neanderthal to create the missing link or the story of Adam's rib, it makes no difference. We are part of the same creation as everything else around us, brought into existence by a force beyond our control.

On a basic level, it makes sense that when we reconnect with other aspects of creation, whether with other people, animals, or nature, we experience a sense of unity and a bond that benefits our well-being. When we bond with animals, like dogs, cats, or even horses, we improve our well-being. These connections are not just with life itself but with something deeper. If you've ever looked into the eyes of a dog or a horse, you understand that there's life behind those eyes, a consciousness with hopes, desires, likes, dislikes, and the ability to express love and appreciation. Even though these expressions might be limited compared to humans, the connection is still there.

I believe the same kind of connection exists between us and nature. We connect to rivers, bubbling brooks, waterfalls, seas, beaches, trees, forests, Bushes, Rock formations, hills, mountains and beautiful views, not just because they are aesthetically pleasing but because they are part of the same creation process that brought us into existence. We are them, and they are us. This connection is inherent, and it's one that many ancient cultures recognised. They believed that we, as the most developed species on the planet, are meant to be the custodians of nature, not its manipulators or destroyers.

Our connection to nature should remind us of this responsibility. We don't want to live in a world where our only connection to nature is through a computer screen. This disconnection would be detrimental to our health. And, if we continue on our current path, it's only logical that nature might fight back, perhaps even eradicating us to ensure the survival of other life forms on the planet. There's a great movie about this starring Mark Wahlberg called *The Happening*, where human arrogance and mistreatment of the Earth cause the planet to defend itself by releasing hallucinogenic toxins to remove humankind and stop him from destroying life on Earth. Sound familiar?

Tree Hugging Hippie Shit

So, this is a very personal entry, but it's still something that I think is worthwhile mentioning. I tend to find that the deeper I go into spirituality, the more I notice nature. This began when I started doing some Deepak Chopra wealth meditations. Without a doubt, some of his instructions and teachings before the meditation explained that there is no scarcity in nature. They taught me that nature is abundant, something I see living in Andalusia, Spain, where, luckily, I am surrounded by wild bushes, palm trees, beaches, stunning mountains and the sea.

But what really caught my eye was the way vegetation grows. What caught my attention more than the neatly preened and spaced-out planted palm trees was the foliage and the vegetation that grew to the side.

I've always said that Andalucia is a place where everything grows. As you head into the Campo, all you need to do is throw a bunch of seeds anywhere and return in a few months to see that it has grown into a plant or tree.

But then, thinking back, this is also true of my house in South London. I remember when I lived in London, somebody like me, who had absolutely no gardening skills or green fingers, as we used to call them, got a bunch of avocado seeds and threw them in a corner near the apple tree at the end of my garden, just to see what would happen. Within a very short space of time, a bush grew. It didn't immediately bear avocados, but I was amazed at how these seeds had turned into something. There is no lack in nature; even cacti grow in the desert. But on most of the planet, if you find a seed, a piece of Earth, and some water, you will get some kind of vegetation.

But the second, more hippie shit part of this is when vegetation starts to talk to you. This was pointed out to me in one of our conversations by Dr Mahdi Brown. He spoke of George Washington Carver and how he would go out in the early morning and talk to the plants and trees, and they would give up their secrets to him, making him one of the greatest scientists and inventors of his age. Hippie shit. Oh yes, I think so. But let me relate to you an experience that happened to me just three or four weeks ago.

One day, while listening to an audiobook, a tree appeared in front of me. Now, the good thing is, we've already discussed that we are not at a stage where things can magically materialise out of thin air, so let's be clear: this tree had always been there. I was always aware of this tree and its position on my evening walk, but that day, I noticed it because it literally jumped out at me and caught my attention, even though I had known it had been there for months.

I mean, I've lived in this area for years, but all that time I'd been in the area, I paid it no attention, and equally, I think it paid no attention to me. But on this particular day, it just made its presence known. This is the only way I can explain it. I've been walking past the tree for years, and this particular day, if it could have moved, the impression it made on me was that it literally jumped in my way.

I stopped and smiled at the tree, and I said, 'Hello' (in my mind, of course, I don't want the men in white coats to take me away). I looked at this tree, how majestic it was, how wonderfully shaped it was, and I just stood there looking at it, communing with it, thinking to myself and talking to this tree through my thoughts.

Now, this is obviously insane, but this particular piece of insanity goes back centuries and is deeply rooted in indigenous cultures. I do not know if you are a fan of a group called Arrested Development, but if you are, you will know that in their breakout song 'Tennessee', Speech, the main rapper talks about going back to Tennessee, talking with trees and asking them for all their wisdom. Because depending on the type, trees can live for hundreds of years.

I've always thought to myself that trees and tortoises are the two creatures I would love to communicate with because they can live for so much longer than humans; they would know amazing things. They would have the potential to be deeply wise and have a perspective that humans, with their limited lives, couldn't possibly achieve. A way of looking at the world human beings couldn't possibly think of having.

So, there I was, smiling at this tree, feeling that this tree was smiling back at me, communicating with this tree, sometimes thinking and sometimes just feeling its energy. Now, I say hello to it every time I walk past it. Sometimes, It responds, and sometimes, it's not really in a communicating mood. But that's ok because it's made me realise all of its friends now. I realise there's a whole row of trees along that path, all of whom I now say hello to as I go by.

I wrote this part of the book because today, on the way back from my walk, I stopped at another tree.

Now, I have paid attention to this tree in the past because it's grown in a very strange way, which means that if you don't pay attention to it as you walk past it, you bang your head on one of the branches. I know this from experience. The last time I banged my head trying to walk past it, it really hurt so normally, on my busy walk, I passed this tree as an obstacle, as an annoyance and only pay attention to it from that perspective.

Today, while listening to some self-talk and being deep in that state of having my subconscious reprogrammed, I walked up to this tree, stopped, and looked at it. I took in all its majesty and marvelled at how amazing it was. It stopped being just an awkward annoyance that I had to walk past and started being this living, breathing entity full of wisdom and life.

A living thing, full of life and life force. So, I stood there, smiling at this tree. The tree looked at me. It didn't actually have the same pleasant feeling or energy as the other trees, but it had an energy that was intertwined with my energy. It was in communion with me like the other trees had, maybe just not in such a friendly way.

I don't think that this tree was as interested in being my friend as the others. Maybe it remembered me as the idiot who wasn't looking where he was going and had bumped into it.

Now, I'm a city lad. I come from Tottenham in London. This is not an area that's famous for bright, open spaces, ravines, canyons, trees, waterfalls, or anything beautiful like that. In fact, the majority of what I grew up around was bricks and mortar. So, there will be people who grew up on farms or in wide open spaces near forests who have a much deeper understanding of this because this was their normality.

I wrote this chapter because it surprised me that the less spiritual my life is, the less I notice the nature around me. But every time I find myself in a spiritual place, nature jumps out at me, draws my attention, makes me pay attention to it, and talks to me in the same way my dog talks to me, not via a shared language but a shared understanding that we emanate from the same source.

Resistance: The Hapkido Example

I've been a lifelong student of martial arts. The martial art that I first discovered and really got into was the Northern Praying Mantis style of kung fu (bowed respect to Sifu Isaac, Sifu Brian Barnes, and Master Aleem).

Northern Praying Mantis is a brute-force martial art based on masculine energy. The aim is to be strong with incredible upper body strength; in fact, the whole point of praying mantis Kung Fu is this upper body strength. The key to Praying Mantis is using that strength to brute force and overcome your attacker. This is why its (often disputed) sister art, Wing Chun, is rooted in feminine cutting energy; at least, this is what I was taught as a student of both. Wing Chun is based on getting in close and making quick, swift movements to cut down your opponent. There are art forms like Lau Gar, which are focused on keeping your opponent at a distance, and art forms like Tai Chi, Aikido, or Hapkido, which focus on using your opponent's energy and force against them.

And this is the point I really wanted to focus on. Praying Mantis is based on using your superior strength and brute force against the force of your opponent and overcoming them, whereas Thai Chi, Aikido and Hapkido are based on using your opponent's own brute force against them. I repeat, not your superior brute force to overcome them, but their own force against them. A lot of this can be seen in the guiding movements you see in Tai Chi, where somebody attacks you, and you guide them, using their own energy and force momentum away from you so their power doesn't hurt you but eventually ends up hurting themselves.

'Ok', I hear you say, 'Thank you for the Kung Fu lesson, Felix, but what the hell has this got to do with this so-called practical hippie shit?' Well, in hippie shit, there is a saying that what you want, wants you to. So, once you start your intention to have it (affirmation, visualisation, etc), it starts working its way towards you.

The explanation of these differing martial arts is to give you another example of the difference between believing that you have to use your own brute force energy, effort, and willpower to achieve a thing and the reality that the things you want already exist as energy, and the moment you have the intention to have them, they start making their journey towards you.

If you are like most people, then you are like the Praying Mantis practitioner. You say that you want something, and it wants you too, so it starts working towards you. But you think that the only way to get it is by effort, so you try to overcome it with brute force, and you try to overcome it with the wrong brute force. The brute force you try overcoming it with says, I don't think this is achievable. I'm never going to get this. Things never work out for me. Only rich people get things like this. The only way I'm going to get this is to fight, fight, fight using my strength and power.

This was exactly my mentality towards life and business, particularly the fight part. I went to war for everything I wanted. I researched history and saw that businesspeople like the Rothschilds or Rockefellers most definitely got things by brute force. Andrew Carnegie, too, built his empire by brute force. I saw these examples, and I thought that this was the only way a person from my background could ever achieve anything. The only way to achieve my wants and desires would be by subjugating them with my overwhelming power, overcoming them with my hard work, overpowering them with my willpower, my unrelenting, never-ending hard work, and besting everybody in competition. It worked; I achieved a lot, especially considering what I started out with, but I've come to understand that there is another way.

You see, when I was diagnosed with heart disease, I physically couldn't work. I, as the saying goes, gave it up to God. I could not work, and there was nothing I could do about it, so I just asked the higher power to arrange things and provide for my family and me. And somehow, through some miracle, money came in every single month like clockwork, with very little effort from me.

The money came from something other than sources that I'd worked on or planned out. The money did not come from people I worked for or business opportunities I had hustled, not even from sources that I had even thought of. Money came from sources that I had not expected and never even knew existed. With little input from me, It came in regularly:

- My bills were paid.
- Our living costs were paid.
- Unexpected costs were paid.
- Everything that I needed to survive was paid.

How was this possible? Well, because of the things I wanted, such as to be solvent, to have enough money to pay for my accommodation and my food, the ability to pay for the food and accommodation for my children who were at university at the time and all of my unexpected costs. These things were energy. And rather than having to fight this energy off or overcome and subdue it for it to yield to my wants. It was on its way to me; it wanted to come to me and fulfil those functions in my life. And as much as I wanted it, it wanted me. And all I had to do was stop blocking it on its way to me to receive it. That is what I believe because if it wasn't this, then what was it. If it was dumb luck, then I had dumb luck for a period of about eighteen months which would be considered Hippie shit in itself.

I do know that when I stopped fighting it (because I had lost the ability to fight) and allowed the energy to come towards me, all I had to do was direct it. The directing of it was the small amount of work I had to do to get it, or as Wallace D Wattles put it, 'By your thoughts you create the things that you want and by your actions you receive them.'

I was very sick. I was asleep more hours of the day than I was awake, but I could do the very few actions I needed to receive this money in the small amount of time that I was awake.

This is the Tai Chi version of getting the win. I used the energy of what I wanted, and rather than fighting it and overcoming it, I just guided it and redirected it to me. And I can assure you, it is a much more healthy, sane and delightful way to receive the things you want.

Or, as I said, maybe I was just lucky. How will I ever know?

But as I said at the start of this book, if you have enough coincidence, you cannot fail to find a pattern. Isn't that what scientific proof is? Repeatable coincidence. Repeatable patterns on demand. Well, I cannot prove anything to you. I am just here to tell you what I have experienced and what I decided it was caused by, and I invite you to try it for yourself to see if this opinion can improve your life in any way.

Three to One

Remember the earlier example of how your mind affects physical sensations in your body, such as pain? A back or knee pain, a habitual joint pain, or you stubbed your toe. So, at first, you will be aware of this discomfort, and then maybe a few hours later or even the following day, you wake up and don't feel the pain. And you think to yourself, oh, that's strange, I used to have a pain in my back or knee, or I had this uncomfortable Splinter yesterday; I wonder what happened to the pain? Why is it not hurting? That's really strange. I don't feel the pain at all. And then, the moment you think about the pain that you should be having, the pain returns.

We discussed that this is the power of your subconscious mind. You instructed your body to feel the pain. I don't know why the pain went away; maybe the body part was no longer swollen and didn't hurt. Maybe it was healed, or maybe your brain had just instructed itself to not pay attention to the pain that was still there. But the moment you reminded yourself of the pain, the pain came back.

And what's worse, once you reminded yourself of the pain, it stayed. You tried to tell yourself, oh no, no, no. I was just thinking about it. Go away. I don't actually want this pain back, but by that time, it's too late; the pain is back now, and it stays.

So not only do you have to counteract any negative thought with a positive one. The truth is you should probably counteract any negative thoughts with positive thoughts at a ratio of three to one.

Let me use the example that I just gave you (because I literally just did this to myself). I have habitual back pain, and I was coming out of the shower, drying myself, and thought, 'Well, isn't it great that I no longer have back pain?' Well, the 'isn't it great' and the 'that I no longer have', didn't register with my subconscious? What my subconscious mind heard was 'Back Pain' and took it as a request. Now the back pain that I hadn't felt for months immediately returned. 'Shit!!!' I thought. So, I tried to reverse it by affirming 'I have a fit, strong, healthy body. My back is fit and healthy.' The tightness in my back remained. I did the same affirmation again, then I made another similar affirmation, only after about the fourth affirmation did, I realise that the sensation in my back had subsided.

You see it is a fact that negative thoughts are far more powerful than positive ones, remember why, yep that's right, because they tend to be related to our survival as an entity. So, I think at the very least, you need three positive thoughts to counter act one negative one, but it's entirely possible you might need five or six.

This is why it's so important to start monitoring your negative thoughts. Being aware of how many you have. That alone will start to reduce them. Then secondly, you need to rationally counteract them. If you say or think, 'Bad things always happen to me.' The moment you realise you said it, the moment you realise that you have thought it, tell yourself that this thought is not rational. Tell yourself that statistically, you probably have no worse luck than anybody else. Maybe if you continued to believe that you had bad luck, you could draw it to yourself. But actually, in reality, bad things do not always happen to you. In addition, are the things you are talking about really as bad as you think they are? In reality, it probably was not such a terrible scenario. And think of all the times you had good luck. Recall those times. This was lucky. That was lucky. This happened to your family. That happened at work. Looking back, we were so lucky we avoided that. So, you, at the very least, have average luck, but in all probability, bearing the fact that you're not living in a war zone, having limbs blown off, and scavenger for food, statistically taking the seven billion people on the planet into consideration, you probably have great luck.

Then you have to hit yourself with some affirmations. I'm so grateful for my life, circumstances, and happiness. Hit yourself with those affirmations, and then hit yourself with more, and then some more. And that's just to counteract one negative thought.

Just assume that one negative thought has the power of three positive ones. So, you need at least three positive thoughts to counter act that one negative.

Right Action. It Comes Four Times Before the Word Chameleon.

When things go wrong, we have a proclivity to scream, either vocally or in our heads, 'Why is this happening to me?' Then, the human habit of externalising everything causes us to look for places or people outside of ourselves to blame. We blame our partners, we blame our children, we blame our boss, we blame our parents, and when all else fails, we blame God. We scream out to 'the God' that we don't believe in and blame him for what is going wrong.

Well, here's the bad news. The most likely cause of whatever's happening to you right now is you. This is the true meaning of the word Karma. It doesn't mean the bad shit you do comes back and kicks you in the ass bitch, as most people like to think. It really means the right action. The whole idea is based on the fact that the actions you do today lead to the results you see tomorrow. So, the terrible situation you're going through today is most likely (not 100% guaranteed, of course), but most likely, caused or related to a result of your past actions.

That's why you're broke. That's why your relationship is in shatters. That's why you didn't get the promotion, that's why you ended up in a car crash.

Now, I appreciate sometimes it's very difficult to see the link between what you did in the past and the horrible event that's happening to you now, and that's because the world is very complex. Millions of things are happening all the time, including things, relationships, and causes and effects that we're unaware of, yet everything we do influences them. Think of the butterfly effect as an example of how this works. The tiniest thing you do could influence your future in a minuscule or dramatic way.

So, although we can't unravel all the minute ways we could have affected our future, we can most definitely see the obvious ones.

I'm currently frustrated because a lawyer who did not arrange for the payment of my commission on a deal I worked on will not return my emails. The lawyer won't return my emails because I wrote to their office manager to admonish them for their lack of contact. Ironic right. I had hoped my mild complaint would have spurred them into action and made them more efficient. A short apology and explanation of the situation would have sufficed, but unfortunately, it had the opposite effect. They obviously took great offence, being as important as lawyers like to think they are and decided not to respond to any of my communications anymore. This is a result of my actions. I didn't have to complain about their lack of professionalism. I could have just sucked it up, as suggested in the book 'Ego is the Enemy' by Ryan Holiday. I could have just sucked it up and waited patiently to see when they finally got around to deeming me important enough to contact and pay the money that I was owed. But I didn't; I made it clear that their behaviour was below my standard. I thought I had every right to do so, and I still do, but I can't complain about the result of those actions because the results that I got, which is them not contacting me and dragging the process out for longer, is a result of the action I took, which was to complain to them about their unprofessionalism.

I thought that this was a sensible, balanced email which outlined the major aspects of my complaint, at least a lot more balanced than the 'What is so wrong with you that you can't even answer a simple email, you arrogant imbecile' email that I wanted to write. But apparently, it was taken as an affront and ignored by both the lawyer and her office manager in an attempt to make me suffer by having the gall to question their inefficiency and unprofessionalism.

But here is what will probably happen to these ladies.

One day, they will have bills that need to be paid, and their wages will be delayed, which will cause them much distress. Their wages may even go unpaid, leading them to bankruptcy, or they will need some information which would take seconds to provide, but they will be ignored leaving them frustrated and unable to make informed decisions, or they will have a legitimate complaint and have it dismissed making them feel as if they did not matter, an action that leaves them feeling vulnerable and unimportant. And they will look up to the skies and cry, 'God, what have I done to deserve this?' forgetting that the answer is in their reaction (or lack thereof) to the email I sent them.

If you look at many things that happen to you, you'll see that there is this exact direct relationship. It doesn't always mean it's fair. You could not be promoted because you just didn't suck up at work, but that's why it's happening to you. Other people 'sucked up' at work. You didn't. So, they got promoted, and you did not. Your relationship could be in tatters because you're in the wrong relationship. You got into a relationship because you were lonely. You started dating your partner to stifle your loneliness, and it worked, which was great. But it's only great that you're in a relationship; you didn't really pay attention to the fact that you weren't in the right one, and now your relationship is in tatters, and you're hurt.

So that's why you are in pain. God hasn't forsaken you. Most of what happened to you is because of you. Now, the first time I was told this, I was very offended. So let me be clear, I'm not trying to tell you that if you've been a victim of sexual assault at a young age or a psychopath attacked you, leaving you with near-fatal wounds, you are the cause of this. Even if this was true, it is a level of reality that I am not suitably wise enough to speak about. But I definitely think if we're honest with ourselves, we can look at many things that happen to us and find a direct line between our actions and their results.

Now, here's the good news. It also goes the other way around. It doesn't just work for bad things. It works for good things, too. What that means is that what you're doing right now, today, while you're reading this book or after you read this book, will actually set up the reality you will experience in the future. So not only are you responsible for all the bad things that happen to you in the future, you're also responsible for all the good ones, as well.

So, think very clearly and deeply about the actions you take today and try to ensure that they will lead to the results you want in the future. Obviously, none of us have a crystal ball, and none of us know exactly how these actions will create future results. Life is very much like a pinball machine. All you can do is press the button, shoot the little silver ball, and look at all the different places where it bounces. We really don't have the power to know which of the many obstacles, targets, bumpers, ramps or flippers it's going to bounce off on its way to where it ends up; all we can do is fire the ball with the best intentions possible. And I think that term is the key. With the best intentions possible, we fire our ball, we make our decisions, and we take action. And in doing that, we are taking 'right action'. 'Right action' that will hopefully bring good Karma.

Practical Karma

There is another way to look at karma as opposed to how most people see it: the idea that what you do comes back around to you via unseen forces. So, I want you to think about this for a moment. Telekinesis, although it hasn't been proven to the level of some other scientific things such as Electricity or Gravity, is something science has often researched, and a lot of people believe in. Well, working with the hypothesis that telekinesis exists, a practical result of it relating to karma would be this:

Imagine if you lived in a way that almost everybody you ever met liked you, and many people who knew you or knew of you loved you. Can you imagine the benefits to your life that would invariably spring from so many people thinking positively when they thought of you? Surely there will be some kind of benefit that comes to your life every time somebody thinks of you and thinks what a great person you are, what a kind person you are, what a helpful person you are, how much they appreciate you, how much they Love you, how grateful they are that you exist. Surely, all of those thoughts will bring some kind of positive benefit to your life. Maybe those thoughts will help you maintain your health. Maybe those thoughts would bring positive benefits to you, like abundance in your finances, or maybe the goodwill of others would just bring good luck and fortune to you. But surely all those thoughts must affect you somehow, and it could only be positive.

Now, let's imagine the opposite. Imagine if you lived in a way that people saw you as mean, destructive, unhelpful, horrible, hateful, maybe even evil. And everybody who came into contact with you, everybody who knew of you, had thoughts and feelings of how much they disliked you, how much they hated you, how reprehensible you were, how much they wanted to avoid you; they replayed all the horrible things that you've done to them in their brains and whipped themselves into a frenzy with emotions of anger, hate, dislike and distrust.

Surely, all of those thoughts and feelings about you and directed towards you must also have an effect on you and your life. They certainly couldn't bring you good luck, abundance and wellbeing. If they brought you anything, it would have to be more bad luck, more unfortunate situations, bad health and maybe even just anger and frustration because you're picking up on the feelings of others, bringing more anger and frustration and difficult situations into your own life.

This could be a very practical version of your karma. Maybe the stuff you do to people bounces right back to you based on how they think and feel about you. This is why I try not to take vengeance on people. I used to think that maybe I was an arm of the supreme, and it was my job to take vengeance on those who transgressed against me. But now I genuinely think that people take vengeance on themselves. We simply need to give the universe enough time for that to occur.

Forgiveness

This is a big one for me because I am one of the most judgmental and unforgiving people you'll ever meet. In fact, one of the defining aspects of one of my friendships was that neither of us forgave anyone for anything. So, it should come as no surprise that we eventually fell out. I did something, and true to his word, he didn't forgive me. When I bumped into him five years later, I approached him, offered a handshake, and said, 'Bro, let's let bygones be bygones.' He responded with, 'Fuck you,' and didn't even stretch out his hand. I guess he's still staying true to his words. Respect!

Strangely, there's something admirable about that level of consistency. It's entirely congruent with the way I grew up. I was raised by extremely judgmental parents where forgiveness was non-existent. My parents set standards of their own making, impossible and illogical standards that only applied to us, not themselves. When we fell short, we weren't just children who failed; we were deemed utterly worthless, useless, and valueless. But this isn't about psychoanalysing my childhood. The point is that my lack of forgiveness stems from such an upbringing.

For most people, I think you'll find that those who had forgiving parents who didn't impose unattainable standards grew up to be more forgiving and accepting of the failings of others. On the other hand, children like me often inherit the harsh worldview of unforgiveness and tend to perpetuate it onto others.

So, why is it practically beneficial to forgive? Let's start with the obvious: anger and hate are bad for your health. While this concept might be relatively new to some, I don't think anyone seriously doubts it anymore. On a simple biological level, emotions like fear, anger, and resentment trigger stress responses, releasing adrenaline, cortisol, and other chemicals that were originally designed to help us either flee from or fight off threats. These responses were never meant to be used as often as we do now, reacting to minor irritations like missing the bus or dealing with microaggressions at work. They were meant for survival in life-or-death situations, not for everyday stress.

Forgiveness is key to reducing these harmful emotions and not activating your sympathetic nervous system. Chronic stress doesn't just make you feel bad; it can make you physically ill, amplifying any weaknesses in your body. Everyone knows that disease tends to target areas of weakness, and if you continue to harbour anger, hate, and guilt, you create an environment where illness and disease can flourish.

Why else should we forgive? It's good for your spiritual and mental health. Since this is practical hippie shit, I won't delve too deeply into spiritual concepts. Still, there is an undeniable connection between mental wellness and forgiveness. Emotions like anger and hate aren't just bad for your body; they're also bad for your mind. These feelings were designed to prepare you for physical confrontations, not to be lived in for prolonged periods of time. Living with these emotions can severely impact your mental well-being.

One of the key lessons I've learned is that if you can't forgive others, you can't forgive yourself. This took me decades to understand. I was unforgiving of others, so, in turn, I was unforgiving of myself. I don't have the cognitive dissonance or narcissism needed to hypocritically forgive myself for my own wrongs while hating others for theirs. Holding everyone, including myself, to the same high standards meant that my refusal to forgive others led to years of mental anguish, as I couldn't forgive myself for my own frailties from simply being human.

I refused to forgive myself for mistakes, unmet expectations, and unachieved goals. I walked around with open wounds, refusing to heal because I couldn't forgive others, particularly those who hurt me when I was young. This leads to the real key point: As the famous quote goes, the concept of 'hate is like taking poison and expecting it to kill the other person'. We must keep hearing this because it's hard to internalise and live by. When someone does something to you that you truly believe you didn't deserve, it's difficult not to react angrily. We're not saints; we're just human beings trying to navigate life with our limited knowledge, but here is the key, so are they.

But the reality is that if you don't find a way to forgive, you're only hurting yourself. In the book Psycho-Cybernetics, Maxwell Maltz speaks about 'fake forgiveness,' where you say you forgive, but deep down, you don't. True forgiveness means destroying all evidence in your mind and heart that the offence ever occurred and starting fresh. Fake forgiveness, however, is when you say you forgive someone to please others or even yourself, but you still hold on to the resentment. True forgiveness wipes the slate clean; fake forgiveness keeps the scorecard.

If you say, 'I forgive you, but I won't forget,' then you haven't truly forgiven. You're better off being honest and saying, 'No, I can't forgive you.' If you pretend to forgive, you're only causing a different type of wound, one that festers beneath the surface.

In the end, if you can't forgive someone, it's better to distance yourself from them and be clear about it. At least then, you aren't pretending to forgive and causing more harm to yourself. Forgiveness, when genuine, is a powerful tool for healing, but fake forgiveness is just another way to carry the burden of anger and hate, which does nothing to benefit them or you.

Make Yourself Happy

So, in terms of creating your happiness internally, without needing any external input, happiness without any environmental stimuli. Here's a neat trick: lie on your bed comfortably, or sit in a comfortable chair and do this. Clear your mind of all thoughts as best you can and tell yourself this one word in as childlike a voice as possible. If you can recapture yourself as you were when you were a Child, the way you talked when you were a child would be perfect. If you've ever seen the adverts for the Haribo brand of sweets where adults' voices are dubbed over by children, this will give you an idea of what I'm talking about. Get into this state and repeat the word 'Happy' to yourself. Repeat the word 'Happy' and let all the thoughts and feelings of when you are happy flood you.

You see, the amazing thing is that language was also created to describe feelings in addition to describing situations and circumstances and giving information. Sure, language is key for relaying information, telling other tribe members that a lion is coming, part of the valley is flooded, where there is food, or that you saw members of our enemy tribe. Language was created for all of those things, but it also has the job of explaining our feelings to others as well as ourselves.

You tell somebody that you are happy, or you tell somebody that you are sad, you tell somebody that you are frustrated, or you tell somebody that you are excited. This means we can use the same power in reverse; rather than telling other people what we feel, we can tell ourselves. We can tell ourselves that we are happy. We can tell ourselves that we are happy when we feel happy, but more importantly, we can tell ourselves that we are happy to be happy. We can say the word happy and use it to evoke those feelings. I don't know if this works for everybody, but it certainly works for me.

So, do the same thing. Close your eyes, relax, say 'excited' to yourself, and just feel the feelings the word evokes for you. Understand that you can get in touch with those feelings anytime you want, just by using the word.

This works for most feelings. If you tell yourself you're tired, the first thing you'll probably notice is your voice changes. It changes from the uplifted sound that you said when you said happy and excited to a more downward range or sluggish sound. You might even find yourself yawning a few seconds afterwards. Tell yourself you're horny, and you may very soon find yourself with visions of people who you find sexually attractive and create sensations in certain parts of your body. Men, do not do this before your teacher asks you to come to the front of the class and solve the problem on the whiteboard.

This is an incredibly simple but unbelievably effective technique.

Now, I'm not necessarily suggesting using this technique to change your mood. It would be very hard to overcome an angry or sad mood by just sitting there telling yourself you're happy. Suppose external stimuli make you angry or sad. In that case, you're probably better off working through that emotion using the techniques Dr David Hawkins taught in his book 'Letting Go' to get rid of it before you try to do this.

But if you want your most common state, your usual state of being, to be happy, there is nothing wrong with starting from neutral and doing this practice to invoke happiness in your life. Because the more you invoke happiness in your life, the happier you will be. And the more you are in a happy state, the more natural and normal a state of happiness will be to you.

And the more natural and normal happy states are to you, the more you will vibrate on that frequency of peace and love that brings you closer to achieving your goals and the manifestation of the things you want in your life. Most importantly, remember that you want these things for one reason only; in one way or another, you want them to make you happy. So, although this happy state will attract all the good things you want to you, by using this technique, you would have actually circumvented the need for them. You will have created a shortcut by being happy before you got the things you wanted to make you happy. So, when the things you want arrive, you may still appreciate them but need them less. Because you would have already been happy before they got there. In fact, you'd have used that happiness as the mechanism to bring them to you.

WOO WOOOO!!!!

FYI, this title is a pun. It's written to sound like the whistle of an old steam engine, the kind that you might see in a Western movie. The idea is to tell you that the Crazy Train is coming. So, if you're ready, all aboard the Crazy Train!!!

Talking to the Universe

There is a famous scene that you can find in a lot of comedies where two people who speak totally different languages try to communicate with hilarious results. Examples of this can be seen in English comedies such as the Carry-on movies, Mind Your Language, and Faulty Towers, but I am pretty sure that this universally funny concept exists in comedy from other countries as well. The idea is that one person who speaks English perfectly is trying to communicate with another person who speaks only a few words of English or English as their second language. So, for example, knowing that there was a gas leak in the building, the person who speaks perfect English would say, 'Whatever you do, don't light the fire', and the person for whom English is the second language would say, 'okay, I'll light the fire', pull out a box of matches and strike them causing an explosion. Canned laughter, Soot-covered faces and frizzled hair would be added to aid the comical effect.

The key comical concept here is that due to their poor command of English, they didn't pick up the fact that they were told 'don't light the fire'. They just picked up the words they understood, which were 'light' and 'fire'.

Having lived in Spain for 17 years, I've experienced this many times. When I did not have sufficient command of the language to understand the full nuance of what was being said, I only focused on the words that I did understand, leading to hilariously wrong conclusions.

Well, the first thing you must understand is that the universe does not speak English, Spanish, Arabic, Mandarin or any of the languages we've developed for ourselves on earth.

To my understanding, the universe speaks one language: feelings. This is much better for us because our languages were developed to explain our feelings, firstly to ourselves and then to each other, as well as convey information and other such purposes.

So, because the universe speaks the language of feelings. This is the reason why affirming that you are rich whilst looking at your bills, your late payment notices and your eviction notice, all of which have left you with abject feelings of terror, fear, poverty, lack, and scarcity, will not work. It won't work because although you are saying the words 'I am rich' in your language, please remember your language is a second language to the universe. You are telling the universe in its language, the language it understands perfectly, that 'I am poor. I have scarcity, I have lack, I have need'. And so, the universe says, 'Okay, what you're asking me for is poor, lack, scarcity and need, sure I can give you those things.' The universe probably thinks it strange. 'I don't know why you keep on asking me for these things because you've got them already, but anyway, here you go. Have some more.'

So, we really need to understand that we are having a two-way conversation with the universe and have two options. We can speak to it in its primary language, the language in which it is fluent or its second language, where we are more likely to make mistakes.

If we use its second (our first) language and send our messages in the words or visual images, we prepare in our brains, a language that the universe does not speak fluently. We risk the tragic comedy of saying to the universe, 'Don't light the fire,' but due to the universe's limited understanding in those languages, having it interpret our words and images as 'light the fire'. Boom!!! There goes your manifestation.

This is why when using its second language, we have to use terms such as, 'I feel happy and healthy', which are definitive and fully stated in the positive so they unmistakably explain what they want the universe to produce. As opposed to, 'I don't want back pain', a statement which will almost invariably have the universe only understand the words 'back' and 'pain', causing it to give you pain in your back. The 'I don't want' part will be lost in translation.

In the same way, when I speak Spanish and someone says to me, 'No mi quiero patatas', I understand the word 'quiero', which means 'I want', and the word 'patatas', which is 'chips. So, I gave them chips because I didn't have a good enough grasp of the language to understand the 'No mi' part, expressing their preference of if they did or didn't want said chips. So, this is the first way that our translation gets lost.

The second way is when we speak the universe's language, which most of us don't really understand. You see, we think that we can lie to the universe in the same way that we lie to each other. I've never seen the movie *The Invention of Lying*, I don't think I need to. I think the title has told me everything I needed to know about it because I've often thought it would be an amazing world if we couldn't lie to each other? Well, that's the world you live in with the universe. You can't lie to the universe. You can't tell the universe that you're fit and healthy if you feel unfit and unhealthy. You can't tell the universe you're in a wonderful relationship and live with love and sexual satisfaction if your feelings are that of loneliness, sadness, dejection and sexual frustration. You see when you're dealing with your feelings, you're talking the universe's first language, and it understands its language perfectly, so there's no point trying to lie to it. It will pick up on what you're telling it through your feelings. This is why we focus so deeply on beliefs, because your beliefs often dictate your feelings in any situation.

When communicating with your feelings, the universe will understand exactly what you're saying to it, even if you don't want it to. It will take what you've said as a command, as a request for more of the same, and give that exact thing back to you.

This is why we need a combination of two things. If we want to talk to the universe, we need to talk in our language but use specific and correct terms stated in the affirmative. No 'I don't want' allowed. We must only express the thing that we want and not express any version of the thing that we do not want so that the message cannot be misconstrued.

Then, we also need to talk to the universe in its language by feeling what we want, even if we don't have it yet, or our current reality is the complete opposite. I totally appreciate that the latter is very, very difficult. Learning how to do this takes mental hard work and practice. I know I'm still working on it, and no, I have not mastered it yet. These are the rocks which lead most people to shipwreck when on the seas of manifestation, leading them to believe that it's all bullshit and doesn't work. Even if they believe that it does, this makes so many people think that it's impossible for them.

As I previously stated, I'm still a student, not a master. But yesterday, in a meditation, I was told something that assuaged my feelings as a novice. While meditating after feeling frustrated writing this book, a voice told me, and I repeat the exact words: 'I'm writing this book.' So, I feel a bit better about my position as a novice since I'm clearly just channelling what you're reading from another source.

As such, I truly believe that just like anything else that requires practice, with practice, you and I, a novice at these techniques, will learn how to create the feelings of what we want, even when we are physically experiencing the opposite. We can communicate clearly to the universe the things that we do want, as opposed to the things that we don't, and have the universe deliver to us the correct and desired reality.

As Below Above

One of the very first hippie shit concepts that I paid attention to was a simple picture of a tree. This picture of a tree showed that the roots of the tree below the ground were about the same distance as the branches of the tree above the ground, and it had the simple words over it: 'As above below.' This always stuck with me as one of those Socrates-type 'learning is remembering' statements because somehow, I knew the truth in this statement, even though I didn't know how or why it was true.

As you go through this book using the examples I've provided, I think that you'll start to understand the truth of this statement. But I would like to give you another more specific example which demonstrates this concept just to keep things simple and practical.

An example is how your mood might affect the people around you and how the people around you might affect your outcomes. I mean, there's a great statement which says, misery loves company. If this is true, then the opposite will be true, i.e. happiness and joy will love company too.

I mean, have you ever met somebody who's so happy and joyful that they just make you sick. They are so excited at seemingly nothing that they get on your nerves, so much so that you don't want to be around them because you just find them so annoying.

Well, what that tells you is that inside you is the opposite. If you were happy and joyful, you'd have no problem being around them, but you were not happy and joyful at that time in your life. You were stressed out, you saw the world as a difficult place, you had problems and difficulties, and this person's happy, joyful, reckless abandon was so contrary to you that it caused you anger and frustration.

This is the most practical way of realising the 'As above below' concept. You see, if this person is genuinely happy on the inside, then it's easy for them to express this happiness and joy on the outside. It will attract happy people to them. Not in a woo-woo law of attraction way, but in a practical, I'm happy, so I want to be around other happy people's way, and surprise, surprise, joyful people want to be around me, too. So, as I see this happy and joyful person in my environment, I am attracted to wanting to be around them in the same way.

Now, if you're miserable, sad, frustrated, dejected, and seeing the world in those terms, If you have a caustic view of the world or a dark-cutting sense of humour which focuses on demeaning people and situations. Guess what? The probability is your friends will be the same, and as you surround yourself with negative people who like to put everything down, what do you think your world will look like?

It's not going to be happy, joyful and full of optimism; it's going to be negative, cynical and waiting for disappointment. A world full of darkness and disillusion, giving you more things to complain about. That is what your world will be. So, 'As above below'. What you have as the predominant feelings and thoughts inside you cannot help but be the predominantly spoken words and actions you express, which will usually lead to the types of people who group around you, the situations you find yourself in and the reality you experience.

Fear Addendum

If you were to ask my opinion of the one thing that has stopped you from having everything you want in life, my guess would be fear. It is not just fear that stops you from doing what you need to do to achieve what you want, such as asking out that attractive person in your office or accepting the offer to give that speech at the conference. I mean the inverse fear that lives deep inside of you. The fears that nobody else knows about, fears which drive your every action and dictate your every decision.

Examples of this type of fear are the fear of walking away from situations that aren't good for you. The fear that you're not going to have the things you want to have, so you hold that feeling of lack, preventing the things that you want from working their way to you. The fear that you're going to lose the things that you have, so that you hold on to them tightly and smother them until they try to escape from you. The fear of losing things that you don't even want but feel that you must hold on to for guilt or shame, for your public perception or just because you can't stand the thought of losing. Fear of losing that job you hate or not getting a client you don't want. Fear of not being in a relationship you know isn't right for you, but you are too afraid to leave. Fear of hurting someone you love more than you are hurting them by staying in a loveless relationship. Fear of not being accepted by the group of people who constantly put you down and make you feel bad about yourself. I call these inverse fears because they are not 'fear' of doing something proactive, such as a bungee jump. They are fears that keep you inactive, fears that hold you trapped where you are, and most of all, fears that keep you trapped in feelings of lack, want, desperation and shortage. Because if you did not believe there was a shortage in supply of the shit pile that you were desperately holding onto, you would toss it at a moment's notice and walk into the wilderness confident that something better would come along.

Once you relinquish yourself from all fears, particularly the inverse ones that I've just described, spend some time away from the toxicity that they bring into your life. Once you confront those fears and give yourself space to live without them constantly looming over you like a dark cloud. Once you do this, you will see that new and better opportunities appear in your environment. Things that are much more aligned with what you really want in life. You will see that things you thought were impossible for you actually come into your life because you've removed all the negativity and the destructiveness that those relationships, connections and fear created.

As they used to say, when one door closes, another one opens. The key here is that you must close the old door first before the new door to what you actually want opens for you. And the key to closing that first door is to acknowledge and root out those internal inverse fears.

Weight Control

Have you ever encountered someone who eats whatever they want and never puts on weight? If you're someone like me who struggled with their weight for years, you most definitely paid attention to this person. Not because there was anything to learn from them, more because they just pissed you off. You thought to yourself, how is it that this person could eat the same things as me, all the things that are supposedly bad for you, and they never put on an extra pound, when everything I eat goes straight to my stomach or straight to my hips?

Well, the obvious medical reason for this comes down to genetics. Your body's genetic makeup is passed down through successive generations, and then there is your weight set point, meaning that people have different metabolisms, causing them to put on or shed weight more or less than other people. Your metabolism is another one of those things on the long list of bodily functions performed completely absent of your conscious agreement or control.

I have already laboured that we do not tell ourselves to breathe, secrete hormones, or regulate our blood vessels. We have absolutely no part to play in the thousands of functions that our body performs every single second. But if we were to play a part, how would we do it?

Conventional science suggests that all of these functions aren't random. They are part of an extremely complex system, and an extremely complex system cannot run by accident. It has to run by some kind of causation. It has to be controlled by some kind of systemisation. Put simply, it has to be controlled by some form of mind, and the current belief is that this system, all of these processes, and all of these activities are run by what we call the subconscious or the impersonal mind.

So, if you were to try to have some influence over this system, the only way that you could do it is through access to the impersonal mind, access to your subconscious mind. Interesting, isn't it?

Have we already discussed that there are ways that you can access your subconscious mind? I severely hope so. This is the point of all that visualisation, affirmation, vision boards, tactile experiences and meditation. So, if you could access your subconscious mind, surely you should be able to influence it in the activities it performs on your body. I mean, we have already discussed this. We've spoken about pain and how we can instruct our body to, at the very least, feel pain or stop feeling pain.

So let me give you another example. Have you ever had one of those days, if you're at a stage of your life, where you need to pay attention to your diet? You know that you have eaten all of the wrong things, and now you need to weigh yourself. You step on the scale with trepidation because you expect your weight to go up, and yet, for some reason, although you ate all the wrong things, your weight came down. Or alternatively, a day when you were so strict and good on your diet, and you know you did all the right things, but you stepped on the scale, and your weight went up. Either way, you would be like, What the hell?

Many other complicated biological reasons might exist regarding how and where your body processes food. Still, it's clear that the subconscious mind partially dictates how you burn calories, secrete hormones, and generally run your metabolism. These are all aspects of weight gain or loss, so weight loss will be under its domain. It's perfectly possible that changes in your metabolism rate, or the rate at which your body burns fat and how it processes the food as fuel inside you, how much it stores as fat, and how much it burns away, all functions of your body controlled by your subconscious mind would influence how much weight you gain or lose.

So, I think it's very possible that when you ate the wrong things and didn't put on weight or when you ate the right things and did put on weight, this was due to changes in these functions, and control over your subconscious mind would give you the ability to make changes in those aforementioned functions.

Now, most of us aren't scientists or even nutritionists, so I wouldn't recommend you learn scientifically exactly which functions control what and then try to use your subconscious mind to give your body instructions. The process could be much easier than that because the whole concept of identity rears its very useful head again, because if you see yourself as a fit and healthy person, and you transmit that to your subconscious mind, then it will take the appropriate actions in terms of burning fats or introducing a higher metabolism rate to assist you with obtaining your new self-image. Be Do have.

Now, don't get me wrong, although I'm sure it's totally possible, I'm not saying that you should eat anything you want in a gluttonous display and expect to be as wafer thin as a model. I think your actions must also be congruent with your image and beliefs. At the very least, if you say you're fit and healthy, you should act like a fit and healthy person.

But we can come full circle and look at the existence of the people who seem to completely ignore all of these rules, live in the complete opposite, and yet still get the result. Somehow, their bodies are ignoring the rules that we all live by, and as such, surely there must be a way to replicate this. Surely, there's something in this that we can learn from. It might just all be down to genetics, and that is that. Or there might be some way of programming ourselves with the right thinking and taking the right actions, which must help us get the result we want.

Happy Accidents… No, Not What You Think

I was working furiously on getting the sale of one of my properties completed by the agreed date, but a problem occurred, and it had to be delayed for another week. I was extremely frustrated about this delay but took it on the chin because these things happen in business. Then, a few days after the delay was announced, somebody I knew had an emergency and was going to be made homeless. They needed a place to stay for a few days until they could find long-term accommodation. Since my long-term tenant had already vacated the property in preparation for the original completion date, I said they could stay in the property I was selling until they sorted themselves out, as long as they promised to leave before the new completion date.

That is how they ended up staying in my property for a few days and avoiding being homeless, and I thought to myself, if this property had been completed on time, I wouldn't have had the opportunity to help them. If things had gone to plan, if I had gotten what I wanted when I wanted it, they would have been homeless and in great difficulty, and I would not have been in a position to help.

Has anything like this ever happened to you? I bet it has. As I said, the majority of having these Hippie Shit experiences are not about them occurring because they do, regularly, for everybody. The key really comes down to your perception of them. If you think they are a coincidence, you will think, 'Oh, that was interesting,' and shrug it off. If you see them for what they are, you'll take a deeper look at what occurred, and hopefully, examining it for what it was will help you to see more and more of the same in the future.

This type of thing has happened to me numerous times, too numerous to mention. Often, something that I'm working on that doesn't happen or doesn't work out when I want it to, or how I want it to, leaves the opportunity for that problem to resolve something else. For example, sometimes, money that I was working hard to earn or should have been paid to me is delayed so that it comes at a time when it's needed to resolve an unexpected problem, one I would not have been able to resolve if I was paid on time because I had already allocated the money to something less important. Sometimes, I'm fighting to get somewhere on time, and I don't make it, but the delay allowed me to see something that I needed to see or do something that I wouldn't have been able to do if I wasn't late.

I like to call these things happy accidents. They're accidental because they were not planned, but because of the delay or the change in plan, due to something beyond my control, because of the change in circumstances from the thing that I wanted, something that I didn't want, some unexpected benefit occurred. An Unexpected benefit not just for myself but often for someone else. This is what I mean when I talk about the jigsaw of the universe. I am aware of how slight changes in my plans have allowed the manifestations of others, and I am sure all of my manifestations were realised through the changing of other people's plans.

This is another time when you really need to look at what we call coincidence a little bit deeper. Analysing coincidence will allow you to build the habit of seeing and understanding these happy accidents. It will help you to stay calm and look for the unexpected benefits in things that happen against your will. Because it's easy to see the correlation or link between your misfortune and the unexpected benefit when they happen a few hours, weeks, or days from each other. But what about delays that happen years apart?

What about the degree you didn't finish? Maybe you admonished yourself for wasting all of that time, yet it is not finishing, which allowed you to change direction, work in child services, and save a child's life. Or the investment portfolio you lost in a market crash, which left you distraught but caused you to leave investing and pursue a career in science, taking you down a path where you would work with the team that improved the early detection of cancer.

You might not be able to see these elongated happy accidents, but you most definitely can see the short-term ones and recognise them for what they are. Armed with this knowledge, you can feel secure that your current difficulties just might be another one of these happy accidents.

Do Bad Things Really Happen?

I left this topic for the end of the book because it's quite an out-there philosophy. To some of you, this will be as woo woo!!!!! as the horn on a choo choo train. But since you've stayed with me all this time, let me try this one out on you: Does anything bad 'really' happen? The practical answer is, of course, yes. Very simple, mundane bad things happen, like crashing your car and writing it off, failing an exam you really wanted to pass, or the person you were deeply in love with breaking up with you. And then there are the truly traumatic bad things that happen, such as being sexually assaulted, losing your business and all your money, or suffering a terrible accident that results in the loss of a limb or the death of a loved one. So yeah, bad things do happen.

So, I'm not going to deny that bad things happen 'in the moment.' But, as Kendrick Lamar famously said in his song, 'Not Like Us', 'Here's the real Ninja challenge'. Let me say at the outset that this philosophy isn't for everybody, and I mean no offence. But having lived through bad experiences for over 54 years, I've come to see that, after a short or long period, there can be positive results from things that seem utterly devastating at the time. Even things that are traumatic and life-changing can eventually lead to positive outcomes.

I'm fortunate enough to have avoided some of the more traumatic, life-changing and horrible events I mentioned earlier. Of course, losing a loved one remains painful no matter how much time passes; I have never celebrated the death of anyone. But that doesn't mean nothing positive has ever come from these experiences. So, to avoid re-traumatising anyone who might still be grieving, allow me to give you some less traumatic examples to illustrate my point.

One recent experience involved a business venture in which I was deeply involved. I was a salesman trying to sell a financial product I believed in

100%. I was invested in the product myself and was convinced that it was amazing and would benefit anyone who bought it. But for some reason, my sales just weren't closing. I tried everything, but no matter how many people I pitched or how many changes to the pitch I made, it was an abject failure, and this completely destroyed my self-confidence.

Yet, two good things came out of this failure. Firstly, I decided to invest the money I didn't have to spare in a sales course. That course turned out to be one of the best decisions I made in my life. It contained the missing pieces that solidified my sales techniques into a holistic approach. It resonated with me and was so effective that I earned back the course cost within my next two sales. So, while I had failed in selling that particular product, the failure pushed me to become a more successful salesman in the end.

The second benefit came about a year later when I discovered the product I was trying to sell was a scam. It was an extremely elaborate and intricately constructed Ponzi scheme that had not only evaded my extreme levels of due diligence but also the due diligence of my lawyers and hundreds of other investors who had lost millions of pounds before it eventually crashed.

As someone who is often relied upon by his clients to conduct due diligence on investments that they have found themselves, I was extremely embarrassed that my own due diligence had failed and to have been caught up in this swindle. Yet, far from being an abject failure, my inability to sell it had saved me from embroiling others in this fraudulent scheme and dragging them into the financial loss I experienced. In hindsight, what seemed like one of the worst failures of my life turned out to be a blessing. Not only did it lead me to solve one of my biggest business challenges (developing a holistic and successful sales system), but it also saved me from unintentionally harming others.

Do you see how this brings me back to my initial question: Do bad things 'really' happen? I have experienced times when I was head over heels in love with someone, only to be devastated when they didn't feel the same way. But two things often happened afterwards: Firstly, I would discover that the person wasn't as perfect as I had imagined. In fact, in hindsight, I would realise that the pain of rejection was far less than the pain I would have experienced in the toxic relationship that would have resulted had we actually dated. And secondly, I would later meet someone who was far better suited for me. Moreover, the rejection would spur me to improve myself in ways that I hadn't considered before, whether by becoming more confident or getting in better physical shape, all of which formed part of the preparation for me to meet 'Mrs Right' (Well at least 'Mrs Right Now' at the time).

So, while these events may have felt like failures and were extremely painful at the time, they ultimately led to positive changes in my life and a net gain rather than a net loss. This is a life philosophy of mine. I don't claim to have worked it out entirely on my own. However, I have noticed a pattern: bad experiences often push me to improve myself in unexpected ways. This isn't something I planned, just a genuine response to the challenges I faced. Looking back, what I thought was a good thing at the time often turned out to be bad, and what I thought was bad turned out to be good.

As Pollyanna-ish and 'hippie shit' as it may sound, these are genuine examples of how bad things might not really be bad in the long term. They only feel that way in the moment. Now, I want to leave you with just one last example because I don't have anything stronger than this. I was watching a business webinar where the speaker, to my surprise, talked about the death of his daughter. Even more surprising was his assertion that as traumatic as it was, he truly believed it set him on the path he needed to be on, to leave a job he felt was meaningless and start a business focused on helping others.

I can't speak for him, and I never want to experience anything like that myself, but I can say that he seemed genuine in his belief. So, do bad things really happen? In short, they do, and I'm sorry for anyone who has to experience them. I hate seeing people unhappy, distressed, or in pain. But I'm grateful to have lived long enough and been blessed enough by whatever you want to call it, whether God, the universe, Infinite Intelligence, dumb luck, or coincidence, that the bad things in my life have usually, eventually, turned out to be in some way beneficial.

When bad things happen, I definitely don't say, 'Hey, this is going to be great!' I allow myself to get mad, but once I've allowed myself to vent, I put the best positive spin on it that I can and then get on with my life. Because unless you have a crazy-eyed genius, a suped-up Delorean and your name happens to be Marty, you can't go back in time and change things.

At this point, I need to redirect you to the teachings of Dr David Hawkins in his seminal work 'Letting Go.' In this book, he explains a practice where you allow yourself to get as angry as possible about the thing that has gone wrong. This can include screaming in your head or maybe out loud. Shouting and screaming, visualise yourself smashing things up, blowing things up, punching people in the face or worse, and continuing to do it until the anger that you feel been released. And if the anger comes back later in the day or even the following morning and you are still mad about the issue, he recommends going through the process again until the anger leaves you. As a person with anger issues, I have personally found this to be a lifesaving process. This process has been my salvation in terms of dealing with anger and I highly recommend it.

Of course, you should be sad when things disappoint you, get mad when things are frustrating or unfair, and grieve when terrible things happen, and in doing this, you should take as long as you need. But I'm also saying that you should live your life as best as you can every single day. Grieve if you're grieving, be sad if you're sad, and if the problem requires your attention, give it your best effort to solve it. Because whilst you 'keep on keeping on,' hopefully, you'll find that, in the long run, something good comes out of the bad.

I want to leave you with a paraphrase of something a Polish tenant once told me: 'Things always work out well in the end. So, if things haven't worked out well yet, it's not yet the end.' I genuinely wish you all the best in your life. If you're in a moment where things aren't great, then you're welcome to adopt this belief that you're just at some point in the middle of the story, but you're most definitely not at the end of it.

The Rights and Wrongs of Right and Wrong

What's the difference between right and wrong? As I said in the introduction to this book, religion has never been a good barometer regarding making decisions about right and wrong. Religions are constantly disputed to the point of war. Most religious texts are a myriad of things, derived either from stories carved in stone or communicated millennia ago by people whom we have no proof of their true identities, aims or agendas in writing the texts. These texts were then transferred, transcribed, written in different languages, edited, removed from, added to and passed down in a series of interpretations, then filtered through various cultural lenses until, like Chinese whispers, we get what we are now told is what God does or does not want us to. You only have to look at the world we live in, a world full of social media lies, misinformation, and alternative facts presented by groups of uneducated and unrepentant followers, to understand and not take the word of eyewitnesses for anything. You can barely believe the reports of an event that happened yesterday, so excuse me for my scepticism regarding events that occurred 2000 years ago.

An example would be the suggestion that the 144 negative confessions were the source material, which was eventually whittled down to the 10 Commandments. If you don't believe this suggestion, take it as an example or demonstration of what the religious doctrines we have now could have gone through before they reached their current form.

So, how do we define what is right or wrong? I've always said I don't need a teacher, an imam or a priest to have a connection with God. If God exists, and he is not an absent landlord, as Al Pacino said in the movie Devil's Advocate. I can contact it, and if I have any questions, I can ask it directly. So, I suggest that you work on building a personal relationship with God, so when you have a question, concern, moral quandary or dilemma, and you need to make the right decision, you can go directly to the source and ask for guidance from the answer. This is the time for meditation, prayer, or any other practice you use to contact the Creator. I am not saying you will get your answer from a booming voice, burning bush or lightning strike. It might send you to a priest, an Imam, or a friend to find your answer. Still, it is just as likely that your answer will appear in the book you are reading, an advert on television or the song on the radio. Just be sure that the direction to your answer comes from your direct connection with the Infinite Intelligence and what this guides you to, not from somebody's opinion.

Prayer and affirmation

The Bible says, 'Use not a vain repetition, as the heathens do. Your father knows you have need of these things before you tell him.' This is interesting and actually brings out an obvious point. If God is omniscient, why do we need to pray to it to tell it what we want? I mean, you can pray in reverence, but it certainly doesn't need your reverence. But if you pray to ask for something, as an omniscient god, it would already know what you wanted, probably before you did. So, if you pray for something like health, wealth, or love, it already knows you want those things, too.

So, if he knows already, and it doesn't require you to beg it for its own benefit, ego, self-esteem or maniacal power lust then why do you need to pray?

I'm sure many priests and preachers will have their own answers for this, but it would appear to me that if God truly is an omniscient being and already knows what you need and want, then the greatest probability is that because it gave you those needs and wants, your prayer is for yourself. Your prayer (although an outreach to God), the true purpose is for yourself. And this brings prayer much closer to the concept of affirmation. If you continuously tell yourself with 100% belief that you can have it, your subconscious mind will be embedded with it and push you towards the situations, circumstances and actions needed to realise it. Through its abilities as a broadcasting and receiving station, you can find the people, circumstances, activities, and opportunities that bring what you want towards you.

Dreams

My number one fascination is dreams. When I was younger, I did a lot of dream interpretation. People would tell me their dreams, and I would tell them what I thought they meant.

I wasn't taught this, and I don't follow any of the usual lines, such as dreaming of fish means that you are pregnant or anything like that. In fact, I've no idea where this ability came from; it's just something somebody asked me to do. One day, someone told me about their dream; I told them what I thought it meant, and they agreed. The next thing I knew, I was being recommended and asked to interpret dreams by other people. Quite fitting since my surname is Joseph, I suppose.

But on reflection, I guess where it really comes from is the fact that I've always had a very, very special relationship with dreams. I've never regarded them as just nonsense that your brain throws up at night, nor a representation of your worries and concerns of the day appearing in your sleep. I've always been 100% certain that they're much more than that. So, I think it's not only interesting but very important to remember your dreams and analyse them. Personally, I've had everything from the usual batshit crazy dreams where I meet Michael Jackson, well just his head and shoulders on a skateboard, to prophetic dreams where I dream something that 100% comes true, as in the case where I dreamt that my ex-boss, offered me a partnership to start a new business, and a week later, my ex-boss called me out of the blue to tell me that he was starting a new business and offered me a partnership in it.

This is why I think it's important to remember and analyse your dreams because they are either; A: Bat shit crazy and don't seem to relate to anything. B: Genuinely a representation of your psyche, something that's going on deep within you, something that concerns you, that you're scared of or worried about. (If this is the case, then these dreams deserve analysis and thought to help resolve whatever is so deep in your psyche that it is represented in your dreams.) or C: They may actually be some kind of communication from a higher power related to what's about to happen in your Life. If this is the case, then it is better to be forewarned, and this may even, on occasion, help you make decisions and avoid problems.

So, the best way to do this is to use the method suggested by Jim Kwik in his course Super Brain. I've been doing this for years, but I like the way he explains it. Get a pen and paper, or, if you're like me, a Dictaphone, and keep it by your bedhead.

If you wake up from a dream, it probably means that the dream was strong enough for it to break your sleep consciousness. So, make a note of what happened in that dream as quickly as you can before you forget it. Then, go straight back to sleep. Do this as many times as you dream, and definitely do it when you wake up in the morning because you may be dreaming right before you wake up.

If you wake up in the morning and then go off back to sleep again, write that dream down, too. Then you'll be able to have a look at the dreams you had in the night and work out which ones were just absolute nonsense and which ones have something to tell you or something that you maybe need to think about.

Your sleep state is probably the most important state you would have in the day. As well as dreams, I know of many people who have had astral projections or other experiences when they sleep. The most interesting fact to me is that when you go to sleep, your consciousness obviously leaves your body. That's kind of the whole point of sleep, right? While you're awake, you're conscious. If something knocks you out or you go to sleep, you're unconscious. So when you go to sleep, your consciousness leaves your body. The big question that no one's ever answered is, where does your consciousness go? I used to believe that your consciousness goes back to join the supreme soul, but the more I experience different dream states, it seems to me that when you go to sleep, your consciousness will go to many places, different dimensions, alternative realms or alternate timelines for all I know. This is the most fascinating question to be answered. And if we ever get an idea of the answer, it will open up a whole new way of looking at existence.

Aliens

I have two thoughts on the existence of extraterrestrial beings. My first thought is that there are not only extraterrestrial beings but inter-dimensional beings,

The information provided by the Hubble and James Webb telescopes about the size of the universe and the number of galaxies within it makes it statistically impossible for other forms of life to exist in it.

In answer to people who think extraterrestrial beings don't exist, I believe that our knowledge and exploration of the universe is akin to a small colony of ants living in the Amazon jungle, having no means of exploring beyond their part of the forest, believing that nothing other than their part of the forest exists. I mean, how could they be aware of the Tower of London, the Great Wall of China or the Empire State Building in New York?

Lastly, in terms of our level of intelligence when compared to extraterrestrial or interdimensional beings, I look at my much-loved and adorable dog, Rocky. I think human intelligence, compared to the other intelligence of this universe, would probably be about the level of the average household pet—not totally unintelligent, but by no means at the level of their intellectual superiors. No street-smart Captain Kirk outwitting new species in my reality.

When I close the door, my dog cannot get through it until it is opened again. He gets scared if he hears a sound he doesn't understand. My dog has no idea of the complex commercial process through which we work to earn money to provide a home for him, buy his food, and put it in his bowl. Regarding our relationship with our extraterrestrial and interdimensional family, if we were as intelligent as the average dog, I would be surprised that our intelligence was so comparatively high.

Time

Now for some totally impractical hippie shit, ready for it…Time does not exist. There's only now. My favourite version of this is the joke I heard from Bashar (who claims to be an extraterrestrial being from a distant planet, hence my waiting to include him until the woo-woo section) about time where he says, 'What's the time' and then answers 'Now', and then waits a few more seconds and repeats 'Ok, what's the time now then' and proceeds to answer 'Still now!!' I'm not sure if he really is an extraterrestrial entity. Still, it's hard to disagree that he gives pretty good advice.

I'm still struggling with this concept of time being non-existent. I probably shouldn't even be writing about it because I haven't fully come to terms with it myself. This is a big one for me, so I apologise if this explanation isn't sufficient.

The closest I've come to understanding it is this: To me, it's all rooted in the idea of multiple parallel universes and multiple dimensions. I'm deeply rooted in the concept that time is linear, even though much of science suggests that it almost can't be linear. If we look through certain telescopes, we can practically see back to the Big Bang, which throws a curveball at the concept of time as a linear process. There are also various scenarios in quantum physics, the most notable being Einstein's theory that if one twin brother took a spaceflight travelling at the speed of light, he would return to Earth younger than his brother.

The closest I get to understanding this is through the idea that, as science posits, there are infinite parallel universes. In each parallel universe, every single possibility is a reality. To simplify, think of it like in science fiction TV shows and movies. There's an infinite number of universes with an infinite number of 'yous' and 'mes', living infinite different lifestyles in infinite different versions of the world. There are versions where the grass is blue, and the sky is green. Versions where the Allies lost World War II, versions where Genghis Khan never lost power—versions where the song 'Friday' by Rebecca Black was an international smash hit, launching her into a career which went on to dwarf that of Taylor Swift. Just endless differing versions of reality.

In that way, every possible outcome of your life exists in one of these different worlds. But more importantly, the closest I get to understanding is that every single outcome of your life has already happened in one of those different worlds. So, if every outcome of your life has already happened, then time obviously can't exist because there wouldn't be a linear version of time; everything that will happen has already happened.

This is how I understand time or get through the concept of time as an illusion. It's an illusion 'to me' because I live in a confined part of the all where it seems like time is progressing. But in the actual 'all,' every single possible outcome has already happened. It's not that I can't choose what I'm doing; it's just that I've already chosen what I'm doing with every possible outcome, in every possible dimension, and in every possible parallel universe. So, because I've chosen every single outcome, and every single outcome has already happened, time doesn't exist. It's just an illusion that I experience. Narr!!, I'm not really buying it either, but it's all I got.

Admittedly, this isn't a very good explanation, but I've listened to many more learned gurus explain the concept and left none the wiser. So this is the best I can give. At the very least, let it be food for thought. I'm sorry for including it if you don't find it helpful. I included it just in case it helps, but it is pretty out there, and that's why it's in the woo-woo section.

Parallel Universe Surfing

Close to this concept of the nonexistence of time is the idea of parallel universes and parallel universe surfing? Well, you can't blame this one on the hippies; it's your quantum physics scientists again who posited the idea that parallel universes exist. Where every single possibility for every single person is a reality. But this leads to the obvious follow-up question: if parallel universes exist, can we surf between them. Can we change from one parallel universe to another? Countless sci-fi TV shows and movies would love this to be true, and if it is true, it would certainly explain the Mandela Effect. Could it be possible that you were brought up in a world where Nelson Mandela actually did die on Robbin Island? The actor and comedian Sinbad actually did star in a movie called *Shazaam*. Then, at some point, you flipped into another universe where these things never happened. Is it possible that I grew up in a world where Bill Cosby wasn't a rapist, Sam Bankman Fried had a real Crypto exchange, Stephen Collins wasn't a sexual abuser, Lance Armstrong was not caught doping, Bernie Madoff ran a genuine investment fund, and John of God ran a Hippie commune that guided adults and children in their faith rather than sexually assaulting them. Maybe I started in a universe where these guys were all just American pie-eating, wholesome famous actors, singers, athletes and businessmen and through my own negativity, jealousy, small-minded pettiness, and hate, I transformed myself into a universe where all of the former and none of the latter were true. Who knows!!! This shit's a bit too woo-woo even for me to deal with. I've got no practical explanations for it. But quantum physics suggests it's possible; they are even trying to build computers based on it. So, I will leave them to continue their scientific research and you to decide where you stand on the issue.

The Matrix

It's amazing how so many current internet influencers are busy telling you that you're living in 'The Matrix', usually announced to the theme tune of *The Twilight Zone*, trying to make their revelation sound exciting, sexy and spooky. However, they're only repeating exactly what ancient Indian Yogis have been saying for the last few thousand years, not just in India. You find versions of this belief system in Indigenous people all over the world, from the Native Americans, the Koori (known by most as the Aboriginals), Egyptians and many other ancient civilisations. These Gurus, Sadhus, holy men, priests and enlightened souls have been saying that this world is an illusion, and that real existence lies in a world beyond our senses for centuries. Yogis call this duality Maya, and it is not a new concept based on the late 90s/ early 2000s Movie series.

The Projector Example… All the Way Down the Rabbit Hole

Okay, so since we started this journey down the rabbit hole, let's go all the way down. Wouldn't it be interesting if everything you experienced was a projection from inside yourself? In fact, it is not just a projection from inside yourself but, specifically, a projection of everything you hate. I just got away from talking to somebody who, whilst I was talking to them, mid-conversation, started checking their phone. I've always hated this kind of behaviour ever since I was a child. I always figured that if you talk with somebody, you should pay attention to them. So, when people talk to me, I try to pay attention to them, and if I get distracted, I apologise and ask them to repeat what they have said when they have my full attention.

Yet over the last 20 years, distraction has become a full-time habit, almost an obsession with people. Nowadays, it's very difficult to get anybody's full attention. They're either half watching the TV, half working on the computer (this is the one that I am most guilty of, but in my defence, if you see me concentrating and working hard on my computer, why would you think that this is a good time to strike up a conversation with me), half looking at their mobile phone, or half doing something else. Having somebody's full attention is now so rare.

But imagine if the fact that I hate this difficulty to get people's attention is why the world is like that. In a similar vein, I hate intolerance. I've worked for many years in many different political movements and organisations to try and stamp it out. Yet somehow, the world is definitely more intolerant now than it ever seemed to be in the 80s or 90s. Wouldn't it be amazing if my hate of intolerance was what is being projected from me out into the world, creating more of it?

If this sounds like something from a sci-fi novel, I severely hope it is. Because we are now all the way down the woo-woo rabbit hole. But I will say this: Richard Dotts gives a wonderful analogy of an old-school film projector in his book 'Dollars Flow to Me Easily'. He explains that if you are looking at, for example, the titles of a movie being played by an old-fashioned projector. For you to see that title on screen for thirty seconds, they have to replace the image of the title however many times it is necessary for it to stay on the screen long enough for you to read it. So, although the film is physically rolling through the projector and the frame is physically changing every second, it seems like the title isn't moving. But in reality, it is moving; it's moving constantly; it's just constantly being replaced with the same image. This is not the same thing as the projector being stuck and that image being stuck on the screen; the projector is moving and replacing each frame projected with a new frame, just of the same image.

What's being shown changes every single second. It's just that what's been shown is repeated over and over and over again. So, it seems like the movie title stays on the screen for thirty seconds, and then as the movie progresses, different frames are displayed to show different parts of the movie sequence.

I love this projector analogy. The point is that your life is what you're projecting onto the screen. You make the images on the film, and it's your job to change them if you want something different to be projected on the screen.

This is the root concept that I am adapting here. It just seems to me very much that all the things I hate or dislike are the things that I see more and more of in the world. Maybe that's because I'm projecting them onto the screen and making more of them in reality. This goes deep into the whole Matrix, Truman Show simulation vibe, and I am aware that it sounds surprisingly narcissistic. This idea that I think that I am somehow in control of the whole world. But that is a theory like the movie Maniac, which features Jonah Hill and Emma Stone. I could be strapped up to a machine, with everything I'm experiencing just the projection of what I think and feel. And if that's the case, then it would make perfect sense that the simulator just projects into my world more and more of everything that I hate, and that becomes the reality I face.

If this were true, it would make sense to hate fewer things, be less judgmental, and love more things. So, when the projector ran out of things that I hated to project, I had no choice but to project the things that I loved.

You can see that in this chapter, I went reverse. Rather than going from a practical approach to the woo-woo, I have started with this woo-woo version and then tried to show that it indeed has a practical side.

The reverse of this concept, the practical view, simply takes us back to our old friend, the reticular activated system. We have already discussed that you see more and more of the things you focus on. If I have a real aversion to sweaty people and I'm at a party where half of the people have been dancing and are sweaty, and half the people are hardly dancing and have no sweat whatsoever. All I'm going to say when I leave that party is, 'Oh my god, I couldn't stand being in there; it was full of sweaty people', not paying attention to the fact that it was divided equally between both types of people. That's how your brain works.

So, because your negative emotions are your stronger emotions, you don't have to believe that you are strapped up to a machine in 'The Matrix', that's playing you a hologram which you perceive as the real world, where everything you hate is being projected out there for you to experience. You can simply acknowledge the very real-world concept that you pay much more attention to the things you dislike and, as such, see them everywhere. If you could find a way to reduce your focus on what you dislike or eliminate the number of things you dislike, and therefore, by default, focus more on things you like, then more things you like will be projected into your world.

This is what I'm working on. I don't have to believe I'm strapped into a chair with wires and nodes attached to my brain connected to a machine in a matrix that is projecting a hologram for this to make sense to me. All I have to do is try and reduce the stuff that I hate and try to react against the stuff I dislike less vociferously so that I can focus more on the things I like, love, and enjoy and have them play a bigger part in my life.

If It Is done, Then What Should I Do

Ok, so I left the biggest woo until last.

What if I told you that you didn't have to do anything? I mean literally. What if I told you that there was a way that you could manifest absolutely anything you wanted in your life without taking any action whatsoever? Yep, just like the Genie in the Lamp, you could sit on a magic carpet eating grapes and command infinite intelligence to bring you everything you desired.

Well, I would guess that once you've got through telling me how much of a lunatic I was, if you decide to examine the idea any further, you will probably say, 'Well, if, in some parallel universe, this hypothesis were true, what would I do all day?' Obviously, once you discovered the power, you'd start your new life by ordering every whim and desire into your existence as if you were ordering from Amazon. Next-day delivery, please!!!

But at some point, you will surely get bored and need an activity to occupy your time. What would you do then? Well, my suggestion for what you should do is to do the thing that interests you. Do the thing that you are passionate about. Do the thing that you care about. Do the thing that you really think needs to be done and do the thing that you think you'd be good at doing it. Do what you think is important, but most importantly, do what you want to do. When you close your eyes and ask yourself, what do I want to do most? This thing that comes to your mind or to your heart more than anything else. Do that.

This is the true root cause of why people say to follow your passions in business, follow your passions in your career, and follow your passions in life. Because if this Hooji Paloogi woo-woo shit is correct, and you can actually draw the things that you want into your life without taking action to get them, then surely you should spend your time doing the things that you are passionate, care about and really want to do. If it were true that God has created a world where we can access him or his higher levels of creation to bring the things we want into our lives, then we wouldn't have to work for them; we can manifest them. So if we can manifest them without having to work and toil and struggle and fight and slave or trick and cheat and lie and war to get them, then what should we do with all that energy, all that time that we've been using to study and qualify so that we can work and compete and fight to get promoted and ask for a raise to get these things? The obvious answer is we should do what we want. We should do the things we care about. We should do the things that are important to us. We should do the things that make us feel happy, make the people around us feel happy, and do things that we think will be important to the world, important in the world.

You see when you hear someone say that your career choice should be what you really want to do, and you think, ok, that sounds great, but how the hell can I do what I want to do and make money? If you are willing to follow this philosophy, you will understand that this is how it works. Because the provision of all the things you want can be done without the work. So based on that, if you're willing to go with this belief, this paradigm of reality, then it doesn't really matter what work you do because you will get the money you want whether you're doing 'safe work', 'pleasurable work', or nothing at all.

The fact that money comes through the work is just incidental. The two are separate. The money comes because you 'will' the money into existence. You 'will' the experiences, the comfort, the finance, the joy, the security. You 'will' the house, the car, the boat, the jewellery. All those things were brought into existence from your wishes, so regardless of where you worked, they would come to you anyway.

They were going to come anyway, and since that is the case, it didn't matter whether you become the lawyer, the doctor, the dentist or the administrator that your parents wanted you to be, based on their beliefs that these are good, steady jobs and would give you financial security. It didn't matter if you followed these 'safe' professions or started a potted plant business, the one you always wanted to own, because ever since you were a child, you were just in love with plants. It doesn't matter since money and financial success would come anyway; it doesn't matter what you do. We are linking two things, which are pretty much separate. If this sounds unlikely, just remember that someone made themselves a millionaire right now by allowing other people to watch them play computer games.

That's why you should follow your dream and passion and do what you want.

One last and possibly the most important point. You should do this because, as previously stated, the happiness that comes from doing the thing you love will greatly improve your ability to manifest the things you want to have. This is your magic Lamp, your happiness and joy while performing the acts you love is how you rub it, and the hippie shit practices detailed throughout this book are how you make your wish for the Genie(us) in you, the part which is connected to the infinite intelligence, to provide to you with your every wish.

Author's note: This was written with thanks to 'Dollars Flow Easily to Me' by Richard Dots, which I was reading while inspired to write this chapter.

Life

From the moment you are born, a clock starts ticking, a countdown to the moment you die. An hourglass being started is a better description, where the grains of sand represent your life force, and you watch them deplete from the side that is full until it is empty. When you're young, you get to ignore this clock, as if the sand of the hourglass will never empty from one into the other. I mean, how could they? The hourglass has only just been turned over, and it seems so full. But as you get older, or if you are unfortunate enough to have an experience that reminds you of your mortality, you're made to pay attention to this ticking clock, for whom nobody knows when hands will stop. You're made to pay attention to this hourglass and realise that, although you don't know when the last grains of sand will fall from one end to the other, it inevitably will happen.

I suggest not wasting your time being preoccupied with the ticking clock or the Sands of Time; just be aware that if they are there, you have been given this miracle of life (as described In the science section). The best thing you can do is use this life to its absolute maximum. Do as much as you can with it, explore all your interests, exhaust all your abilities to their limit, all the natural abilities that you were born with, develop and explore them, and then exhaust them until you can do no more with them. Do good and send good vibrations out into the world, and therefore, receive good vibrations from others. Love the people who you love fiercely and without restriction. Be kind, be generous, create, and in bad times, just do the best you can.

Because I don't know if anybody will ever work out the meaning of life. So, in my opinion, the best thing you can do is to get the maximum enjoyment, happiness, and peace that you can without causing any detriment to others. That's my definition of life. And if it matches with yours. I suggest you use your life as much as possible before the last grain of sand falls out of the timer.

Conclusion

So, after all this research, If you were to ask me, Do the practices in this book allow communication with an Infinite Intelligence or God? My answer would be that, scientifically, I don't know. But spiritually and from experience, I know that they relate to forces outside of ourselves. I've concluded that the benefits of the practices in this book are for you. They will work for you if used open-mindedly and with enough faith to be done without constant disbelief.

The visualisation of meticulous details, the bringing in of your senses to your visualisations, the smells, the feeling, the touch, making them as real as possible. The affirmations and the self-talk in the positive language.

The tactile experiences of sitting in the sports car you want to own or taking for a test drive. The vision boards or putting up postcards of the place you want to go on holiday.

These things are for you. They're not necessarily to attract anything to you. They're not to tell the omniscient God or universe that you want these things and implore it to bring them to you. They're there for you to release the blockages that you have put in place, that your environment has put in place, that your belief systems have put in place, that your mentality has put in place, that your thinking has put in place, that your actions have put in place. Your stubbornness, anger, frustration, fear, and worry have been put in place. You have put up a thousand barriers to your own good, and your constant indecision and changing of mind would make it very difficult for you to receive anything from the Infinite Intelligence, especially if it's going to come through the normal channels of industry, which cannot be instantaneous and so will unusually take some time.

So, I believe these activities and techniques help the process. If you can visualise the same thing repeatedly, it is the equivalent of being able to ask for the same result without wavering. And if you can ask for the same result without wavering, then the entity delivering it to you can give you that one thing without being confused as to exactly what you want. If you ask for something different every single time, it will be very difficult to give you what you want. The best you'll get is an approximation or amalgamation, such as my Car, which was a mixture of Cars A, B and C, all of which I requested at some point in my visualisations. The same would go for affirmations.

If it's true that you can't receive anything that you're not in frequency with, then there's no point asking for a million pounds when you spend all of your time at the frequency of poverty or debt. If you spend your day worrying, complaining, and angry about how poor you are, then you'll be on the wrong frequency to send out the request. I mean, do you think that these are the predominant thoughts and feelings of the average multi-millionaire?

But if you affirm that you are something better, someone richer or at the very least becoming richer, and this allows you to change your frequency because you affirm it with belief, then you can send out that request. It can be heard, and if you hold the belief that you are those things, it can be sent back to you on that frequency, and you can receive it.

The same will be true of the Kinaesthetic approach. You can visit places, sit in cars, and touch things that you want to own. All of this will change your frequency due to your proximity to these things. They will no longer be items far away from your reality that you could never hope to see or own; they will be things in your world and potentially in your grasp. It will change the frequency of what you believe and what you think is possible. It will change the frequency that you live in, that you sit in, that you experience. And if you can change frequency as previously explained, then things on that frequency can be sent into your life.

So don't think so much of this whole Law of Attraction stuff as you sending out your mind to the music of the Twilight Zone, allowing your brain to go searching for the things that you want and manipulating people by taking control of their willpower body snatcher style into bringing them back to you.

There is no coercion, no tricking, no ordering, no cajoling. Think of it more in terms of the idea that everything you want wants you, so the only thing stopping you from being together are the obstacles and barriers you put in place to having them. Your thoughts, your beliefs, your doubts, your fears, your constant worry. In short, the frequency you send which was formed by the mental environment you grew up in and never chose to challenge and change. Or the mental environment of the friends, work colleagues, and political affiliations you now choose to live in and believe.

These are the blockages to receiving the things you want, and unblocking them is the work you must do to receive the things you want. As Wallace D Wattles said, 'This is the proper use of the will, to teach yourself how to think and what to think, and then to think those things. You think those things by visualisations, affirmations, self-talk and kinaesthetic experiences, or preferably a mixture of all of the above. This will bring you closer to the attainment of the things that you want and greatly reduce the time taken for these things to be delivered to you.'

PRACTICES & EXERCISES

PRACTICES

Invoke Happiness

Here are some practices to consider. The first practice revolves around the idea that the ultimate purpose of everything we do while we are alive, one way or another, is to be happy. Therefore, it's essential to practise being happy. As mentioned earlier, feelings of happiness are independent of everything else; they are not simply a response to stimuli. They can be, but they don't have to be. So, practice stimulating happiness within yourself. This stimulation doesn't have to come from external sources; it can be internal.

One of the best ways to do this is by creating a mental vault filled with all the things that have made you happy in the past, joyful experiences you've had, people you've loved, people who love you, your successful moments and triumphs over adversity, and your celebrations. Replay these moments in your mind, sinking deep into the memories and the feelings that they engender feelings. Whether you visualise them vividly or not doesn't matter. Just replay those experiences and recapture that feeling. Relive those moments, rekindle that joy, excitement, and wonder, and do this as often as you like. Try to maintain that feeling for as long as possible and see how quickly and effectively it lifts your mood.

Segment Intending

Another practice that I find valuable and I append to the morning gratitude practice is a form of 'segment intending'. I first heard about this from Ester Hicks (yes, the 'I am possessed by an alien intelligence called Abraham' that Ester Hicks). But like much of her advice, I have used it and found it incredibly effective. So as dubious as I am about its Alien Possession origins, I find Abraham Hicks an example of following the message, not the messenger. This version I am suggesting is a blend of the many versions of segment intending that I have learned from different sources. Still, I will explain the basic concept here. When you wake up in the morning, take a moment to decide what you'd like to happen that day. Please note that this is definitely not a to-do list. Instead, it's a list of things that would make you happy if they happened that day. You don't have to write it down; just reciting it is fine. Just think about the day ahead and muse on how you would like them to go if it were in your power.

For example, instead of writing, 'Give the presentation,' you might say, 'Wouldn't it be great if my presentation went really well?' Instead of just thinking about your commute to work, consider, 'Wouldn't it be nice if my commute was peaceful, with no traffic?' This 'Wouldn't It Be Nice' list allows you to focus on things that would make you happy if they occurred.

You can also add unexpected items to your list. For instance, 'Wouldn't it be nice if I met someone new and interesting today?' or 'Wouldn't it be nice if some unexpected money arrived in my account?' Just include things that would bring you happiness.

Gratitude List

The essential counterbalance to the practice of segment intending is to make a 'gratitude list' at the end of the day. This practice again combines elements from several sources. It is a powerful practice and can be done in the morning, but it's probably best done at night. Write down or mentally recite every good thing that happened to you that day. It doesn't matter if you had a terrible day—even if it was the day you were declared bankrupt, signed your decree nisi, or dealt with a sick loved one.

I'm not suggesting you ignore these events, but something good must have happened at some point during the day. Maybe someone showed you kindness or compassion during a tough moment; write it down. If you went bankrupt and were frustrated but enjoyed an amazing hotdog that reminded you of life's simple pleasures, write that down, too. List every good thing that happened that day. This practice is powerful because it pushes your Reticular Activating System (RAS) to focus on the good things in life, even if it's just appreciating a particular tree you love. The purpose of this exercise is to teach yourself to remember and acknowledge not just all the good things that happened that day but that no matter the problems or obstacles you face, good things happen every day. As such, you always have something to be grateful for.

These two practices combined, which only take about 5-10 minutes a day, create a positive cycle. You start your day by thinking about all the good things that have happened and by expressing gratitude for these best moments in your life; this can generate happiness within you. Then, you move on to the 'Wouldn't It Be Nice' list, identifying all the things that would make you happy if they happened that day. Finally, at the end of the day, you list all the good things that did happen again, expressing gratitude for them.

Even if nothing from your 'Wouldn't It Be Nice' list comes true, you still have a list of positive things from your day. This ensures that no matter what happens, you always end the day with a list of good things in your life. The magic happens when you start to see things from your 'Wouldn't It Be Nice' list coming true. Maybe you did get a call from a friend you hadn't heard from in a long time, or perhaps your meeting went better than expected. Once this starts to happen, hold on to your hat, you have now entered the realm of the hippie shit.

By combining these practices, you begin to understand that sometimes the things you want, do manifest in your life. This is an excellent starting point for understanding how manifestations, things from outside yourself that you don't actively create, can be real and come true.

Listen to Self-Talk at Night.

I have already explained that the best way to listen to self-talk is in the background while you go about your everyday activities. The other best time to listen to self-talk is at night.

Put the self-talk audio on right before you sleep and leave it playing, allowing yourself to fall asleep with it playing. This is so powerful because as you go to sleep, your brain waves go from Beta through Alpha and Theta to Delta. Your Alpha and Theta brainwaves are when your brain is most susceptible and receptive to suggestions. These brainwaves are believed to allow you to access your subconscious mind. So, if you leave the self-talk playing while you fall asleep, then it will be playing when as your brain enters into these different states and can access your subconscious mind at the times that it's most malleable.

I'm sure Dr Helmstetter says something about self-talk not working if you aren't fully awake, but I very much disagree. I have played self-talk all night while sleeping and found that the result is quite life changing. After a few months of this practice, I woke up with increased confidence, positivity and a happier outlook. The best thing about this practice is that it is the perfect counterbalance to the hours of negativity that most people experience in their waking hours. Just imagine, after 16 hours of intermittent negativity from other people, the media and the world around you, you allow yourself eight hours of positivity and confidence using no extra time from your day while you sleep.

EXERCISES

Rewire Worry Exercise

These are a few exercises to help you to rewire worry.

How do I rewire worry? I rewire worry by thinking too many good, healthy, positive and productive thoughts to ever have any time for worry, doubt or uncertainty. If a worrisome thought tries to find its way in and will not go away, I write it down along with one or two possible solutions. By doing this, I rob the worry of its energy and often find the solution in front of me.

First, stop yourself whenever you have a worrisome thought and analyse how realistic it is. If you are anything like me, sometimes we see a movie, and it sticks in our brains. Then, months later, when our child goes off on holiday or to a nightclub and doesn't confirm their arrival, we replay a scene from the movie where an international terrorist organisation takes over the nightclub and holds everybody hostage. Once you let a thought like this in, you can run a scenario like this in your brain for ages, getting more and more worked up and terrified as to what could happen, how helpless you would feel, and all the horrible things that could happen to your child while in this situation. But, luckily, it's all bullshit. It hasn't happened, and based on the probabilities of life, 90% of the time, nothing like this will happen. Yet you've given all this energy to it, and all the energy you've given to it, as unlikely as it is, makes it more likely that this or something else negative will happen. Because your focus and emotion mean that you were essentially praying for it.

So, when you have a thought like this, it's very important to stop it immediately, right in the middle of it. Stop it right away; don't let it continue. Stop it and do one of the rewiring worrying exercises below.

Number One

Ridiculouise it (yes, I did just invent this word)

Ridicule the thought by replaying it over and over again but changing it to make it more and more ridiculous. Do this by changing the images, blurring the colours, exaggerating the features of the protagonists, and playing warped or comical music to accompany it. Make it seem comical or stupid, whatever works for you to show how ridiculous it is. Then replace it with the image you want, which in this example will be of your child going out and having a safe, fun time at the event.

Number Two

Analyse it.

Allow your rational, sensible brain to analyse how likely it really is. Maybe Google the statistics and get proof of how often the thing you are panicking about has actually happened or, even better, has happened in your area. Use this to prove to yourself how unlikely it is to happen, and then use that information to tell yourself to stop worrying about it.

Number Three

Write it down and counteract it

You can write down the potential worry and use this to criticise it. Use the potential problem you have written down as a source of analysis, and then write down three ways to solve this problem were it ever to occur. This way, although it is highly unlikely to happen, you now know that even if it does happen, you are prepared for it, you have a plan to mitigate it, and you have options that you like to resolve it. This preparedness should give you options that make you happy, that make you confident, and that make you feel peaceful. Ways that you would react if it were to become a reality, which takes the fear and panic out of the possibility.

Of course, there are more ways to rewire worry, and I suggest that you find as many as possible. Most importantly, find the ways that really work for you so that you can reduce the amount of unnecessary worry in your life and spend that precious energy on positive thoughts, which will lead to productive actions and positive results.

Counteract Your Negative Thoughts.

This is probably the most important exercise in this book, so although I have already covered it in an earlier chapter, I have repeated it here as a separate exercise.

You need to create a system where every time you have a negative thought or feeling, you automatically teach yourself to counteract it, neutralise it or replace it with a positive one.

The idea is that you create an alarm in your brain that goes off every time that you have a negative or discouraging thought. As soon as that mental alarm goes off, you do not continue with that thought, if it goes off halfway through the thought you stop the thought immediately, so you don't allow it to lead to another negative thought and then another negative thought as human brains are prone to do.

Every time you have a negative thought. You don't fight it. You don't resist it. You don't say that won't happen. You acknowledge that it has occurred, and before you have another thought, if you are based in rationality like me, you may want to counteract the thought with a realistic objection as to why it is incorrect and then, once challenged, replace it with a positive one.

Every time you have a hateful thought, don't try to fight it; definitely do not try to suppress it. If you do not have the need to rationalise everything, then you don't even have to negotiate your way out of it. Let it play out, and then replace it with a loving one.

The aim here is for you to create an automatic system where your negative thoughts don't lead to more negative thoughts, they lead to positive thoughts and your positive thoughts lead to positive thoughts.

This way, you can guarantee that you will spend most of your time in positive thought.

Like anything, this will take quite some time to perfect but even if you could perfect it to the level that you think in positive terms 50% more of the time, what you would have done is diverted your brain from constantly thinking negatively and removing the worry, upset, pain and hurt that the negative thinking brings.

This is not the same as automatically believing that bad things don't happen. It's just being aware that you're thinking negatively, stopping it immediately, challenging the negative idea like you would if you were debating yourself, and then going to your happy place to think something positive.

This is not delusionary. You are not pretending that things are not happening; you are just redirecting what your mind is doing. If bad things are happening, you are just not dwelling on them or allowing them to magnify and grow.

Rather than dwelling on the bad things and letting them magnify creating more bad thoughts to accompany it, you acknowledge the bad thing has happened and then redirect your mind to something that you like, something potentially totally unrelated, totally unrelated to the bad thing, difficulty or unpleasant situation.

So that your mind can spend most of its day in happy pleasant places which will be beneficial for you firstly, in the most practical way because happy thought leads to a happy day and then secondly in more esoteric ways as your vibratory signature will be closer to one of joy which will attract more joy to you.

Be Less Reactive

So, this is another exercise. This one is to help you to be less reactive in difficult times and to control your anger and stress.

First, think of a minor stimulus that you dislike but usually react to, such as a notification on your mobile phone or a loud TV in the next room when you are trying to study. Now, envision yourself not responding to your mobile phone, telling yourself, 'I'm not going to react to the stimuli.'

As you start to see yourself having greater control over the lesser stimuli, you should see this play out in your responses to these things in real life.

Once you start to get results, you can start to imagine yourself reacting calmly and controlled in more challenging circumstances and even imagining the worst-case scenarios of current events.

For example, imagine somebody being abusive to you, somebody giving you bad news, or your partner doing that thing that always makes you react in anger and shout at them. Just visualise yourself not responding to any of those problems, staying calm, not reacting at all, or, if you do react, reacting in a manner that allows you to stay in control of your feelings and emotions.

The idea is not to visualise bad things happening to bring them into reality but to visualise yourself being composed in difficult situations and seeing yourself as resilient and calm when times are tough.

So, if you have a strong enough mind to ensure that you don't take yourself down a rabbit hole where you start visualising bad things and feeling the fear and worry that will draw these bad things towards you, then this technique is a powerful way to teach yourself how to stay calm and keep it together when difficult times arise.

Get 'the Happy' Feeling

Try this exercise adapted from the seminal book psycho cybernetics.

Start by getting into a relaxed state. Go through the yoga process of mentally relaxing every part of your body. From your head to the bottom of your feet. Tell yourself to relax your head, shoulders, stomach, waist, hips, Thighs, knees, calves, ankles, and feet. Relax absolutely every single aspect and part of your body.

You start the process by choosing an experience to remember. Think of a previous achievement—it doesn't matter how big it was. Just remember yourself at a time when you succeeded at doing something—it doesn't matter what. Visualise it and try to recapture the feeling. Try to recapture the feeling of satisfaction, the feeling of achievement, the feeling of happiness or joy, and whatever feeling was associated with that moment.

Then go from the happy thought of what you achieved, take that thought and particularly the feeling and move it into thinking of yourself the way you want to be, visualising yourself being the person that you want to be, seeing yourself behaving the way you want to behave, or achieving the things you want to achieve.

Shadow Boxing, aka Mental Rehearsal

This exercise has been mentioned in several sources, but it is most famous in Dr Joey Dispenza's works. It has many names. Due to my martial arts background, I call it 'shadow boxing.' For ease of remembering, you might prefer to call it roleplay or mental rehearsal, but it is undoubtedly the same thing.

This is the physical and mental rehearsal of whatever you would like to achieve. For example, as a salesman, you might want to roleplay a sales call. Get a partner and roleplay, like actors, the whole scene of you making the call, you talking through the sales script, and them, as the client, giving you answers and objections.

Another version of this would be a scenario where you practise on your own but focus only on what we call 'the sales objections', where you make a list of all the objections (reasons that they will give you not to buy), and then visualise yourself or physically practice answering these objections out loud with confidence.

I call this shadow boxing because great fighters watch their future opponents to learn their fight styles, strengths, and weaknesses. They cannot practise on their opponents before the actual fight, but they can shadowbox them. They can pretend to fight with them, actually shadowboxing them as imaginary opponents.

If you watched the person who you will be fighting live or on recording, then you can mentally run through the attacks that they will do. So, you will know how to defend yourself from those attacks and how to counter them. You can physically move your body going through the attacks, how to respond to them in terms of defence and how to counterattack.

Similarly, Dr Joey Dispenza gives examples of tests conducted on people learning how to play the piano, shadowboxing or mental rehearsal of playing the piano improved their skills. The same thing has been shown with golf: practising your swing without the ball, three-pointer shots without the basketball, or even your backhand stroke in tennis, and practising in your mind without the racket all improve the results. All these forms of shadowboxing, mental rehearsal or roleplay are effective in increasing the participant's skill level and leading to greatly improved results. It should be something that you do.

Tell Yourself You Love Yourself.

One of the most fundamental needs for all human beings is to be loved.

As children, we are born helpless, and we need our parents' protection. They protect, care for, and nurture us because they love us (chemically induced as part of the human survival instinct, but love nonetheless). So, when taken from a child's perspective, the lack of love for us means death. There is no Tarzan baby abandoned by its parents and raised by gorillas or feral child raised by wolves. These make great stories, but in reality, both of these babies would be dead.

Much has already been made in numerous psychology and pseudo psychological writings about the change in the life of a child between its infancy when love is given regardless of what it does, and its teenage years where all of a sudden, love must be earned and is now only given depending on his adherence to rules or his behaviour, and then finally adulthood where all love and attention must not only be earned but fought for by competing with others.

I believe that this has a devastating effect on the human condition because although the rules and requirements for gaining love change drastically as we age, our biological craving for it does not, leading many to follow destructive paths such as controlling others or taking drugs to get or feel love if none is forthcoming.

The saddest part of this story is that once parental love has become conditional, we are not taught how to go to the only other guaranteed source of love available, one which we can rely on and, if nurtured correctly, will never fail to provide us with all of the love we need. That source is us.

So, tell yourself that you love yourself every single day. This way, if you don't get it from anywhere else, at least you get it from yourself. This is important, so indulge me and allow me to repeat it: tell yourself that you love yourself every single day, so if you don't get it from anywhere else, at least you get it for yourself.

Many practices will get you into the habit of doing this.

Mirror practices are the best as they involve looking at yourself as you express love for yourself. Eye gazing, literally gazing into your own eyes and saying I love you is very effective, although this can be a little disconcerting when you first try it.

Another way to make it a routine is to do it in the bathroom after you wash your hands. As you wash your hands, just give yourself a sincere compliment, for example, how great you look or how well you handled that meeting this morning, and then finish the statement with, 'I love you, man, or I love you, girl, or whatever meets your vocabulary.'

Lastly, treat yourself like someone you love. Think of all the things you would or actually do for someone you love, and then do them for yourself. Buy yourself gifts, go for treats, book a sauna, massage or tickets to the game. Show yourself that you love and value yourself, so regardless of whether anyone external shows you this affection, it is not lacking.

Got a Problem? Ridiculise It

We've already discussed that worrying is like praying for what you don't want, and If you're anything like me, you might also think you can't visualise. It's challenging to bring up images and pictures in your mind's eye of the things you do want, the things that would empower you. Yet somehow, when you're worried about something that hasn't happened and probably never will, you have no trouble conjuring vivid images and feelings of exactly what that terrible thing would be like.

So, here's a technique that I believe I first heard from Anthony Robbins, and it's incredibly powerful. Since you're undoubtedly thinking about something that hasn't happened (because if it had, you wouldn't be worrying about it; you'd be dealing with it), the key is to use the same methodology for the thing that hasn't happened, as you would if it had: destroy the image, debunk it, and take away its power by mocking it and showing it for the stupidity that it is.

Here's an example, let's say you're sitting there, thinking your company presentation is going to bomb, and you're imagining how you'll feel when it all goes wrong. You visualise how the office snob who always looks down on you is going to mock you, your boss looking at you with a look of expected disappointment (there goes your promotion for another year), and the person you are attracted to and really want to impress trying their best to ignore your disastrous performance. All of this Is already happening in your mind, and the presentation isn't until tomorrow. The key is to catch yourself in the middle of that visualisation, in the middle of that feeling, and then mock it.

First, brighten the images in this visualisation, then distort them in any way that suits you and your personality. You might turn them into a black-and-white film, transforming it into a Charlie Chaplin movie or a Keystone Cops scenario. The characters putting you down can be morphed and made to look stupid, unattractive, dumb, and ridiculous. Then, throw something absurd into the image, like a golden elephant flying through the office. Anything that makes the whole scene absurd and will ruin it. The point here is to highlight to yourself that not only has the thing that you are worrying about not actually happened, but the thing that you are worrying about is ridiculous, so you will treat it with the ridiculousness it deserves. One minute, it's a very real scene of a trauma you're imagining might happen; the next minute, it's an absurd vision of something that could never happen because, come on, a golden elephant is not going to fly through your office tomorrow morning.

This is a super powerful tool. I've used it effectively to destroy traumatising images and memories from the past. Whenever I used to replay them in my mind, I would suffer terribly as I re-traumatised myself with their gravity and seriousness. Then, I learned to use this tool to distort and destroy them, freeing myself from their power to upset me. How you choose to distort and destroy these images is up to you. I've also used things I enjoy, like anime, in this process. I might take an image and turn the whole thing into anime, changing the characters into exaggerated animated versions. Once they're animated characters, I can jump in and destroy them, stopping them from doing things that hurt or humiliate me. I often turn my tormentors into circus clowns to remove their power and authority. In these visualisations, I can become the powerful person I want to be, and as that powerful person, I no longer suffer embarrassment and mistreatment. Instead, I'm treated with respect and deference.

Now, I don't want to turn you into a narcissist. Still, if needed, you can change yourself from the image of someone who is put down and mistreated into someone who is respected and treated well. It's your imagination, dude; remember, you control it. It doesn't have to be reasonable. I repeat I don't particularly advise you to become a narcissistic lunatic, but at least you can take power to balance out the negative and self-deprecating feelings you might be having, feelings where you get put down and feel lesser, and change those feelings to you being powerful and strong.

Why is this a powerful way of doing things? Well, here's the real key: if I tell you to sit down in the morning and visualise good things happening, there's probably less than a 30% chance you'll do that. It will feel hokey, corny, silly, all of that. That's why hijacking the thoughts that you already have is so powerful because, well, you're already having them. You don't have to set aside time to put yourself down, worry, panic, or think about all the things that could go wrong; you're already doing it. So, all we're doing is taking the time you're already using to visualise and feel, running conversations, accidents, disagreements and negative possibilities through your head, and changing them.

First, change the negative possibilities into comical absurdities so that they no longer seem like a possible reality to you. Then, change them into wonderful positive possibilities, where instead of that horrible thing happening or the absurdity occurring, the same scene replays but becomes something positive, beneficial, and uplifting for you and your life.

Authors note: These exercises draw on several sources, including, but not limited to, the works of Dr Maxwell Maltz, Anthony Robbins, and Dr Joey Dispenza, as well as my own experiments and experiences.

Gratitude Questions

Are you grateful to be alive? Are you grateful that all your limbs work? Are you grateful that you can use your hands? Are you grateful that you can use your legs? Are you grateful that your brain is functioning correctly? Are you grateful for the people that you love in life? Go through the people you love in life and name them. Are you grateful for your daughter? Are you grateful for your son? Are you grateful for your husband, wife, or significant other?

Are you grateful for your friends? Think about them. Name them one after the other. Think about what you're grateful for, your friends for? Are you grateful for your job? I didn't ask if you like your job. I asked if I was grateful for it. What would your life be like without it? Are you grateful for the money it provides you with? Are you grateful for the ability it provides you to have a home? Now? Why would you prefer to be homeless on the street? If you don't have a home but you live in your car? Are you grateful for your car? Are you grateful that you don't have a debilitating disease? Are you grateful that you haven't been diagnosed with just five weeks to live?

Gratitude is the frequency that brings us closest to the Supreme Being, the infinite intelligence, the universe, God, whatever you want to call it.

Many things are happening in your life, but I'm sure you can make up your own list of all the things you can be grateful for. Even if some of the things on this list aren't true for you, whatever on this list is not true for you, something that you can't be grateful for, I'm pretty sure there's something else you can think of that you really can be grateful for.

The key to this kind of gratitude is to think of what life would be like if these statements weren't true. If your legs didn't work properly, if you couldn't use your arms, if you didn't have a job and couldn't pay your rent if your children weren't healthy, or if you just broke up with your partner who annoyed you so much, and you had nobody to love in your life. If you'd lost all your friends and had nobody to confide in or talk to.

But I doubt all of these things have happened to you simultaneously, which means you've got a lot of stuff you can still be grateful for.

The problem is that because our brain is a deletion machine, we don't practice enough gratitude for these things every day. Just like we learn how to brush our teeth and take a shower without having to concentrate on it, we learn that we have a functioning body, a functioning brain, wonderful children, and a job that gives us enough money to pay for our housing and our lifestyle, and we take it all for granted, too.

It's just something that we have, part of the routine of our normal life, just like brushing our hair. But we shouldn't. We mustn't. Gratitude is the frequency that brings us closest to the Supreme Being, the infinite intelligence, the universe, God, whatever name you like.

All the great teachers say gratitude is the frequency, and if we broadcast on that frequency of gratitude, we are broadcast on the frequency closest to God. If you were really grateful for something, you would want to thank the person who gave it to you.

So, if you really are grateful for any of these things, you will want to thank the infinite intelligence, the universe, God, whatever you call it for it. And the frequency that you can thank is the frequency of gratitude.

So don't take these things for granted. Be grateful for them every day. Choose something to be grateful for every day, or better, still run through a list like this and feel that gratitude every day.

Don't just say gratitude; feel the gratitude. Think about the thing. Think about how grateful you are for it. Think about how horrible your life would be if you didn't have it and how wonderful it is that you do have it.

Even mundane things should be broadcast out on that frequency so that you can connect with infinite intelligence. That frequency not only gives you those things, but if you build a communication with it, it will give you all the other things that you wish for, want, desire, visualise, affirm, and pray for.

MY PERSONAL EXPERIENCES WITH THE WOO WOO

My Personal Examples

As a practitioner of practicality and real world-ism, I expect you to listen to the words of this book with much scepticism and, after a long pause, say something along the lines of 'prove it'. So, I think it is only fair to share a few examples of how these concepts and practices have helped me in my own life. But before I do, I want to make one thing clear: I'm definitely a baby student of this material, not an expert, not a Guru or teacher, so my own personal experience is all I have to share.

On one hand, I sometimes struggle with feelings of inferiority, wondering if I should be writing a book on something I'm not an expert in. But on the other hand, the fact that I'm not an expert might be the very reason I should write this book. If I were an expert, I might be so committed to the process that it would be hard for me to step back and look at it from a sceptical, pragmatic or practical perspective, one that might resonate more with people who aren't 100% sold on these beliefs and the perspective for which this book is written.

That said, allow me to explain that I've always been good at one thing: noticing the magic in my life. What I mean by this is that I've always had a knack for acknowledging when miraculous things occur, although my biggest challenge has been fully accepting these events as more than just coincidences. This reluctance has often held me back from manifesting the way I know I should. I think my ability to notice these things started after reading John Redwood's book, 'The Celestine Prophecy', where he stated that nothing is a coincidence. That concept struck a chord with me, shifting my mindset and making me realise that the things we often dismiss as coincidence, serendipity or luck couldn't be so easily explained away.

With that realisation, I began paying serious attention to these occurrences. I'm not asking you to agree with my interpretation of these experiences as something beyond hard work; I'm just sharing what I've observed. I hope that by looking at some of this 'woo-woo' stuff through a practical lens, you might start your own journey, applying some of these ideas to your life without turning into a stereotypical long-haired hippie type. Instead, you can use these principles to benefit yourself and the world around you.

Let me start with my move to Spain. I don't remember every detail, but I do recall one significant aspect. When my son was very young, we were living in the UK. We already decided to move to Spain, so we were constantly researching all aspects of our move. In this period, it was my duty to put my son to bed. I would sit with him on the bed, read him a story, and then once we finished and I had tucked him in to sleep, I would stay with him until he fell asleep and during this time, waiting for him to fall asleep that I would take a few minutes and use the silence to do some visualisation. I would visualise the home I wanted in Spain, its view, and even my future kung fu teacher, who I'd read about in a magazine. I didn't know where this teacher was based, but I knew he was in Spain, teaching the same style of kung fu I was learning, Praying Mantis, a martial arts style which is not easy to find.

When we eventually moved to Spain, a few weeks after we settled in, I was talking to an English-speaking builder in my area who told me about a kung fu teacher in the next town. To my amazement, it was the same teacher I had visualised learning from. The builder and this Master were friends, so he made the introduction, leading to a student-master relationship and a friendship between myself and this teacher that lasted for years. But the truly crazy part was this: after living in our new apartment for five or six months, I sat down one day, looked at the view, and realised it was *exactly the* view I had visualised years earlier. Right down to the smallest detail, including the fact that my sea view was partially obscured by a building near the swimming pool, just like in my visualisation. Yet even then, it wasn't enough for me to fully believe.

Next, let me tell you about my Mercedes. I had built a vision board with a picture of a Mercedes ML 300, a car I promised myself I would have. I kept my eyes open for opportunities to buy it, but something went wrong every time I found one. The seller wouldn't get back to me, the car was sold before I could act, or it was too expensive. I was frustrated but kept believing that something would come through.

Then, a friend of mine decided to move back to the UK because of the recession. He had a Mercedes, not the ML I wanted, but a classic model, and he offered it to me for €2,000, half of what it was worth. He even let me pay just €400 upfront, with the rest to be paid later when I could afford it. It wasn't the car I had originally envisioned, but it was a Mercedes, and I was happy with it. This is where I differ from some people who say you should hold out for exactly what you want. I believe in accepting something good enough if it meets your needs.

Holding out for exactly what you want can sometimes lead to disappointment or even mental stress. You might pass up perfectly good opportunities because you're fixated on an ideal that may not come in the form you expect. This reminds me of that joke about the guy stranded on the desert island praying for God to rescue him, who refuses the help of a boat and plane and then when he dies, God admonishes him, telling him that he sent the plane and the boat, to rescue him, so why did he refuse them. Although I know that good is the enemy of great, I'm practical enough to say that if something good enough comes along, I'm willing to take it. This car was good enough, and I was grateful for it. Later, when my friend found a job in the UK, he told me to keep the car without worrying about the remaining payments. So, I got a €4,000 car for just €400.

There are many more examples like this, where things manifested in my life not exactly as I envisioned, but close enough. These examples might not be as clear-cut as you'd like, but that's the point, I'm sharing my practical experiences. The last story I'll tell you is about my previous apartment. We lived comfortably when the landlord told us we had to move because he was selling the property. We didn't want to leave the area, but no rentals were available nearby.

We eventually agreed to move to a place in a town that I wasn't excited about. Even as we started planning to move to an apartment away from the area we wanted to be in, I kept calmly believing that something better would come along. Then, just weeks before our move, a good friend came to us with a property in the same complex where we were living and wanted to stay. It was a bit of a mess because the previous tenant had wrecked it. Still, the owner wanted to rent it out quickly to a reliable family.

It turned out that the person managing the property was someone we knew, a cleaner we had hired before to work for us. We both laughed when we realised we'd been communicating without knowing it was each other on the other end of the message. Even more surprising, the actual owner was someone we had met and shared a friendly conversation with the previous year while walking around the grounds.

The property wasn't available immediately, but I wasn't ready to give up. We contacted our agent and explained that we wanted to stay in our current urbanisation and asked if they would be willing to delay our move. They agreed, and two months later, we moved into our newly renovated apartment, right where we wanted to be, without having to change our surroundings or lose touch with our friends.

This reminds me of a story I read in the book 'You Are a Badass' by Jen Sincero, which explains how she found the perfect place to write her book. The author trusted that something would come along, and it did. Reading that story, I didn't fully believe it would work for me, but now I have my own experience to reflect on. Although I still don't have the unwavering faith I'd like, every one of these experiences adds to my faith and level of belief.

I've also had moments when I desperately needed money and believed that the universe would provide it just in time. And it did completely out of nowhere, with no connection to any work I'd done. Money arrived right before my bills were due. At this point, I can't ignore the evidence that something beyond my efforts is at play in delivering what I want and need.

These are just three examples. If I took the time, I could probably give you 30 more. But these are the ones that stand out to me. As I said, infinite intelligence or whatever you want to call it (insert your favourite title here), is an experience good; I cannot or wouldn't even want to try to convince you that it exists, but having experienced this higher power for myself you would have great difficulty talking me out of my belief in it. My wish for you is that you start by looking at the practical benefits of some of these beliefs and activities expressed in this book. Once you begin using them and getting personal gains, you'll start to see improvements in your life, leading you further down the path of self-improvement and connection with whatever higher power is out there, guiding you to better things.

The Mr Maph Experience

My good friend and internationally successful singer Mr Maph, called me one day and said he wanted to come and visit me. We'd always got on well, ever since he had moved his family to Spain, where we met, and I was always happy to spend time with him.

The Problem was that it was in the recession of 2008, and I had no money. But he was quite insistent and said he would drive all the way down from where he lived to my town for the visit so we could spend some time together and have a coffee.

As it was a recession, my business wasn't going very well, like most of the western world my revenue had plummeted, so I was preoccupied with one thing. I needed to go to a job interview the following day, but my finances were so low I did not have the money to put petrol in the car to get there. So, I decided to abandon my problems and spend some time with my friend. Maph arrived, and we spent a couple of really cool hours together catching up on each other's lives, etc. At the end of the meeting, he insisted that he paid the bill, as I was broke, I didn't complain. He went up and paid the bill, and then, as he came back, he thrust 40 euros in my hand. I looked up at him bewildered, and I said, 'What's this for?' He responded to me, 'I don't know, bro, something inside me just told me to give you this money'. Now. I've always known Mr Maph as a devout follower of Jesus Christ, but I'm telling you, I sat there with my mouth gaping, and I said to him, 'Bro, I just have to tell you, I got a job interview tomorrow, and I had absolutely no idea how I was gonna put get the money to put petrol in the car to go and get this job. The recession is basically killing off all of my business, and I really need this job to provide for my family.' He replied something to the effect of 'Obviously, I didn't know that. But as I paid the bill, something just told me, Hey, you know what? You need to give Felix this change.' Nevertheless, to say, I thanked him, he went his way, and the following morning, I put on my best suit, put petrol in my car, drove to the job interview, and got the job which allowed me to provide for my family for the following 12 months.

Hippie shit, yes, but trust me, it happened. Don't believe me, just ask Maph. Anyone with any spiritual belief will be aware that you can be used by the creator at any time, and in my opinion, if you are chosen in this way, you are most definitely blessed and highly favoured.

My Early Warning System

Here's another experience from the realm of practical hippie shit. Whether you believe it or not, I understand. If you don't, that's okay; I wrote this book to share my experiences, not to convince anyone. But if you're still sceptical, just hear me out. This one was particularly odd.

I was driving down the road, listening to music, when a random thought suddenly popped into my head: *I wonder where the horn on this car is?*

I thought that because I was driving a car that I wasn't very familiar with. I'd only driven it a few times before and didn't know where the horn was located. So, while watching the road, I quickly glanced around the steering wheel and realised the horn was in a very unusual place. Most car horns are on the centre of the steering wheel, but in this car, the horn is on small buttons on the side. Having located the horn, I thought, *Great, I know where it is now*, and continued to concentrate on my driving.

Within 60 seconds of figuring out where the horn was, a car flew straight at me on my side. In their impatience, someone decided to overtake the car in front of them on a blind bend. As they came around the bend, they were heading straight towards me. I slammed my brakes and hit the horn to ensure they saw me. They swerved out of my way just in time, avoiding a collision. I managed to stop in time and drove off, trying to shake off the fact that they had nearly caused a serious accident. As I passed the car they had overtaken, we exchanged looks, shaking our heads in mutual acknowledgement of how reckless that driver had been.

After passing that car, I'm not ashamed to admit I burst into tears. We all ask the big question, *what am I here for? Is there a God? What happens when I die?* And rarely do we get clear answers or signs. But when something warns you about imminent danger, something that tells you that danger is ahead and you're not meant to get hurt or die, even if you don't fully understand it, that's a glimpse of something more.

To me, it's proof that there's something beyond us, something that prompted me to wonder, *Where's the horn on this car?* a thought that popped into my head minutes before I would actually need it to avoid a potentially fatal accident. That's the experience of God I'm talking about.

You can take it or leave it. I'm not here to convince anyone. I'm sharing these experiences because they, along with what I've studied and learned, however limited my knowledge may be, have guided me to write this book.

Felix Joseph

About the Author

Felix Joseph is a serial entrepreneur and business consultant, starting in entrepreneurship at the tender age of 13. After graduating from Economics Hons Econ, he has run multiple businesses, including an events promotions company, a property investment company, a digital marketing company, a property consultancy, a coaching and mentoring company and a not-for-profit organisation for musicians, to name a few. Along this journey of multiple business and entrepreneurial ventures, he has taken a keen interest in the mindset required to be successful in business, and this led him to deep investigations into all of the concepts that help people perform at their best and get the most out of life. This book is a combination of those studies.

Printed in Great Britain
by Amazon